CIVILITY AND ITS DISCONTENTS

Bruce L. Gary

Reductionist Publications, d/b/a
5320 E. Calle de la Manzana
Hereford, Arizona 85615

Other Books by Bruce L. Gary

ESSAYS FROM ANOTHER PARADIGM, 1992, 1993 (Abridged Edition)

GENETIC ENSLAVEMENT: A CALL TO ARMS FOR INDIVIDUAL
LIBERATION, 2004, 2006, 2008, 2011, 2014

THE MAKING OF A MISANTHROPE, 2005

A MISANTHROPE'S HOLIDAY: VIGNETTES AND STORIES, 2007

EXOPLANET OBSERVING FOR AMATEURS, 2007, 2009, 2014

MIDNIGHT THOUGHTS, 2014, 2016, 2018

QUOTES FOR MISANTRHOPES, 2016

Published by Reductionist Publications
5320 E. Calle de la Manzana
Hereford, AZ 85615

2019 February 11

Printed by CreateSpace, Charleston, S.C. 29418; USA

Cover picture: "Carnival in Rome " by Johannes Lingelbach, ca. 1650, depicting fools mocking the elite and celebrating vulgarity, as only the *hoi poloi* and Roobs know how.

"Anacharsis laughed at him [Solon] for imagining [that] the dishonesty and covetousness of his countrymen could be restrained by written laws, which were like spiders' webs, and would catch, it is true, the weak and poor, but be broken by the mighty and rich." Anacharsis, 600 BC

"Anyone who is stupid enough to trust or believe me deserves the consequences." A sentiment summarizing John Grambling's attitude toward the many banks that he defrauded.

"A great civilization is not conquered from without until it has destroyed itself from within." Will Durant

"Good news, oh beautiful planet, the accursed race of Man is not immortal." Robinson Jeffers

In a democracy the people get the government they deserve!

CONTENTS

INTRODUCTION

I've always been intrigued by "taboo topics." The first one was religion: why can't people question the legitimacy of religion?

When I was older, I wondered why everyone cheered for the "home team" when there was no obvious reason that the home team deserved to win. In college I wondered why the nature/nurture debate was so skewed in favor of nurture. Why was eugenics such a horrible idea starting in mid-20th Century America (yes, there are "humanitarian" versions)? Why is it forbidden to state the incontrovertible truth that half of Americans have a below-average IQ?

As my understanding of physics advanced, I wondered why there was so much resistance to viewing living organisms as automatons. I was puzzled by the reluctance to view criminality as adaptive. Later, I became intrigued by the idea that an organism could be genetically enslaved to the advancement of something unrelated to individual welfare, such as the genes that assembled it, or a group of similar individuals. In mid-life I wondered why everyone assumed the human race would exist forever.

But the most important taboo, or at least the most urgent one for a society to confront, is the lethal effect of psychopaths on a society's prospects for survival. Psychopaths hijack every institution where rewards of money and power exist. Some occupations are dominated by psychopaths, and even some academic disciplines lose their discipline when unethical people (with PhDs) work to hijack them for nefarious reasons. The greatest dangers are when psychopaths hijack a government, and morph it into a tyranny.

It never occurred to me that the rest of humanity was justified in ignoring these taboo topics. Why are humans so timid? Are they simply stupid, as Einstein once suggested to a reporter who insisted on an example of infinity ("Two examples, the size of the universe, and human stupidity; and I'm not sure about the first one.")

The key to understanding all of these taboo topics comes from sociobiology. This scientific discipline explains why the topics are taboo, and provides explanations for them.

Let's briefly consider just one of these taboos: that an individual organism can be genetically hijacked into the service of promoting some other goal than individual welfare. A honey bee will attack an intruder too close to its hive even though this attack will lead to certain death of the attacking bee. As my beehive remover guy casually explained, "the bee can be thought of as just another cell of the beehive body." In other words, the bee exists merely to serve the hive.

Introduction

Human behavior is mysteriously irrational, and some of the same insights gleaned from the study of bees and other species can be used to understand human behavior. After all, like every other individual organism we humans are assembled by genes, and our lifetimes are miniscule in relation to the lifetime of the genes that assemble us. This must be significant, yet only sociobiologists have studied the implications of this fact.

As a scientist in the physical sciences (astronomy and atmospheric science), I admit to reliance upon "reductionism" for understanding almost all things, even those related to human behavior! One of the humanities has "met" reductionism, and embraced it: sociobiology. The reductionist sociobiologist has a way of describing and explaining human nature, which I'll illustrate in this book.

Our ancestors were civil with people they knew, i.e., fellow tribesmen. With strangers, i.e., other tribesmen, uncivil behavior was not only normal but expected. This so-called "tribal mentality" evolved in response to the competition of tribes for territory and the fate of tribes on their success in securing and maintaining territory.

During the Holocene climate warming, starting 11,700 years ago, territorial needs changed because an acre of land could sustain a larger population. Tribal territories shrank, bringing tribes into closer contact, and since old hostilities could not be curbed the stage was set for increased inter-tribal conflict, and in response to that, the joining of tribes to form invincible super-tribes. But this meant that some of every person's fellow tribesmen were strangers, for whom loyal fellowship was unnatural. This is when a new form of "civility" was called for. Humanity is still in a transition to a civilized state, yet human nature evolves too slowly for us to easily accept the new requirements.

Sigmund Freud's *Civilization and its Discontents* (1930) captured something essential about the vulnerability of a civilized society to individual discontent. Later writers neglected to translate these discontents into terms of present-day sociobiological understanding. The time is overdue for righting this oversight.

In 1929, when Freud wrote *Civilization and its Discontents,* Hitler was considered a buffoon. Few people feared his rise to power because it seemed an absurd possibility in the most educated society in the world. Elites were held in high esteem by most people, and the malcontents who railed against an entrenched governing elite were a political fringe that wasn't taken seriously. However, pervasive poverty in Germany, and a sense of betrayal by those in power, created a discontent for the many jobless, and they had open ears for anyone who promised to improve the German economy.

A similar discontent has grown in America in response to economic dislocations caused by new technologies, large corporation outsourcing and a U.S. Congress that no longer cares about little people. The rise to power of Donald Trump has caused many thoughtful people to wonder if America is ripe for a transformation from democracy to tyranny, as happened in Nazi Germany in 1933. I am one of the people bothered by such thoughts.

Hitler hated the elites probably partly because they threatened to undermine his message, aimed at the uneducated. This must have contributed to his hatred of Jews, for they dominated academia and journalism – a traditional bastion of elites. Trump hates elites for the same reason, and this explains his obsessive criticism of them and his invention of "fake news."

The specific event that led to this book's beginning was a faux article submission to a humanities journal. The journal's e-mail invitations annoyed me, so as a joke I wrote something that I knew would be rejected by any reviewer with today's insipid humanities perspective. A week later the journal e-mailed acceptance "according to two reviewers," which proved to me that the journal was a scam, meant for collecting a $200 publication fee.

It was fun writing in a way that I knew would annoy timid "snowflake" thinkers who had hijacked and converted a once disciplined academic discipline, sociobiology. That's what prompted me to write this book. It is aimed at those who are no longer welcome in that once vibrant field, and who no longer have an outlet for their writings.

Sociobiology has its origins in E. O. Wilson's seminal book *Sociobiology: The New Synthesis* (1975). A year later Richard Dawkins published his "interpretation" of sociobiology: *The Selfish Gene* (1976). The field was born, and other books tumbled out, and books published prior to 1975 took on new meaning as laying the ground-work for sociobiology.

A backlash grew, mainly from Marxists down the hall from E. O. Wilson's office at Harvard, who feared that sociobiology's emphasis on genetics would undermine their activist social meddling designed for reducing discrimination against Jews and other "minorities." They poured cold water, literally, on E. O. Wilson and his message. This scared the West Coast sociobiologists at the University of California at Santa Barbara. The timid UCSB group renamed their field "evolutionary psychology" in order to keep a lower profile than E. O. Wilson's at Harvard. This stratagem worked, but it conveyed a message that those in the young field could be intimidated. After a couple decades the "wild thinkers" were banished, and the field of evolutionary psychology, EvPsy, became as tame and feckless as the fields of anthropology and psychology had been during the previous century.

I was never a participant in the glory days of sociobiology, for by then I had an established career in astronomy at Caltech/JPL. NASA funding was great during the 1960's and 70's, so I easily changed fields a couple times, but always within the disciplines of the physical sciences: radio astronomy, atmospheric sciences and aviation

Introduction

safety. All the while I kept an eye on what was happening to my "first love" field of sociobiology. I would occasionally attend EvPsy conferences (HBES), and subscribe to an EvPsy journal. It saddened me to see my favorite sociobiologists fade away, and I knew that I was watching a field being hijacked from heroic thinkers by timid thinkers.

I knew how federal funding agencies work from my decades as a "principal investigator" with funding success in the physical sciences, with funding by NASA, NOAA, EPA, Navy, Army, Air Force, etc. It seemed likely to me that the part of the National Science Foundation (NSF) that had funded sociobiology, and later EvPsy, had been infiltrated by do-gooders who felt that their social agenda was threatened by the bold sociobiologists.

It is ironic that sociobiology has within it an understanding of the forces that inevitably doomed its acceptance in academia, as this book will make clear. I sometimes wonder if E. O. Wilson understood that his new field was destined to be banished from academia within his lifetime. I have also wondered if Sigmund Freud anticipated that someday all of his writings would be categorically discounted as outdated by newer "understandings." This book's title is of course a play on "Civilization and its Discontents" – which I view as one of Freud's greatest contributions.

I'm retired now, and living off a pension and part-time consulting as an astronomer with a productive backyard observatory (described at Wikipedia). I'm not dependent on NSF, or other funding sources that have abandoned sociobiology. So I'm free to write unfettered, and that's what this book is all about!

At the end of this book I'll review the "sampling theory" argument I employ for predicting that there's a 50% probability that humans will cease to exist in two or three centuries. Sometimes, as I contemplate the demise of humanity, I feel like the imaginary person at the bow of the Titanic, shouting "Iceberg!" while no one pays attention.

Chapter 1 is the mock article that I submitted as a joke to the non-legitimate humanities journal. It can be viewed as an outline of the major themes of this book. Each "section" of the joke article is worthy of chapter-length treatment, and that is my plan.

If this book shocks you with its ideas, then good! Only idiots cannot be shocked by ideas! Whether or not you're shocked, or even amused by the ideas, it doesn't matter. After all, humanity is likely to cease to exist in a few centuries – so nothing really matters for long!

Introduction Supplement

The first version of this book was written hurriedly, during a 5-month recovery from a serious car accident. I didn't know if I would recover, so my writing was "hurried." After publication of the first version I was gaining strength and was able to correct typos and add a chapter, which became a second version. It has now been 8 months, and I am 95 % recovered, so I have had more time for review and writing a third version that is closer to my traditional writing standards. The basic message of my book is unchanged:

Human nature was forged during millions of years living in small tribes during the "ancestral environment" (AE). Inter-tribal competition for territory began before our lineage separated from the chimpanzees. The shift of allegiance from individual to the tribe, a transition referred to as eusociality, has been underway throughout this time. The evolution of increasing intelligence (in the brain's posterior lobes) during the past million years has posed a threat to the eusocial transition because a thinking person can theoretically ask why it should be patriotic. A check on this individual self-serving temptation was needed, and this led to the evolution of "conscience" (a pre-frontal lobe mental module).

During the simultaneous evolution of eusociality and conscience, a certain amount of nastiness was needed for the small percentage of tribesmen serving territorial border patrol duty. The strength of the conscience mental module was therefore unevenly distributed among every tribe's population. Another winning strategy was to maintain tribal population size within the range of 100 to 200 individuals (which includes the Dunbar Number of 150). This assured a sufficient amount of interpersonal interactions for assessing trustworthiness among the group of adult male tribesmen, which in turn enhanced warrior performance during inter-tribal conflicts.

When the current interglacial climate warming began 11,700 years ago the land became verdant and tribal territory shrank in order to be no larger than needed by 150 individuals. This closeness led to inter-tribal warfare, and tribes that coalesced with other tribes were winners. This forced all tribes to grow, leading to many super-tribes competing with each other.

Super-tribes had an unforeseen flaw: the nastiness that yielded the right number of merely nasty but needed tribesmen (sociopaths) yielded a smaller percentage of double-dose nastiness, called psychopaths (i.e., lacking "conscience"). Psychopaths were a liability for every tribe because their version of nastiness was whatever rewarded the psychopath, regardless of harm to tribal harmony and survival. Whereas the occasional psychopath in small tribes could sometimes be dealt with by banishment or murder, the

Introduction

psychopath in a super-tribe could merely relocate within the same super-tribe after he was discovered. Super-tribes had no experience from the AE that prepared them for dealing with mobile psychopaths.

New niches in super-tribes were naturals for psychopaths to occupy, and eventually super-tribes were being hijacked and led by psychopaths. Whereas civilization could in theory be a collection of harmonious societies, uncorrupted by psychopaths, the ascendance of societies led by tyrannical psychopaths betrayed the promise of what a civilization could be. America was founded on democratic principles, and for over two centuries it held a promise of defying the appeal of psychopathic takeover.

However, the wealthier the society, the more confidence voters had in their inner-directed search for truth and the less respect they had for their "betters" (the elites). The psychopaths played on this naïve voter, and the time arrived, in the year 2016, when a psychopath became president of the once great United States of America.

Europe is undergoing a similar descent. Asia has very little experience with maintaining a democratic form of society. Africa has even less experience. I'm holding out hope that New Zealand (and possibly Australia) will hold strong. When America collapses, and Europe follows, the prospect of recovering civilization from the tyrants may be lost. Humanity's future is precarious.

To answer the question posed by this book's title:

> **Discontent with civilization is produced by 1) having to encounter and politely tolerate strangers on a daily basis, and 2) feeling the frustration of living in a society dominated by psychopaths.**

Sociobiologists have a new opportunity and challenge: providing a credible account of the origin of sociopaths and psychopaths in the (pre-historic) ancestral environment. Sociobiology rose to prominence during the 1970s, and began to be eclipsed by entrenched and timid anthropologists during the 1990s. Neuropsychologists, who can work with sociobiologists in solving this mystery, began their rise to prominence at about the same time, during the 1960s, and began to be overcome by entrenched and timid psychologists also during the 1990s.

It is appropriate that I now acknowledge a book that has inspired me for two decades: *Sick Societies: Challenging the Myth of Primitive Harmony*, by Robert B. Edgerton (1992). When I bought the book 20 years ago I wasn't surprised by the subject matter, but I was surprised that such a book hadn't been written decades earlier. I knew my society was somewhat sick 50 years ago, and I assumed all societies were at least equally sick. I agreed with the suggestion, probably made in the 1960s, that what our society judged as "normal" was actually flawed in so many ways that anyone who was free of these flaws would be judged so deviant that they must be sick. This perspective has been a common theme of my non-professional writings during my entire life. A couple of my books even include the word "misanthrope" in the title, which is meant to convey my profound disappointment with human nature. For me, a misanthrope is also hopeful that someday a better nature will evolve. I believed that most of my life, but now I don't.

My disappointment with humans must have started in early childhood while browsing picture books of World War II atrocities (I was born in 1939). In elementary school I became puzzled about people's religious beliefs. Every year since then my disappointments with human nature and human stupidity have increased. Evil in some people, and stupidity in most people, are found in every society.

Some societies are sicker than others. Consider the following one: 1) 1/3 of women are raped before the age of 35 (8 times the rate in Europe), 2) 1/5 of children born are sired by some man other than the family father, 3) 1/5 of adults can't find their home country on a world map, 4) 1/5 of the people think the sun revolves around the Earth instead of the Earth rotating once per day, 5) the society is headed by a psychopath, and 6) more people know the names of the Three Stooges than the three branches of their government (74 % vs. 42 %). Oops! With that last factoid I just revealed that this society is America!

Apologists for America, and human nature, are found from pulpits to academia. Academic intellectuals form a broad spectrum, from the highly disciplined physical sciences, such as physics and astronomy, to the undisciplined ones, such as psychology and sociology. Anthropology is somewhere in the middle, with a "physical" branch and a "cultural" branch. Cultural anthropologists believe (following the sloppy field work of Margaret Meade) that the ills within modern societies are due to the corrupting influence of civilization. If only the people could be "left alone" there would be social harmony, as found in primitive societies. This belief justifies social activism to change governance. There's a tiny grain of truth in this position, but it overlooks the fact that all primitive tribes, where there is no governance, are even less harmonious than civilized societies (as Edgerton's book documents). By overlooking this inconvenient fact, sociologists are allowed to claim that crime is a failure of society to provide families with opportunities for a healthy nurturance of children. The adult criminal is therefore not evil, he just has scars left over from an impoverished childhood – and the impoverishment is due to a governance that needs meddling by the all-knowing social activists. The academics who promote these beliefs have a social agenda, and they won't let Truth get in their way.

One of the most stubborn truths that defy sociology is that a small fraction of men are evil at birth. They have genes that destine them for evil behavior in adulthood, and we refer to them as "psychopaths." The most commonly used method for identifying the psychopath is Robert D. Hare's *Psychopathy Checklist*. It is a list of 20 items that include

Introduction

such things as "callous lack of empathy," "manipulation of others" and "pathological lying." Because of the subjective nature of scoring someone on these matters the incidence of psychopathology has not been accurately estimated. The range is between 1 and 4 %, and the most cited value is 1 %. Men are more often identified as psychopathic, and I will adopt about 1.5 % for discussion purposes.

Each of the Hare *Psychopathy Checklist* items can have a score of 0, 1 or 2. The maximum score is therefore 40. A score of 30 or higher has been in common use for identifying someone as a psychopath (although a score of 27 or higher has been used with equal validity). Many more people have scores below 30 (or 27), and above the normal person's score of 0 and 1. These people are technically not psychopaths, so what are they?

These people have a remarkably similar personality profile to those technically identified as having a "borderline personality disorder" (BPD). The incidence of BPD has been established to be 5.9 % in the USA (Hyde, 2010). There are slightly more women with BPD than men (approximately 6.2 % for women and 5.6 % for men). The most salient personality trait for BPD is "manipulative." I refer to the BPD person as a sociopath. Combining sociopaths and psychopaths we have an incidence of about 8 % for both men and women.

In this book I ask the question: *"What is the origin of psychopaths and sociopaths, and what is their effect upon contemporary societal strength and the fate of our civilization?"*

My answer can be summarized thus: *Sociopathy is an evolutionary adaptation, and psychopaths are the unforeseen and unfortunate result of too many sociopath genes. Ironically, present-day psychopaths are more successful than others in achieving positions of power, such as tyrannical leadership of a society. Their hijacking of societies is a threat to the survival of a civilization (that consists of like-minded societies, such as Western Civilization). The psychopath is therefore analogous to a cancer cell in an individual; it has no prevision of the ending it produces, which in this case is the death of the societies that it infects, and therefore the eventual death of the civilization that related societies comprise. Humanity, as we now know it, is destined for an ending caused by a population collapse during the next few centuries (as predicted independently by Sampling Theory). The only way to theoretically avoid this catastrophe would be the extermination of all psychopaths. Since there's no feasible way for this to happen, the outcome of humanity's demise in a few centuries is inevitable.*

This matter is important, and it puzzles me that so few people have addressed it. Is there some taboo about acknowledging the existence of badness in some people's nature, as if it would be impolite to do so? Maybe there's some justified fear among people who ask about these matters, as if a tyrant leader will declare "Your curiosity is unpatriotic! Off to my gulag you go!" Or maybe there's some connection to the twin facts that women are attracted to psychopaths and men secretly wish to be one?

We shouldn't expect answers for this neglect from academics, because most of them simply blame poor childhood experiences (somehow related to modern life) as leading to adult criminality. There's an opening for non-academics to play a role in speculating about the origin and present effects of psychopaths upon society.

I'm a non-academic on this matter, and I cannot stop myself from offering my thoughts on the subject. This may be taken as a warning to the reader, which I advise for the readers of any book, or any human utterance: be skeptical of everything! This book is one person's speculation, and aside from the factual statements, which I think can be taken as true, the speculations are mere "suggestions for consideration." They may have some merit, or they may be completely without merit. I offer this book to the reader with that proviso.

Finally, I want to note that this book poses a minimal danger in case it is totally without merit. The First Edition sold only one copy, as did the Second Edition. I anticipate that the readership of this Third Edition will also be close enough to zero that it cannot influence legitimate inquiry into this important matter regardless of its merit.

Chapter 1. A Joke Article

Psychopaths and Cancer Cells

B. L. Gary, 2017 Oct 29
Hereford Arizona Observatory, Hereford, AZ, 85615, USA

ABSTRACT

A person with cancer, and a society that tolerates psychopaths, are headed toward the same ending: death. In both cases a fault at a lower level of organization undermines performance and survival at the higher level. The immune system does an amazing job of identifying and disposing of cancer cells. A civilized society, however, was so dependent upon the embrace of tolerance for its rise (requiring the coalescence of tribes, and eventually civilization), that the culture of a civilization is incapable of the requisite <u>in</u>tolerance of psychopaths needed for its survival. Psychopaths pose the same threat to a civilizations that cancer cells pose to the multi-cellular organism. It is ironic that sometimes the prerequisite for something's rise is also a fundamental flaw that leads to its collapse.

Key words: eusociality, psychopathology, sociopathy, sociobiology, evolutionary psychology

E-mail: BLGary@umich.edu

INTRODUCTION

Most academic publications are focused on tiny issues of proximate causation; only the sociobiologists (and their timid imitators, the "evolutionary psychologists") are concerned with "ultimate causation." Anyone seeking an ultimate cause for animal behavior, and especially that of humans, faces the challenge of arousing angry resistance from established experts.

These "experts" act as if they are living in the "ancestral environment" where enforcing conformance on all matters was needed for preserving tribal cohesion, which in turn determined the fate of the tribe and all its members. This accounts for a fundamental flaw in all the "soft" academic disciplines, such as the humanities: they are led by charismatic leaders and are therefore undisciplined.

The following was written by someone with experience adhering to higher standards of truth-seeking, i.e., the "hard" academic disciplines of astronomy and the atmospheric sciences. My approach therefore ignores the shackles of political correctness, and it will surely annoy anyone who is accustomed to innocuous discourse.

GAME THEORY PERSPECTIVE

Any game theorist would regard the following to be self-evident: whenever living elements come together to form groups that compete with each other, and when the losing group is devastated, the constituent elements will behave as if only the group's welfare matters. In other words, for the elements forming a group the element's welfare only matters to the extent that they can serve the group. Thus, when the evolution of single cells brought them together to form multi-cellular life, single cell behavior evolved to be devoted exclusively to the welfare of the multi-cellular entities they formed. One could say that "whereas the genes of single cells had been enslaved to the cell, the genes of multi-cell life enslave the cell to serving their multi-cell entity."

As illustrated in Fig. 1, the next evolutionary step was for the coming together of multi-cell individuals to form a group, or tribe. These tribes compete with each other in such a manner that the individuals of the losing tribe had the shared fate of extinction. According to the same game theory pattern identified by the previous coming together (single cell to multi-cell organism) we should be prepared to expect that the behavior of individuals in a tribe will be devoted to tribal welfare, with regard to individual welfare limited to whatever serves the tribe, i.e., "Individuals of a tribe should be enslaved to the tribe."

EUSOCIALITY AND A DILEMMA

This last stage has a name: "eusociality." E. O. Wilson lists 4 ½ groups of species that have made the eusociality transition: ants, termites, honey bees and bumble bees (Wilson, 2012). Ants have been perfecting their eusocial lifestyle for 120 million years, so when an ant attacks an intruder it does so without hesitation or any thought to its personal demise.

Humans are the ½ species; we started on a transition to eusociality thousands of generations ago, but our evolution of individual enslavement to the group has just barely begun. When a human attacks an intruder, or joins his tribe in waging war on a neighboring tribe, he may briefly think about personal consequences. (This is because of a rapid evolution of left brain capability, with insufficient control by the right brain: but that's another story.)

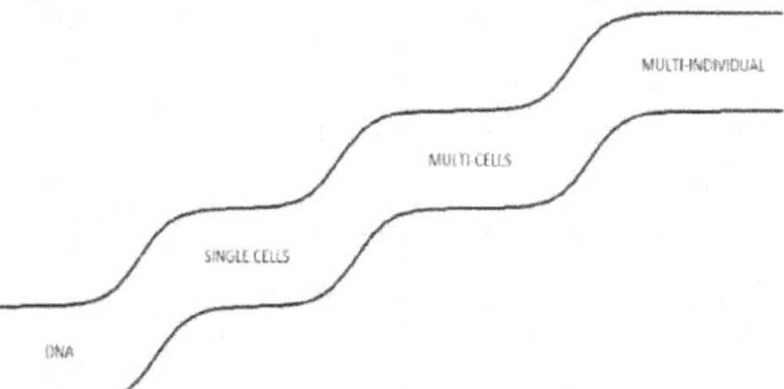

Figure 1. *Stages of complexity for living things.*

Humans are an imperfect eusocial species, but we are eusocial enough to dominate the world. We are imperfect in a way so profound that we have trouble acknowledging the imperfection. Our flaws are twofold: on the one hand we have too many "rogue" individuals who victimize the majority of eusocialized individuals in each tribe (in present-day society), and on the other hand all of the others (the eusocialized normaloids who are dutifully enslaved to the group) suppress intellectual inquiry into any matter that might reveal how enslaved most of us good ones are and how un-enslaved the bad ones are!

To understand how this dilemma might be resolved, maybe we can learn something from how the analogous problem was solved by the transition of single-cell life to multi-cell life.

IMMUNE SYSTEM TO THE RESCUE

The early life forms that were multi-cellular must have had to deal with old-style cells that remained loyal to their single cell destinies. The transition in progress needed a way for the organism to identify the old-

Joke Article

style "selfish" cells that threatened the organism by stealing resources and interfering with how the new cells were trying to serve the organism.

Their solution was to create an "immune system" whose task was to identify the old-style rogue cells and mark them for destruction. Every cell had a program for self-destruction, called "apoptosis," and when an immune system killer T-cell marked another cell, an internal program for apoptosis was activated and the DNA inside the cell was chopped-up into tiny, non-functional pieces.

TRIBAL IMMUNE SYSTEM

Could something similar have evolved for a species of multi-cellular organisms on a path to eusociality? Yes, in the case of humans it takes the form of "intolerance for non-conformance." Each tribe has a customary way to dress, a manner of speech, rituals to perform, mythologies to believe and patriotic behaviors to execute. Any individual who is detected to depart in even the smallest way from conformance is under suspicion. When such an individual has been identified he is either shunned, banished from the tribe or murdered.

These instinct-driven cultures play a role for tribes that is analogous to the immune system's role for the multi-cell organism. Rogue individuals are therefore analogous to a cancer cell, and at both levels mechanisms are in place for identifying and getting rid of the rogues.

PSYCHOPATHS AND SOCIOPATHS

The person who poses a threat to the tribe for his disloyalty and self-centered behavior has a modern name: "psychopath"! Psychopaths are the un-enslaved rogues who victimize their enslaved, i.e., eusocialized, fellow tribesmen. Psychopaths are social parasites. Today, 4% of Americans are psychopaths (according to the 20-question Hare Psychopathology Checklist).

Another 6 % of Americans are sociopaths, also referred to technically, and somewhat euphemistically, as having a "borderline personality disorder." (I view BPD as a milder form of psychopathology, as if caused by fewer psychopath genes; thus scoring in the range 15 to 29 on the Hare test instead of the 30 and above for psychopaths). Sociopathy (a catch-all term for sociopath and psychopath behavior) threatens societies by victimizing cooperators (stealing resources) and usurping control of societal functions (despots).

TRIBAL SIZE, THE DUNBAR NUMBER

Did the tribal counterparts to modern societies have the same 10 % of internal enemies of the social order? I claim "no." Consider the fact that tribal size was essentially always smaller than the Dunbar Number of about 150. For fewer than this number it was possible, even necessary, for each adult to know every other adult in the tribe. A tribe requires mutual trust for survival in its competition with other tribes. If a fellow tribesman can't be trusted to serve the tribe in many ways, such as in defense when attacked by a neighbor tribe, that tribesman is a liability instead of an asset to everyone in the tribe. This is why "patriotism" is such an important measure of men, even in modern societies.

This may be why tribes that became large nurtured a charismatic leader who would create a following of fellow tribesmen that he could lead to a "promised land." In this way all tribes would be small enough for cheaters to be identified and dealt with.

TRIBAL-COALESCENCE

Now consider what happened starting 11,700 years ago, when the Holocene climate melted glaciers and created verdant land that could sustain a higher density of game and more food for gathering. Tribal territory could shrink and tribal population could grow at the same time, and this brought competing tribes closer together. Old instincts required that they engage in inter-tribal conflict. However, the coalescence of tribes became more feasible and the rewards for size may have overcome the penalties for not knowing everyone within the home tribe (Gary, 2014, Ch. 19).

I argue that the super-tribe that won battles was also a place where sociopaths and psychopaths could flourish. In other words, could the pre-Holocene incidence of sociopathy (sociopaths and psychopaths) have been much less than today's 10%? If so, is the incidence now rising? And what could be the consequences for civilized societies if the level of internal enemies is 10%, and rising, at a time that our cultural tools for dealing with psychopaths has failed to evolve?

PSYCHOPATH OPPORTUNITIES

A tribe that has been hijacked by a psychopath creates within itself a new social setting, one in which other sociopaths and psychopaths have greater opportunities. Possibly the most famous psychopath is Genghis Khan. Imagine him taking over a tribe in 12th Century Asia, and inviting like-minded tribesmen for marauding, raping and massacre adventures. It has been estimated that 1 in 200 men throughout the

world have a Y chromosome derived from Genghis Khan. From the standpoint of the genes, psychopathology was a winning ticket to a future presence in the human genome.

A reading of history reveals that societies are most often ruled by ruthless tyrants. Adolf Hitler, Attila the Hun, Genghis Kahn, Joseph Stalin, Henry the VIII, Ivan the Terrible, Maximilien Robespierre, Augusto Pinochet, Pol Pot – these are just some of the world's notorious tyrants who gained control of their society and ruled with ruthless, psychopathic zeal.

With this history in mind, can one imagine a civilized society remaining uncorrupted by a psychopathic leader? Psychopaths are present in every society, and they are opportunists. It is common knowledge that the CEOs of most large companies are psychopaths. They climb the management ladder using "sharp elbows," and they discard loyalties that no longer serve them while feigning loyalty to the next level up – the victims in their sights.

HUNTER-GATHERER LESSONS

A famous observation of a hunter gatherer society records what happened to a tribesman who was too big for his britches. On a hunt he was ambushed and murdered. That's how our small-tribe ancestors, before the Holocene, may have dealt with psychopaths.

Why are we, today, unable to deal with psychopaths with the same resolute dispatch? Why do we tolerate them?

TOLERANCE IS THE PROBLEM

Tolerance! That's what was needed when the early Holocene tribes coalesced into super-tribes. After a joining of tribes there must have been widespread suspicion and resentment of those strangers who the tribal leader decreed had to be trusted. They dressed differently, spoke with a different accent and phrases, practiced different rituals, and believed in different mythologies. Yet, this large and cumbersome tribe was victorious over all smaller tribes. So all tribesmen had to keep their instinctive intolerance in check, and feign tolerance.

Some super-tribes made the transition more smoothly than others, and presumably they were rewarded with more victories. In this awkward manner the Holocene was evolving tolerance, or at least a cultural reluctance to be publicly intolerant of those who were a threat to society. (As an aside, this is the origin for political conservatism and liberalism.)

IS INTOLERANCE THE ANSWER?

We cannot be sure of the relative importance of cultural influence versus genetic influence in determining today's hyper-tolerance. Genetic evolution is much slower than culturgen evolution, but the former keeps a flexible "leash" on the latter (Lumsden and Wilson, 1981). Maybe there's a clue in the global distribution of tolerance, which peaks in Scandinavia and is rare in the Middle East.

There are many theories for why this global pattern exists (Gary, 2014, Ch. 19), but there is a more important question: Does an intolerant society protect itself from tyranny? The answer is "no," and the evidence is that the Middle East is also the historical center for tyrannies while Scandinavia is the antipode for tyranny.

So the level of a society's tolerance or intolerance, whether achieved by genetics or culture, does not inoculate a modern society from rule by psychopath, i.e., tyranny.

PRESENT PREDICAMENT

What is our present predicament, especially in America and Europe?

Reading the newspaper, or watching the TV news, provides a seemingly endless list of examples of sociopathy at work. Essentially every criminal act is by a sociopath or psychopath. Every white collar criminal act, including political scandals, is due to sociopaths and psychopaths. If all sociopaths and psychopaths could by some magic disappear, what a wonderful world this would be!

At some level of conscious thinking, this is the goal that has inspired utopias. The universal failure of all utopias may be rooted in their cluelessness of the root cause of failures of traditional societies: unchecked sociopathy.

Idealists, or at least the progressive idealists, are really aspiring for transforming their American or European society into a utopia. They preach an old sermon, that the road to "a more perfect society" is more tolerance. How ironic that this is, in fact, the opposite of a path to a winning place. More tolerance just widens opportunities for rule by psychopaths.

HERE'S THE ANSWER

A logical conclusion of my arguments is that there is no path to a winning place! All present societies, like all past ones, are doomed! Among the hundreds of civilizations in recorded history, a median lifetime is approximately 5 centuries. That's how long it takes for the psychopaths to seize control, or hijack a rising civilization, and milk it to death.

DEMISE DATE FOR HUMANITY

I've achieved control over my worrying about these matters. It's not because I'm 78 years old, and near my end. It's because the human species is near its end, so things that used to matter will soon not matter.

I am one of the first people to have presented a conjecture (Gary, 1992, Ch. 7) on how to time the end of humanity using "sampling theory" (which has become known as the Anthropic Principle). It goes like this:

Suppose you're asked to guess the length of a finite sequence, and are allowed to fetch a sample at random. If you fetch the number 62 billion (total number of humans who have ever lived) the logical prediction is that there's a 50% chance that another 62 billion will live. (Any mathematician would understand this, subject to the assumption that the sequence has a fixed length, which in this case relies upon the belief that the universe is a gigantic pinball machine, governed by the laws of physics, i.e., F = ma, so that all past and future configurations are inherent in any one configuration.)

Plausible world population scenarios for the future call for another 62 billion people to be born during the next two centuries. In other words, sampling theory analysis predicts that there's a 50% chance that humanity will come crashing to an end in a couple centuries, i.e., about 2250 AD.

Things aren't all bad, however. Consider the famous lament by the conservationist Robinson Jeffers: "Good news, oh beautiful planet, the accursed race of man is not immortal." (ca. 1925).

REFERENCES

Gary, B. L., 1992, *Essays From Another Paradigm*, (eventually published as *Genetic Enslavement: A Call to Arms for Individual Liberation*, referenced below)

Gary, B. L., 2014, *Genetic Enslavement: A Call to Arms for Individual Liberation*, Hereford, AZ: Reductionist Publications, Amazon.com.

Lumsden, Charles J. and Edward O. Wilson, 1981, *Genes, Mind, and Culture: The Coevolutionary Process*, Cambridge, Massachusetts: Harvard University Press.

Wilson, E. O., 2012, *The Social Conquest of Earth*, New York: Liveright Publishing Corp.

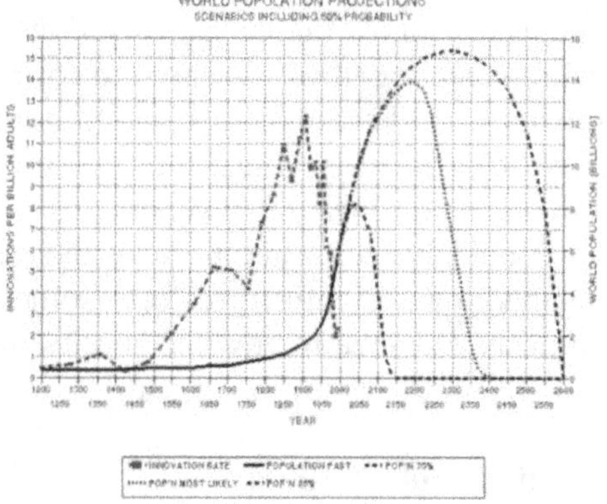

From the cover of Gary, 2014 (described in Ch. 29)

ADDENDUM

OK, it was obvious from the Introduction that this "mock article" was a joke! It illustrates how I tease my humanities friends for being afraid of ideas! It was a fun little romp! Ha, ha!

Chapter 2. Single Cell to Multi-Cell Transition

When living elements join to form a new living thing, the elements evolve new ways of behaving. How will an assembly of entities behave when it consists of entities that had previously never been assembled together? The once separate entities will forego concern for themselves and instead act on behalf of the new assembly. In essence, their enslavement switches from "unto oneself" to "unto the group." Let's consider what must have happened when the first single-cells came together to form multi-cellular organisms.

In the beginning, before multi-cellular life existed, and even before single cell life existed, there were molecular strands (resembling RNA and DNA) that by luck thrived in a pond with "food" and which reproduced themselves. Since these strands replicated we have to call them "life." The reproducing molecular strands that reproduced faithfully, and prolifically, would obviously dominate the pond.

Coming Together to Form Cells

Because we know that cells evolved there must have been events in which these strands of life came together somehow to form a "cell." The cell lives or dies on how well it functions, so the cells that came to dominate the pond were controlled by strands that served cell function. Either the first cell was constructed by a single life strand, or more than one. I don't want to dwell on this evolutionary step because I'm ignorant about how this could have come about. Nevertheless, this may have been the first step in a "coming together" of life entities to form something bigger than itself and more complicated, requiring a change in how the entities that came together functioned. I prefer to use the next step in the evolution of complexity to illustrate a basic concept of game theory.

Forming Multi-Cellular Life

There must have been a first occasion when single cells divided and stuck together instead of separating and going their separate ways. Such a stuck-together pair of identical cells might have been less vulnerable to predation by predator cells. If sticking together had some such advantage, then a genetic predisposition for it would have evolved; this would have led to the appearance of cells that were genetically identical and genetically-driven to stick together. A new mutation could then have changed the properties of the outer layer of cells, affording additional protection from predators. This would have entailed the invention of DNA methylation, or the covering of DNA strands so that only some of the DNA was uncovered and active in producing proteins that defined the cell's properties.

This may be how "organs" originated, and how a multi-cellular organism evolved. Because methylation of DNA could change what proteins a cell produced, some cells could combine with like-methylated cells to form an "organ" that functioned in a way unique to it. This is the essence of a "division of labor" and it is only possible because all cells of the multi-cellular organism are joined together in a "one for all, and all for one" manner.

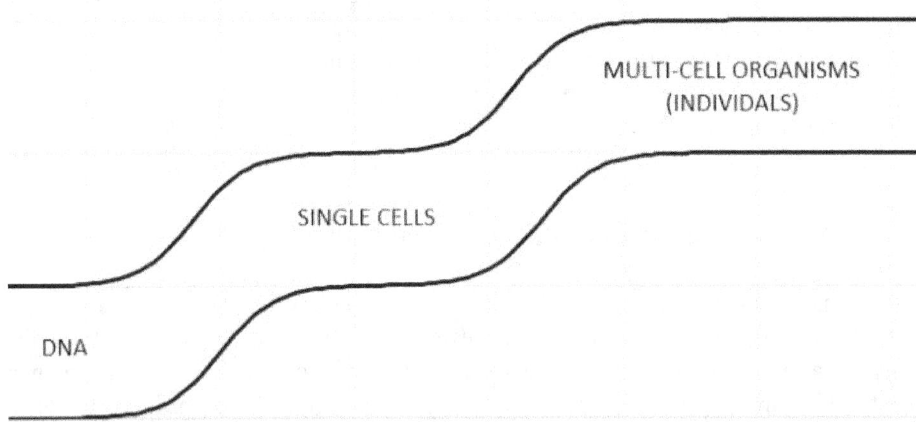

Figure 2.1. *The first two stages of living things coming together to form more complex life.*

Figure 2.1 illustrates the first two transitions from simple life elements to more complex life: 1) RNA or DNA strands to single-cell life, and 2) single cell life to multi-cellular life. During each transition the component entities had to change their "allegiance" from self to the new thing that they formed.

Requirement for an Immune System

Notice that all cells in a multi-cellular organism have a shared fate. This is an important precondition for other things to happen, as any game theorist would recognize. Cells in a body are rewarded by the success of the <u>body</u>, and the only measure for any such cell is how well it contributes to the body's performance.

This is such a simple-sounding statement, but it hides unseen subtleties. For example, if a cell is a liability to the body, because it is under-performing its assigned function for whatever reason (injury, mutation, etc.), the cell's most important contribution to the body is to self-destruct! A cell may not be in the best position to know if it's a liability, so that's the job of the immune system's killer T cells. These immune cells scour the

2. Single Cell to Multi-Cell

body for under-performing cells that need to be marked for self-destruction in order to maintain the body's performance.

There's one other cell type that needs to be marked for self-destruction: a cancer cell! Such a cell behaves in a way that doesn't have the body's welfare "in mind." It's as if the cell is oblivious to the body's needs and reverts to an ancestral self-serving behavior. If such a cell is able to multiply and start to form many of itself (a tumor), it may stimulate "angiogenesis," which is growth of capillaries for diverting extra blood to the tumor, i.e., stealing resources meant for other cells (those still functioning on behalf of the body). A cancer cell has no pre-vision of its future demise by causing its host body to eventually die due to uncontrolled metastasis of cancer cells; the cancer cells just do what they do because they are somehow programed to change allegiance from the organism to itself.

Three Cell Types Needing Destruction

I can think of three reasons a cell should be marked for destruction: 1) it loses its ability to function through injury or a mutation that destroys its ability to function on behalf of the organism, making it "in the way" of the other cells, 2) the cell can "revert" to the way of its ancestors, before they transitioned to working on behalf of the organism, rendering it self-serving and a threat to the other cells, and 3) the cell undergoes a mutation that causes it to re-invent itself as a self-serving cell that steals resources and threatens the organism-sustaining function of the other cells. Every day the human body, for example, has to deal with 1000 to 5000 cells that mutate to a pre-cancerous state. This may be a tiny fraction of the 30 trillion cells in a typical human body, but the efficiency of the immune system's killer T-cells to locate them and mark them for apoptosis is nevertheless amazing!

Chapter Summary

So here's a summary of the "lessons learned" from this chapter. When a life element joins with others to form a new entity, and the elements of that entity live or die together ("shared fate"), the behavior of the elements must evolve from serving themselves to serving the interests of the newly-created entity.

This evolutionary transition requires many generations, and during the transition there will be a mix of elements that behave in the old, un-evolved way and those that behave in the new way. A mechanism is needed for identifying the un-evolved elements, and destroying them. A multi-cellular organism achieves this with an immune system whose killer T-cells identify and mark the old-style rogue cells (cancer) for self-destruction by a process called apoptosis.

The same mechanism is employed to identify and destroy any cells that spontaneously change to resemble the cancers cells. Finally, this mechanism is used to identify and destroy "worn out" or defective ("senescent") cells that are "in the way" of the functioning cells.

These actions by the immune system of an organism illustrate the game theory principle that when elements join to form an entity with a "shared fate" for all elements, a mechanism is required to assure that all elements are functioning on behalf of the new entity instead of themselves.

Chapter 3. Individuals to a Social Collective

There's one more transition to consider: individuals joining to form social collectives with a "shared destiny." This is the most interesting and possibly difficult transition for a species to undertake. Ants, honey bees, bumble bees, termites and naked mole rats have completed this transition. Humans started the transition too recently to have completed it. In fact, it may be theoretically impossible for humans to proceed very far with the transition.

A game theorist will naturally wonder if every coming together of elements to form something new, with a shared fate, will be subject to the same challenges as the evolution of multi-cellular organisms from single cells. Consider that the coming together of individual multi-cellular organisms to form a collective of them is another level in the hierarchy of life, as depicted in Fig. 3.1.

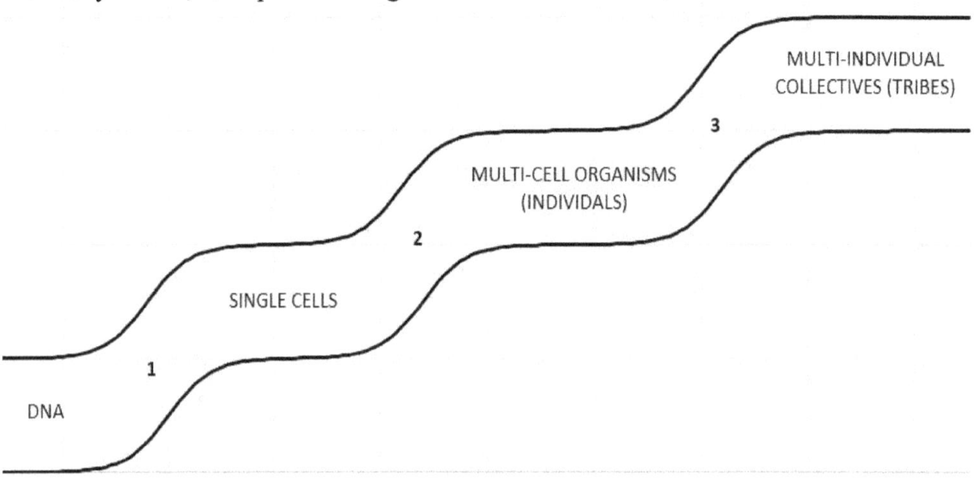

Figure 3.1. *The three transitions connecting the four levels of the coming together of living things to form a more complex living thing. Transition #3 is referred to as a "eusocial" transition.*

In theory, there might be an analogous relationship between a flock of birds to an individual bird as the relationship between a bird's body and the cells that constitute that body. Or consider a bee hive and the individual bees that the hive is composed of. These are possible examples of a collective transition, but we need to invoke the "shared destiny" of the collectives as an additional requirement. If the flock of birds is dispersed by some external intervention the birds may continue to live and prosper without ever coming together again as a flock. Their existence does not have a shared fate. Bees, on the other hand, have a shared fate! A single bee cannot live long without the hive. A hive either survives, or it dies, and all the bees of that hive share in the fate of the hive. Thus, birds have not undergone the last transition, but bees have.

3. Individuals to a Social Collective

Transition#3 Has a Name

The term "eusocial" was introduced in 1956 by Suzanne Batra. The description of eusociality emphasized interdependence of the individual members, and identified division of labor as a salient feature illustrating this interdependence. Eusociality was popularized by Edward O. Wilson in a book, *The Social Conquest of the Earth* (2012). I claim that neither of these authors capture the following essential features of the eusocial transition: 1) the eusocial transition is a repeat of past coming together transitions in which one level of living elements form an entity at a new level of life, and 2) during each transition the behavior of the lower level elements change their "loyalty" to the newly-formed higher level. In spite of these oversights I accept the previously published descriptions of eusociality. I mostly want to emphasize that during the eusocial transition a "selfish perspective" surrenders to an "altruistic perspective," which is equivalent to stating that eusociality repeats a pattern of converting enslavement to a lower level of life to a next higher level of life.

For Transition #1 the DNA or RNA strands changed from serving themselves to serving the survival prospects of the cells that they assembled and lived within. For Transition #2 the cells changed from serving the survival of the cell to serving the mulita-cellular organism that they were a part of. For Transition #3 the individual organism changes its behavior from serving itself (and close kin) to serving the social collective that it is a member of.

In the case for ants, for example, eusocial Transition #3 entailed differences of body type to facilitate division of labor adaptations. In the case of humans the eusocial Transition #3 converted the individual's behavior from enslavement to the individual (and close kin) to enslavement to the social collective. Such a species consists of collectives that compete with each other in a manner that results in the survival or death of collectives and most of the individuals in the collective. For humans, the word "collective" can be replaced by the word "tribe."

Individuals Analogous to Cells

My "Bee Guy," who removes hives from my property, once remarked that bees are so devoted to the hive that the individual bees can be considered like cells serving a body (the hive). They defend the hive in such an automatic way that they are oblivious to the fact that their sting will inevitably lead to their death. Ants are the same. I have been stung a few times while working in my yard too close to an ant colony, and the stinging ants have always done so with a surrender of their lives.

3. Individuals to a Social Collective

It is worth considering the suggestion that "a tribesman is to his tribe, as a cell is to the individual tribesman." Only those tribes prosper that consist of "loyal" tribesmen. As E. O. Wilson points out, the eusocial insect species achieved their dominant position in the world during the past 150 million years of evolution, whereas humans have been on the eusocial path for a much shorter time. It is difficult to estimate how long humans have attempted the eusocial transition; it could be as short as 1/4 million years or as long as 10 million years. In either case, a few thousand generations hasn't been sufficient to produce a complete transition to eusociality, but apparently a ~ 90% incidence of mostly eusocial individuals (as explained below) has been enough to propel humans to Masters of the Planet. Thus, most humans instinctively understand the concepts of teamwork, patriotism, and "my tribe, right or wrong."

Analogies abound between the "single cell to multi-cellular organism" transition and those few species that transitioned from individual organisms to a eusocial society. Just as a body consists of many cells with identical DNA, but with different methylation patterns (leading to different protein production needed to form organs), a species with a eusocial organization has a "division of labor" among individuals.

Communism and Fascism

What would a collective look like if it had progressed further along the path to eusociality? We can only speculate about such experiments by tribes in the ancestral environment. Contemporary tribes, as well as super-tribes (called "societies"), provide some evidence on the matter.

Communism can be summarized by the saying "All for one, and one for all." Each individual is expected to contribute to the collective's welfare to the extent of their ability. In return, the collective is expected to help the individual to the extent of the individual's needs.

Fascism is more extreme: each individual is expected to contribute to the welfare of the collective, but it relieves the collective from helping the individual. An individual's needs are irrelevant to a fascist society; if he can't contribute to the collective, he can be ignored and suffer whatever fate awaits him. World War II illustrated what fascism can produce. For example, Japanese Kamikaze pilots flew their fuel-laden planes into Allied ships to damage or sink them; such actions on behalf of the Japanese fascist Empire were puzzling to the Allies because of their extreme replacement of individual aspiration for service to the collective.

The notion of fascism as a desperate and temporary measure for the survival of a weak tribe under siege is an important theme of this book.

3. Individuals to a Social Collective

Tribal Mentality as an Allegiance Shift

Everyone in a human society is expected to place greater importance on "allegiance to the tribe" than to the self. This is easily stated, but challenging for the forces of evolution to achieve. For the ants, bees and termites this may have been straightforward; after all, it occurred ~ 150 million years ago. However, for humans the evolution of this eusocializing process must have been especially difficult to start – considering that in theory we humans are able to think and question things.

Starting about 1.8 million years ago our ancestors began a dramatic growth in brain size. Since intelligence of the IQ type resides in the posterior cerebral cortex lobes it is possible that this brain growth spurt was for the posterior lobes. Another increase in brain size began ~ 0.3 million years ago. This one may have been for the frontal lobes, where lifestyle strategy and personality reside.

A mainstream explanation for the first growth spurt was that our ancestors were learning to master the environment (fire, cooking food, hunting tools, etc.), and the second was caused by the need for speech. I accept this interpretation, but would like to add the following: The first brain size increase was <u>also</u> allowing for the evolution of ways for the individual tribesmen to be "enslaved" to the tribe, while the second increase was <u>also</u> evolving a conscience capable of overruling logical questioning of this enslavement.

In my book *Genetic Enslavement: A Call to Arms for Individual Liberation* (2014) I treat the matter of every living thing being enslaved to the genes that assembled it, and I specifically identify the human enslavement as being on behalf of the tribes that the genes predispose us to live within. Enslavement to the tribe is actually enslavement to the genes, since the tribal lifestyle is just a "strategy" used by the genes to enhance their own longevity within the species gene pool.

Enslavement to the tribe involves many things: sharing food, cooperating in the hunt, helping others make tools, trading babysitting duties, protecting the tribal territory by patrolling the border and joining other tribesmen in waging war (defensive and offensive). Patriotism usually refers to warrior duty, but it can also refer to sacrificing some personal gain for the greater benefit of the tribe.

Later chapters will return to the role of "conscience" in preserving eusocial transition gains, with arguments for the role played by a "conscience mental module" (in most humans) for assuring automatic personal sacrifice (i.e., incurring short-term loss of personal gain) with results that benefit the tribe, and therefore the tribal gene pool.

3. Individuals to a Social Collective

As our human ancestors evolved along the eusocialized path we developed the most diverse division of labor arrangements of any species. This was achieved with minimal diversity of anatomy and physiology, relying instead on diversity of personality traits. The eusocialized insect species, on the other hand, exhibit extreme examples that involve anatomy and physiology. Among bees, for example, some are "workers" that forsake reproduction tasks. Their body types differ depending on their role in the hive.

For almost two centuries academics have used the term "tribal mentality." It refers to the fact that every tribesman is willing to help fellow tribesmen, but hates and wants to kill men from neighboring tribes. A shorthand phrase captures this: intra-tribal amity, extra-tribal enmity. Or, we tolerate cooperating fellow tribesmen but cannot tolerate any other tribe's men, regardless of how good they are by any objective measure.

These examples illustrate how the individual allows himself to be enslaved to an agenda that contributes to survival of the collective.

Prospect for Humans Completing the Eusocial Transition

Humans may never complete the transition to eusociality for many reasons. E. O. Wilson (2012, Ch. 6) gives reasons for this that are related to the "life cycle" of insects (the role of the queen in founding colonies). Completing the eusocial transition requires that evolutionary forces favoring group selection be more powerful than individual selection forces. I would simply add the following two reasons. Human brains have recently evolved a new thinking capability in the left pre-frontal lobe (see Ch. 5 for a description of brain anatomy and function). This brain region is capable of rational thought, and it is theoretically capable of assessing instinct tricks for serving the genes, and the tribe, that involve a penalty to individual welfare. We can excuse the ant for not anticipating certain death after attacking an intruder, but not humans. The other reason for questioning the likelihood of humans completing the eusociality transition is the questionable likelihood of humans surviving as a species for more than a few centuries. This matter will be treated in the last chapter.

Chapter Summary

Let's summarize the lessons of this chapter. When individuals of a species come together to form a collective that competes with other collectives, and assuming that most individuals of a collective have a "shared fate," evolution will reward tribes consisting of individuals who instinctively exhibit behaviors that serve the collective, regardless of the effect upon individual well-being. When this eusociality transition occurs, it can be said that the individuals are enslaved to the collective.

3. Individuals to a Social Collective

Humans are partially eusocialized: a significant fraction (~ 1.5 %) of human individuals are not eusocialized at all, and the remainder are partially socialized. The un-eusocialized individuals are known as psychopaths, and I refer to those who are slightly more eusocialized as sociopaths (I refer to those who are the most eusocialized as "normaloids"). They are dealt with by the collective in a way that is analogous to the way a body deals with cancer cells: psychopathic and sociopathic individuals are identified by all individuals of the collective and either avoided or removed by either shunning, banishment or murder. This, at least, is how things evolved for possibly a few million years, up to the beginning of the Holocene epoch of warmer climates.

Chapter 4. Three Laws of Life

Gene pools are the level at which evolution occurs. Every coming together of life elements to form a new entity that competes with others of its kind eventually evolves a variety of individual types from what once were a same individual type. Gene pools evolve with no prevision of the end they are achieving.

From previous chapters we can summarize key aspects of life on this planet as behaving according to the following three laws.

Law #1:

Whereas individuals can compete with individuals, and tribes with tribes, it is more useful to think in terms of gene pools competing with gene pools. After all, gene pools evolve on long timescales and the individuals assembled by these genes are short-term combatants for achieving the end of eternal genetic existence. Gene pools evolve, not individuals. The lay person may acknowledge that evolution is something that happened to our ancestors, but no thought is given to gene pool changes that produced this evolution. Genes are mistakenly thought of as serving the individual because they give life to the individual, but the individual serves the genes in ways that are never recognized by the individual.

The uncomfortable truth is that the individual is created by the genes as a way to assure continued genetic existence. Because genes exist for millions of years, while the individual exists for a matter of years, the individual is in fact "enslaved" to the genes! This is accomplished by a brain that is assembled by the genes, with as many as 50 % having influence. The brain is just another organ, like a kidney or muscle, meant to promote survival of the individual long enough to reproduce so that other individuals can carry the same genes into the future.

During most of the ancestral environment (AE) the human species consisted of thousands of gene pools. Sometimes the "other" gene pool belonged to another species. The individuals created by a gene pool are merely a means for the genes to achieve an immortal presence. None of this is "understood" by those genes, nor by their individual creations (with few exceptions).

Law#2:

Whenever like-elements of life combine to form groups that compete with others of its kind, the winning groups are the ones that eventually evolve a diversity of the constituent elements. The previous chapters describe three coming together transitions. After each transition the new entities evolve from "same type" individual entities to "different type" individual entities. This is easiest to understand for Transition #3, when individual organisms came together to form groups of (essentially) same type individuals, such as tribes. Considering the case of humans, and our pre-human ancestors, whereas initially the individuals within the tribe may have been similar, eventually evolution led to tribes composed of individuals who differed from each other in significant ways.

This last transition is the most important one for us to understand, especially for the case of humans. When groups of individuals are joined in winner-take-all competition, and when each tribal gene pool differs in how much diversity exists in the individuals that that tribe's gene pool creates, an evolutionary advantage will usually exist for the tribe that creates a greater diversity of individuals. Every specific tribal need can be met better by the joining of individuals who are better matched to that need than the joining of general-purpose individuals. Because of this "division of labor" we should expect that after the creation of tribal life the pace of evolution should quicken.

For example, each tribe might have a warrior class (analogous to soldier ants). The same tribe might also have artisans who specializes in making weapons for use by the warriors. The same artisans could make tools for use by non-warrior construction workers (e.g., making huts, paths and other infrastructure). Each tribe can be thought of as having a need for a specific percentage of each individual type. If 10 % of tribesmen are needed for warrior duty, another 30 % are needed for construction work, 5 % are needed for artisan duties, etc., tribes that produce individuals with these skills at the optimal percentages will have an advantage over tribes that fail to achieve the optimal percentage. (This is referred to in sociobiology as an "evolutionarily stable strategy, or ESS.)

Law #3:

Living things have no prevision of outcomes. Every living thing exists because its ancestors were successful; pre-adaptations are accidental. For example, a cancer cell has no prevision of its death when the host dies. The same concept applies at a higher level of life, human civilization, as expressed by Bertrand Russell (1903):

Such ... is the world which Science presents for our belief. ... That man is the product of causes which had no prevision of the end they were achieving; that his origin, his growth, his hopes and fears, his loves and his beliefs, are but the outcome of accidental collocations of atoms; ... all the noonday brightness of human genius are destined to extinction in the vast death of the solar system, and that the whole temple of man's achievement must inevitably be buried beneath the debris of a universe in ruins.

The last chapter of this book suggests that the extinction of human civilization may occur sooner.

Chapter 5. Neuropsychology Tutorial

Every brain is assembled by instructions from genes. The brain's posterior lobes determine the many aspects of IQ, and the brain's frontal lobes determine the many aspects of lifestyle strategy. The capabilities and predispositions of the posterior and frontal lobes are quite uncorrelated. Therefore, some sociopaths and psychopaths are gifted with intelligence and talent, while others aren't. Every individual starts life with a somewhat predestined life path.

This chapter provides some useful background for understanding topics treated in following chapters. Whereas this chapter emphasizes posterior lobe function, the next emphasizes frontal lobe function.

In any human population there's a spectrum of traits. When nurture doesn't have an important influence on the expression of a trait in adulthood we can use the term "phenotype" to describe the set of such traits. Thus, a person's phenotype is determined by their "genotype."

Stature is often cited as an example of a genetically-determined trait. For a population in which everyone has the same nutrition stature would be determined 100 % by genetics. (This ignores a few obvious exceptions, such as childhood diseases, etc.) When nutrition varies greatly across a population the opposite can be said: stature is determined almost 100 % by nurture (individual nutrition). This nature/nurture caveat will be assumed to exist for every trait, and I won't dwell on this detail in what follows.

IQ is one of the strongest genetically-determined traits, exhibiting a ~ 70 % correlation for identical twins raised apart. IQ is generated in the "posterior lobes" of the cerebral cortex. Psychopathy is another genetically-determined trait, and it is generated in the "pre-frontal lobes." Figure 5.1 shows where these lobes are located.

Underneath the cerebral cortex is the rest of the brain, consisting of a "limbic system" (where emotions are generated), the cerebellum (located beneath the occipital lobes, responsible for fine motor movement), and the brain stem (responsible for regulating heart rate, breathing, and other basic body functions). Other components exist (such as the reticular activating system, amygdala, etc.) which won't be discussed in the remainder of this book.

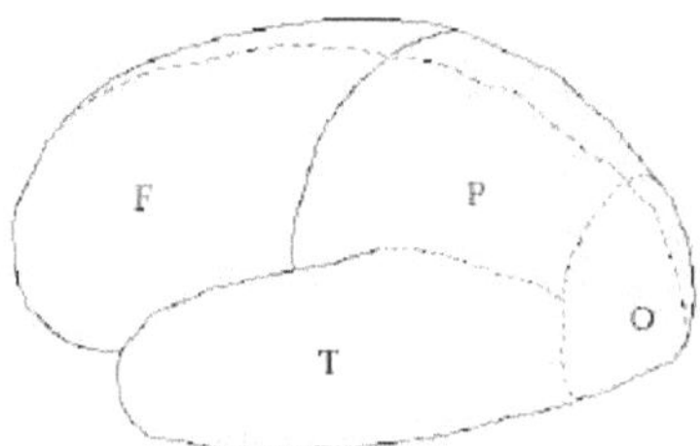

Figure 5.1. *Cerebral cortex brain lobes: Frontal, Parietal, Temporal and Occipital. The P, T and O lobes are collectively referred to as "posterior lobes." The F lobe consists of a "motor strip" along the border with the P and T posterior lobes. In front of the motor strip is the "pre-frontal" portion of the F lobes. The view is of the left side, front is toward the left. The right side of the brain has the same architecture.*

The cerebral cortex is what makes humans human! It has dominated brain evolution during the past several million years of our ancestral evolution. The human cerebral cortex has grown in size faster than any other brain region. The frontal lobes have undergone a growth spurt during the last 1/3 million years.

Specific functions are performed by specific cerebral cortex regions. For example, the production of human speech occurs in Broca's Area, located in the left frontal lobe and shown in Fig. 5.2. Speech reception is performed by Wernicke's Area, located in the temporal lobe of the left hemisphere, also shown in Fig. 5.2.

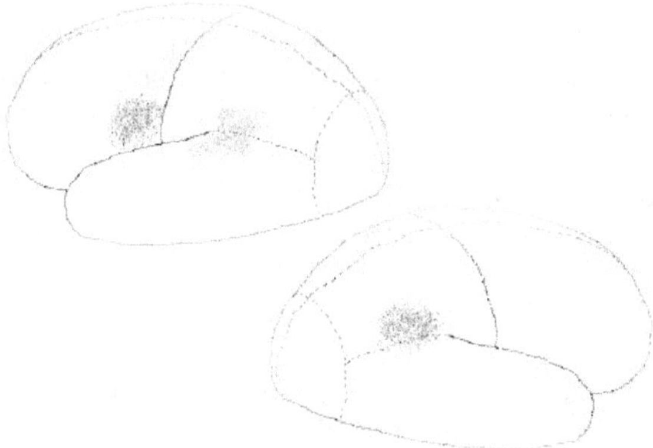

Figure 5.2 *Upper panel shows location of language comprehension area (Wernicke's Area, right-most pattern of dots), and speech production area (Broca's Area, left-most pattern of dots). The lower panel shows the location of the inferior parietal lobule, which monitors the spatial relationship of body parts in relation to the immediate environment.*

5. Neuropsychology Tutorial

The left and right cerebral hemispheres are close to anatomical mirror images of each other. However, they have some functional differences. For example, whereas language reception and production are located in the left hemisphere, spatial recognition tasks are located in the right hemisphere. This is indicated in Fig. 5.2.

Left and right cerebral cortices, which I'll refer to as "left brain" (LB) and "right brain" (RB), have different "wiring." Axons are the connections between neurons. Axons in RB have thicker insulating coverings ("myelination") than in LB. This apparently is an evolutionary response to RB's specialization in "holistic" computing, which requires more long-path connections than needed for "serial" computing. LB consists of many self-contained modules, with short connections within the module, and the modules are connected to each other by a small number of long-connections. LB architecture resembles how common (serial) computers function: subroutines produce an output that is shared with other subroutines. The RB architecture resembles how the rarer type of parallel (neural network) computers function: nodes are connected to other nodes at seemingly random locations throughout the entire network.

Given that LB resembles a serial processor, and RB resembles a parallel processor, it is logical that some tasks are better performed by LB and other tasks are better performed by RB. For example, language production and reception consists of decoding "chunks" of information (phonemes) and combining them with attention to temporal sequence. This computing style is serial in nature, and is therefore found in LB. Facial recognition, however, doesn't have any temporal sequence aspects; it is a holistic task, and it is therefore a capability of RB.

Each posterior lobe is divided into three regions: primary, secondary and tertiary. It's not important to describe this here, except to say that brain architecture is very specific. It is understood, and the genes do an amazing job of creating every aspect of this architecture.

A surprising finding helps to illustrate this. As stated above, performance on an IQ test is completely determined by the posterior lobes. When frontal lobotomies were commonly used on unruly people, changing them from aggressive to passive, it was found that IQ did not change. In fact, some patients had improved IQ.

"Personality" resides in the frontal lobes. A famous split-brain experiment provides evidence for a person's left pre-frontal and right pre-frontal having different life goals (Gazzaniga and LeDoux, 1978). Patient PS, who had undergone full callosal surgery (cutting of connections between left and right cortices) to control seizures, was asked about his job choice; his left pre-frontal answered "draftsman" whereas right pre-frontal answered "automobile race." Another split-brain patient was recorded to be buttoning a shirt with one hand while the other hand was busy unbuttoning.

The most famous example of the "lateralization" of personality comes from an accident in 1848 to an unfortunate Phineas Gage. An unexpected explosion sent a metal tamping rod through his left pre-frontal cortex. After his amazing 2-month recovery he exhibited a totally unexpected personality change. Instead of the friendly person that people knew, he was "fitful, irreverent, indulging at times in the grossest profanity… at times pertinaciously obstinate… he has the animal passions of a strong man." (Harlow, 1868). As I explain in *Genetic Enslavement* (Gary, 2004, pg. 77), where I use the abbreviations RBf for right pre-frontal and LBf for left pre-frontal: *This old example illustrates the well-known finding that RBf language ability is usually limited to profanity, songs and other memorized verbal material, such as the alphabet. A wealth of studies show that LBf is the site of the most advanced human traits, such as conscientiousness, positive social behavior, rationality, strategic planning, and positive affect (mood). LBf is often referred to as the site of executive function. RBf, by contrast, is associated with lack of inhibition, anti-social behavior, emotionality, and negative affect. RBf is more closely connected to the sub-cortical limbic system, the source of emotions.*

Histograms

IQ test scoring is defined so that a population's average IQ is 100 and the standard deviation of the IQ score distribution is 15 points, as shown in Fig. 5.3. Thus, 50 % of people have a below average IQ, and 68 % have an IQ between 85 and 115 (i.e., 34 % have an IQ below 85 and 34 % have an IQ above 115).

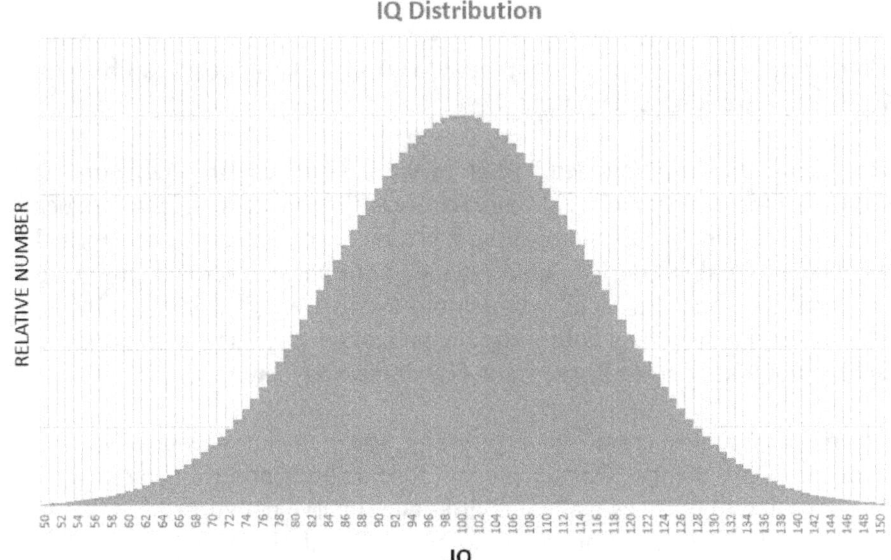

Figure 5.3. *IQ distribution.*

5. Neuropsychology Tutorial

IQ tests consist of many sub-tests; approximately half of them probe performance of the left cerebral hemisphere (posterior lobes), and the others probe performance of the right cerebral hemisphere (posterior lobes). Usually, all sub-test scores have approximately the same score for an individual. Occasionally one sub-test score will be much lower than the others, and in children such a person is identified as "learning disabled." Injury to a specific posterior lobe area could produce such a result.

Frontal lobe performance is more challenging to measure. Several tests exist, but they measure different aspects of "executive function" (e.g., Halstead-Reitan Battery, Montreal Neurological, Luria's Neuropsychological). The Hare Psychopathy Checklist, Revised (PCL-R) can be considered another frontal lobe test, even though it measures a narrow set of behavioral tendencies.

Un-lateralized Brain Architecture

During the 1970's and 80's speculation about brain lateralization was refreshingly wild! Someone wrote an article in *Science* (about 1980) speculating that children with learning disabilities might have had brains that were "wired" with an un-lateralized architecture summarized by the article title: "Two Rights and No Left." The title is referring to the speculation that a brain could have an architecture of RB/RB instead of the usual LB/RB. This speculation was inspired by an apparent correspondence of traits that were often missing for learning disabled children and the traits that split-brain patients exhibited when the left brain was probed.

I have never encountered an article in the neuropsychology literature wondering what a person would be like if their brain was un-lateralized with the opposite architecture, namely, LB/LB, i.e., "two lefts and no right."

About 90 % of people are "right-handed." Most of the left-handed 10 % have opposite brain lateralization. This means that their language areas (Wernicke's Area and Broca's Area) are in the right cerebral hemisphere, along with other capabilities that are normally found in the left brain; and similarly, capabilities that are normally found in the right brain (such as physical maps and facial recognition) are in the left-hander's left brain. For most of these left-handers body control by the prefrontal strips are unaffected (e.g., the left prefrontal motor strip controls the right side of the body, etc.).

This contra-lateral body control cross-over is puzzling, and to my knowledge hasn't been explained by evolutionary theory. The mechanism for this body control means that the motor strip is connected to muscles using a contra-lateral nerve network. About 2 % of people have an "ipsilateral" connection: their motor strips control muscles using a nerve network that is on the same side of the body as the motor strip. (Hooked writing posture apparently improves ipsilateral control, and is a sign of this laterality wiring.) The ipsilateral people are mostly left-handers.

Let's consider the hypothetical LB/LB person. There are two categories of LB/LB, depending on whether the frontal or posterior lobes are involved. Let's first consider the hypothetical case of only the posterior lobes being un-lateralized (LB/LB for posterior lobes only).

With posterior lobes being LB/LB there would be pairs of Broca's Areas (speech production) and Wernicke's Areas (speech reception), one in each hemisphere. Fast-talking, with sometimes incoherent interjections (by a competing other LB), might be predicted. This is common among psychopaths. Such a person can be expected to have enhanced logical analysis skills, or understanding of situations. However, they would be handicapped from a lack of intuitive comprehension of complex social situations (a RB posterior lobe capability), and they would have to overcome this by exerting more conscious analysis. This is in approximate agreement with psychopathy. However, a shortcoming of this hypothetical brain architecture is that the frontal lobes are unaffected, and since "conscience" is likely to be a frontal lobe capability this person would continue to act with a conscience.

So now let's consider the hypothetical person with un-lateralization confined to the frontal lobes (LB/LB for frontal lobes and normal LB/RB for posterior lobes).

For these people thinking and behavior will be influenced by positive emotions and social agreeableness. They will be more logical than normal, and more conscientious. Their control of impulses will be improved. These traits are incompatible with psychopathy, so I think we can rule out this category of un-lateralized brain function as a way to account for psychopathy.

I want to suggest another un-lateralized configuration that may have a better chance of accounting for psychopathy: RB/RB for frontal lobes and normal LB/RB for posterior lobes. (Recall that the previously-cited article for understanding learning disabled children hypothesized RB/RB without specifying whether this was for the frontal or posterior lobes. My reading of the article is that RB/RB was meant to apply to the posterior lobes with no requirement for frontal lobe architecture.)

Considering such a hypothetical person from the perspective of their RB/RB frontal lobes, they would have poor impulse control, poor life-strategy planning and poor follow-through of any formulated plans. They would be anti-social and they would lack a conscience. They would rarely be depressed (because there would be a weak connection with the limbic system). They would lack emotion-driven prosody in their speech, and lack meaningful hand gestures; they would therefore have to learn how to

5. Neuropsychology Tutorial

imitate those emotional components in their communication. All of these traits match psychopathy.

The speculations of this section are really an aside, since they are about "proximal causation" explanations for psychopathy and the goal of this book is a "distal causation" exploration of why contemporaries are discontent with civilization and the role played by psychopaths in producing this discontent. (Notice that I prefer the terminology "distal causation" instead of the pedantic "ultimate causation" version.)

The next chapter is devoted to a description, and definition, of one important aspect to frontal lobe function: sociopathy and psychopathy.

Chapter 6. Sociopathy and Psychopathy

The brain's purpose is to produce "adaptive" behavior. The brain's frontal lobes determine the many aspects of adaptive behavior. When life strategies are disruptive to harmonious group social life, these strategies are sociopathic or psychopathic.

In this chapter I finally present a definition, and description, of sociopathy and psychopathy.

Defining sociopathy and psychopathy are subjective. In any human population there's a spectrum of behavioral traits that constitute life strategies. When nurture has an unimportant influence on the expression of life strategy we can use the term "phenotype" to describe the set of such traits. In this book I will categorize people as belonging to one of four types: normaloid, unreliable, sociopath and psychopath.

The measure I will use for determining these categories is Robert D. Hare's "Psychopathy Checklist, Revised," PCL-R (Hare, 1990). It is the most-used tool for measuring an individual's degree of psychopathology (I'll simply use PCL hereafter). The scoring is based on 20 items (cf. Fig. 6.3), with each item scored as either 0, 1 or 2. The maximum score is therefore 40. Most people score 0, as illustrated in the next two figures.

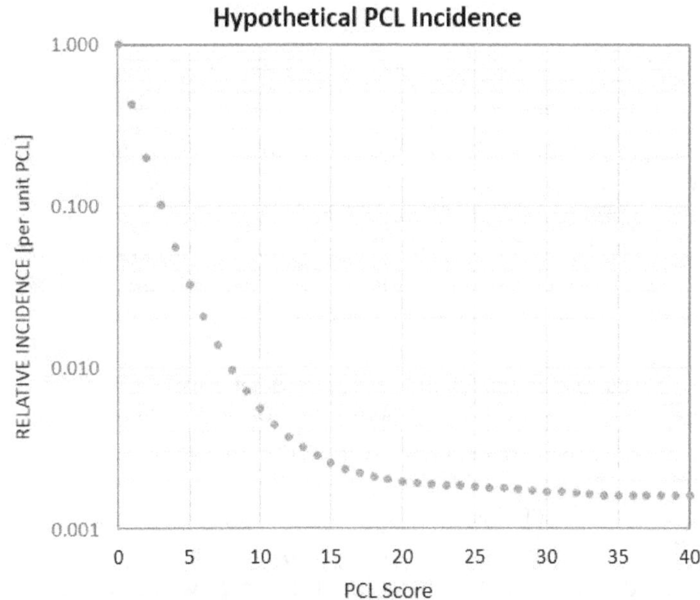

Figure 6.1. *Relative incidence of PCL scores for an American/European population (using a function that is loosely based on data which I devised for illustration purposes).*

6. Sociopathy and Psychopathy

When an individual is evaluated by different qualified people the PCL scores exhibit good agreement (e.g., ~ 3 points). This is one of its virtues. However, it was designed for use with prisoners, not those who have never been incarcerated. Other tests have been created, some specifically for the wider population of un-incarcerated; my choice of relying upon the PCL is therefore somewhat arbitrary.

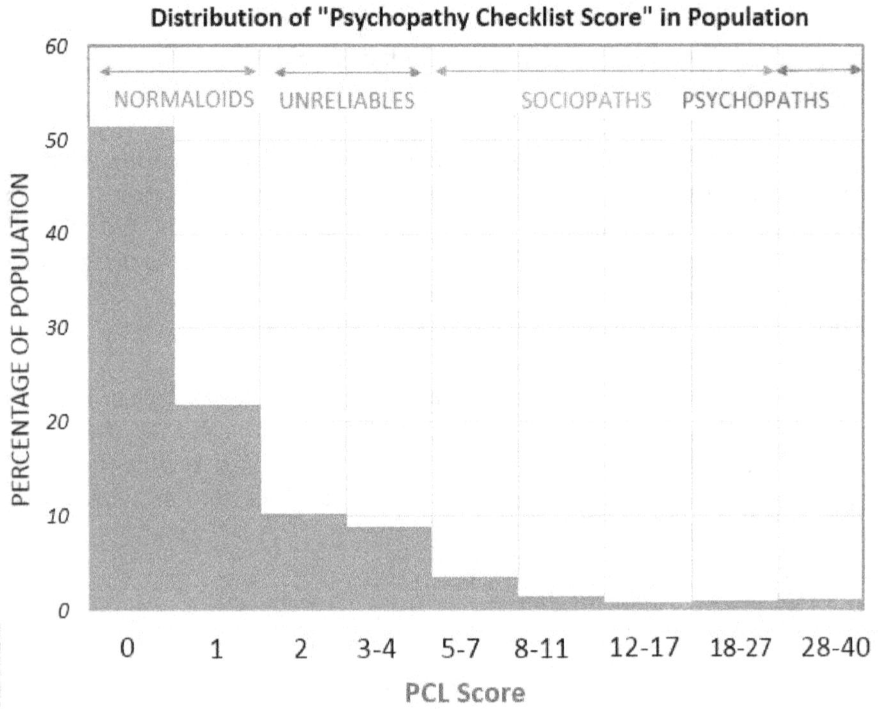

Figure 6.2. *Percentage of a general population with PCL scores in the ranges indicated, based on Fig. 6.1 (for an American/European population, using a function that I devised for illustration purposes). My assignment of a PCL range for "sociopathy" is arbitrary, but is consistent with a measurement of 6 % of the population having "borderline personality disorder" (BPD). Percentages for these four groups: Normaloids = 73 %, Unreliables = 19 %, Sociopaths = 6.6 %, psychopaths = 1.1 %.*

One of the messages of Fig. 6.1 is that psychopathy is a region on a spectrum of measured values. There is no clear distinction between a psychopath and all others since people populate the entire PCL scoring region of 0 to 40. It is therefore somewhat arbitrary where to set the boundary. PCL => 30 is most often used, but PCL > 27 has also been used with essentially the same results. The PCL range for psychopaths is therefore approximately 28 to 40. This PCL range includes 1.1 % of the population, according to the somewhat subjective PCL incidence model I used for Fig. 6.1, which was constrained by adjusting the incidence function (Fig. 6.1) to be monotonic (always decreasing with higher scores) and 2) the integrated distribution between 28 and 40 = ~ 1 %.

Figure 6.3 is the list of the 20 PCL items. Each of the 20 items are scored with either 0, 1 or 2 for the person under evaluation. The scoring is supposed to be done by trained and qualified investigators (not amateurs). Both personal interviews and file records are used in the scoring.

Interpresonal Group

1. Glibness/superficial charm
2. Gradiose sense of self-worth
4. Pathological lying
5. Cunning/manipulative

Affective Group

6. Lack of remorse of guilt
7. Shallow affect
8. Callous/lack of empathy
16. Failure to accept responsibility

Lifestyle Group

3. Need for stimulation
9. Parasitic lifestyle
13. No realistic, long-term goals
14. Impulsivity
15. Irresponsibility

Antisocial Group

10. Poor behavioral controls
12. Early behavioral problems
18. Juvenile delinquency
19. Revoke conditional release
20. Criminal versatility

Miscellaneous

11. Promiscuous sexual behavior
17. Many short-term marital relationships

Figure 6.3. *PCL items, as presented by Hare (2016). The four groups are used for classifying psychopath classes. Factor 1 is based on scores of the first two trait groups (Interpersonal and Affective) and Factor 2 consists of scores for the next two trait groups (Lifestyle and Antisocial).*

6. Sociopathy and Psychopathy

There are high correlations among all items. Nevertheless, a "factor analysis" of PCL scores (Hare, 2003) reveals the existence of two broad categories, or "Factors" (Interpersonal-Affective and Lifestyle-Antisocial). Each of these has been shown by factor analysis to consist of two additional sub-categories (psychopathic, callous-conning and sociopathic, general offender). A specific person will have a PCL profile which will identify them as either psychopathic (and belonging to one of the two Factors, as well as one of the four sub-factors), or not being psychopathic. However, just because someone's PCL score is below the 30 cut-off doesn't mean that they don't share some aspects of psychopaths; they can score very high in one of the Factors and low in the other Factor. For example, whereas 25 % of the prison population are psychopaths, 75 % have high enough scores for Factor 2 to qualify as being "Lifestyle-Antisocial." In other words, whereas only 25 % of a typical prison population can be categorized as psychopathic, another 50 % would be categorized as psychopathic based only on Factor 2 traits. The research about psychopathic profiles is fairly new, and ongoing; speculation about the interpretation of evolutionary adaptive relationships should someday provide very interesting insights.

Sociopaths appear to be a less extreme version of psychopaths. My estimate for the PCL range for sociopaths is 5 to 27. This encompasses ~ 7 % of the population. I'm equating "borderline personality disorder" (BPD) with sociopathy, since the traits for BPD are very similar to psychopathy, but with smaller scores; they have been estimated to comprise 5.9 % of the US population (Hyde, 2010).

The next figure is my attempt to show how a person's inherited IQ and PCL lead them toward specific job categories. I apologize for the highly subjective nature of these speculations, but my purpose is to illustrate a direction for future investigation. Some of the job category placements are inspired by the findings reported by Murphy (2018).

Just as IQ has many posterior lobe components that are lumped into one number, things measured by PCL have many frontal lobe components (and combinations of components, or Factors and sub-factors) that are lumped into one PCL number. Nevertheless, it can be said that when a human embryo is conceived it has a genotype placing it on a life trajectory toward a phenotype that ends up somewhere in the IQ/PCL domain. Rehabilitation of psychopaths is a lost cause, and the same for sociopaths. "The fault, dear Brutus, is not in our stars, / But in ourselves, that we are underlings."

Many parole hearing psychiatrists have been snookered by consummate, smooth-talking psychopaths. Even more lay people who randomly encounter these psychopaths are tricked into trusting them, with a realization that is usually too late. I've been the victim of both types, as has probably everyone reading this book. Psychopaths and sociopaths are a part of everyday life, today; amazingly, everyone seems reluctant to acknowledge this.

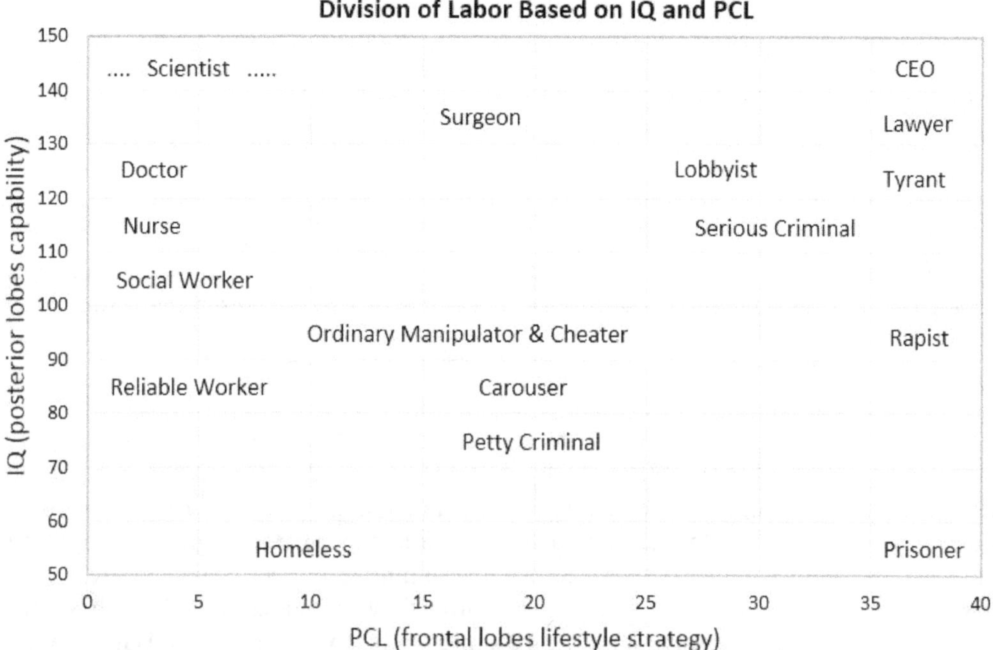

Figure 6.4. *Suggested relationship between job category and a person's IQ and PCL.*

Conscience

The usual description of a psychopath (also frequently equated with "sociopath") is that he or she lies a lot, manipulates others, is charming in the manipulations, likes to achieve power over others, strives to always win, never admits guilt, lacks remorse for victimizing others, has a glib and fundamentally unemotional affect. Most of these descriptions can be efficiently summarized using the phrase: *lacking a conscience.*

The first substantive description of psychopathy was by Hervey Cleckley (1941), who described the psychopath as someone who, in spite of a normal presentation of self, was in fact a master deceiver who had no moral restraints. A few decades later R. D. Hare corrected the impression that psychopathy was a mental illness by clearly stating that the psychopath is untroubled by any of the usual mental illness complaints (depression, anxiety, etc.) because the psychopath had no complaints and no desire to seek treatment for change; the person was simply unencumbered by a conscience! Non-psychopaths had a conscience, and this is what contributed to complaints by some normal people. The title of Hare's breakthrough book reveals how important the concept of conscience is to understanding psychopathy: *Without Conscience* (1993).

6. Sociopathy and Psychopathy

So, what's "conscience"? Consider the following explanation: *"Psychologically speaking, conscience is a sense of obligation ultimately based in an emotional attachment to another living creature (often but not always a human being), or to a group of human beings, or even in some cases to humanity as a whole. Conscience does not exist without an emotional bond to someone or something, and in this way conscience is closely allied with the spectrum of emotions we call 'love.'"* (Stout, 2005). This account illustrates one end of a spectrum of speculations, while the same author describes a speculation from the other end: *"Or is conscience, as more than one sociopath has implied, simply a psychological corral for the masses."* (Note: This author equates "sociopath" and "psychopath," but since she states that 4 % of the present-day population is sociopathic I suspect that she's using a range of PCL scores that includes all psychopaths and the highest scoring half of sociopaths.)

These descriptions of "conscience" are suggestive, but they are missing something. Consider the word "conscientious." It includes "meticulous, scrupulous, careful, principled" and "doing things according to one's inner sense of what's right or wrong." For example, when I conduct astronomical measurements of star brightness using my backyard observatory I adhere to procedures that minimize subjective bias motivated by a desired result. Data cannot be rejected as "outliers" without a credible hypothesis for how they could occur as an artifact (e.g., a cosmic ray hit to a CCD pixel). When I write a scientific paper I am careful to acknowledge relevant publications of previous work, and I am cautious about over-stating results of my work. Being conscientious is a personality trait which probably is genetic (in elementary school a teacher noted on a report card that I was "conscientious").

The conscience, whatever it is and wherever it is located in the brain, is more than Stout's "…closely allied with the spectrum of emotions we call 'love.'" I will leave it to the reader to gradually formulate a fuller understanding of this pivotal concept, which I hope the rest of this book will provide.

This Book's Allegations

With the definition of terms established, I now want to summarize the "sequence of allegations presented for consideration" in this book:

1) Our ancestors started the eusociality transition before our lineage separated from the chimpanzees.
2) A complete transition to eusociality for pre-humans was never possible because of the continuing evolution of "intelligence," a capability of the posterior lobes.

3) The evolution of increasing intelligence threatened eusociality gains (tribal patriotism) because individual enlightenment could in theory lead to individual self-serving behavior.

4) The need to provide a "check" on unlimited self-serving behavior led to the evolution of "conscience," a mental module located in a prefrontal lobe.

5) During the AE only ~ 95 % of humans were fully endowed with "conscience" because ~ 5 % were needed for territorial "border patrol duty," which required uninhibited cruelty to neighbor tribesmen. The ~ 5 % were "sociopaths."

6) During the AE, when all tribes were small (between ~ 100 and 200 individuals), the multi-gene production of ~ 5 % "weak conscience sociopaths" led to ~ 0.5 % of the population having a complete lack of conscience; we now refer to them as "psychopaths."

7) The small incidence of psychopaths posed a negligible threat to small AE tribes because most tribes were too small for them to statistically have a psychopath within the adult male and female population groups (of ~ 50 or fewer adult males and ~ 50 adult females, the two most important constituencies of a tribe with ~ 150 total population).

8) When the Holocene warming began, tribes coalesced into super-tribes, with populations of thousands and more. Civility to strangers from other tribes was enforced, and this led to a discontent with life in the ever-civilizing super-tribe.

9) Those least able to tolerate strangers (i.e., strangers with origins in other tribes during coalescence) preferred living in the countryside, while those more open to strangers preferred living in the super-tribe's city center. This is the origin of "intolerant conservatives" and "hyper-tolerant liberals."

10) The ~ 0.5 % psychopath population was present in every super-tribe, and they could escape detection after disruptive or criminal behavior by simply relocating within the super-tribe.

11) Throughout the Holocene the incidence of psychopaths increased until they reached ~ 1.5 % today. The population of sociopaths has increased to > 6 % (though "sociopaths" somewhat redefined comprise ~ 10 %).

12) Psychopaths achieved dominance in many super-tribe niches, and one of these has been the hijacking of leadership.

13) Hijacked super-tribes are tyrannical, and these societies have had a permanent presence during the late Holocene.

14) Other factors that came into existence as super-tribes became civilized have predisposed the *hoi poloi* in democracies to prefer voting for psychopathic leaders. In "America" this includes: wealth-generated Roobification, blatant

6. Sociopathy and Psychopathy

> gerrymandering (starting in 1988, leading to infiltration of Republican Party by psychopaths and their increasing nastiness starting in the 1990s), internet, Facebook, increasing Russian hackers, Fox News and *National Enquirer*).
> 15) Similar trends exist in Europe. So far our only hope for preserving uncorrupted democracy is New Zealand (and possibly Australia).
> 16) If tyrannical trends continue, global civilizations are at risk of disappearing.
> 17) Sampling Theory can be interpreted as predicting that humanity (as we know it) will cease to exist in ~ 3 centuries (a 50 % probability between 1 and 5 centuries).
> 18) I'm not alleging that psychopaths will be the most important factor leading to the collapse of civilization, but it is worth considering the role they may play.

I conclude with the suggestion for reader consideration that: civilization is threatened by the twin discontents of 1) most people being genetically predisposed to dislike strangers (caused by genes that evolved during an ancestry of millions of years of living in small tribes that were in constant competition), and 2) psychopaths have insinuated themselves into so many aspects of civilized life that everyone else senses their corrupting influence by feeling that the social order favors only those already in power. As general discouragement grows, and as psychopaths gain more power, the continued existence of civilization is threatened. I suggest that there's a 50 % probability that a collapse will occur within the next 3 centuries.

Chapter 7. Poisson Considerations

Whenever a social group, such as a tribe, is dependent upon the presence of at least one individual within a critical category, evolution will provide at least a few such individuals so that there is never an absence of any. When tribal size within the AE is typically ~ 150, and the number of adult males is ~ 50 at any given time, tribal survival requires that 4 or more of all adult males belong to the critical category. This is derived using Poisson statistics. Since 4 individuals is 8 % of this tribe's adult male population, we should consider that it is the sociopaths (~ 8 %) instead of the psychopaths (~ 1.5 %) who protected the tribe from territorial loss by forming border patrol bands.

During the ancestral environment (AE) tribal size was probably within the range of 50 to 200 (tribal fission tends to occur above 150 individuals). Consider a tribe of 60 individuals, consisting of 20 adult men, 20 adult women and 20 children. Assume that every tribe must include a group of at least 3 "ruffians" for patrolling the border (the importance of border patrolling is described in Chapter 9). The same "ruffians" would be needed for organizing tribal warfare. If such a border patrol band cannot be formed the tribe will be at risk of losing territory by challenges from a larger neighbor tribe; it will also be at great risk of being challenged with all-out tribal warfare by a neighbor tribe. Is it feasible that the forces of evolution can reliably produce at least one organizer for the creation of a border patrol (and war party) for a tribe this small?

In previous chapters the reader may have thought that I assigned the role of "organizer" of the 'ruffians" to a psychopath. Let's start with this as a default assumption (overlooking for now the likelihood that a psychopath would perform poorly in this role) and explore its feasibility (spoiler alert: it's not feasible!).

If a tribe with 20 adult males is to have at least one psychopath organizer the percentage of male psychopath births would have to exceed 5 % (and persist for many generations). The term "optimum" implies that more than 5 % would lead to disruption of tribal harmony and less than 5 % would lead to insufficiency.

The first thing to notice is that 5 % is much larger than the present-day best estimate of 1.5 % for the incidence of psychopaths. We can't rule out that during the AE the percentage was greater than today; however, a good case can be made that the percentage is now increasing, so it must have been lower, not larger, during the AE.

The second thing to consider is the possibility that during a generation there could be zero psychopath births among the males who would later assume the mantle of adult tribal protectors. Poisson statistics can be used to assess the probability of this occurring.

7. Poisson Considerations

"Observationalists" are familiar with random event statistics. For "large number statistics" (N > ~ 10) there will exist an outcome probability function, P(N), describing how often repeats of the random events produces the value N. This function will have a Gaussian shape, the 1/e width of which is the standard deviation. The Gaussian width will be square-root of N. For example, if N averages 100 for many measurements, the population of measured values versus N will have a distribution width given by "standard deviation = 10."

When N is small (e.g., N < ~ 10), the Poisson distribution is not Gaussian. This is because negative values for N cannot exist. (Strictly-speaking, even for large N the probability distribution is never exactly Gaussian in shape, because a Gaussian distribution extends from negative infinity to positive infinity.) There is more than one version of Poisson statistics, and the "Geiger counter" version is the appropriate one for the present situation.

Suppose that in the AE there is an optimal number of male psychopaths needed for tribal dominance over others. Consider the case where this number is 1 (for a tribal size of 60, i.e., 20 adult men). Since individual phenotype is determined by individual genotype (for traits with negligible influence by the environment), and since genotype is determined by the random process of the way paternal and maternal genes combine when an embryo is conceived, there is no way that exactly 5 % of male embryos will always be conceived, yielding exactly 1 adult male psychopath in the tribe. During the course of many generations of a tribe there will be differences in N, with departures from the optimum of 1 by different amounts; sometimes N = 2, sometimes N = 3, etc. Sometimes N = 0! Poisson statistics can be used to predict how often a tribe will have different numbers of psychopaths. Figure 7.1 shows this for the case of N = 1 being optimum.

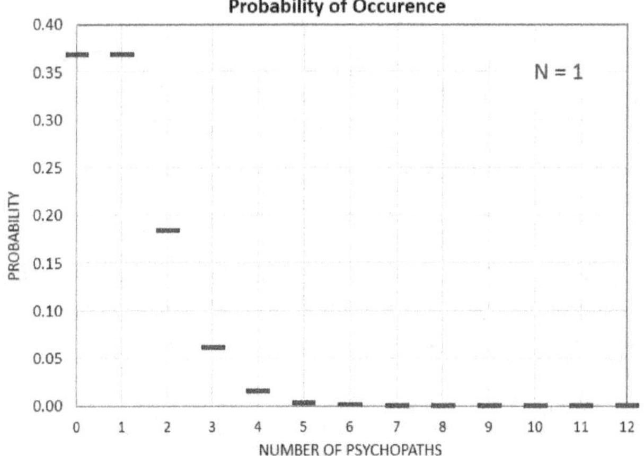

Figure 7.1. *Probability of occurrence of required individual for tribal survival (such as a psychopath) when the optimal number (average) is 1, using Poisson statistics.*

For a tribal gene pool which produces 5 % of the critical individual type (a psychopath, for example), which translates to one critical individual, there's a 37 % probability of producing zero individuals of the critical type, as the previous graph shows. So, in spite of the fact that over many generations the average number of the desired type born is 1, about 1/3 of the time there will be none. Such a tribal gene pool would be doomed!

For this tribe (of 60 total size) to have 3 male psychopaths, for example, the optimal fraction of male psychopath births would be 15 %. The P(N) function for N = 3 is shown in the next graph.

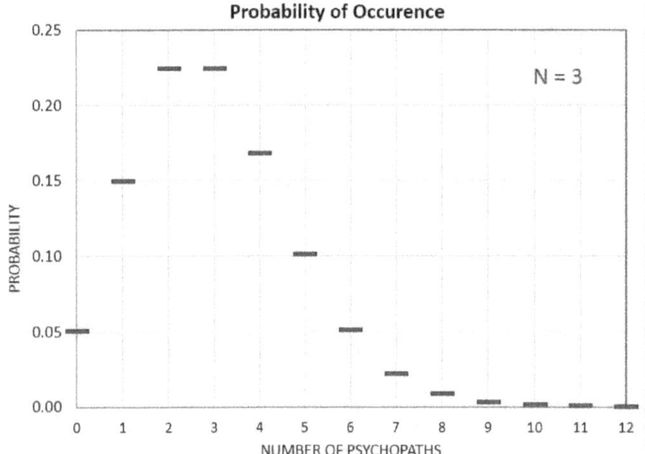

Figure 7.2. *Probability of occurrence of psychopaths when the optimal number is 3, using Poisson statistics.*

This figure's message is that ~ 5 % of the time the sequence of tribes under consideration will have <u>no</u> psychopaths! This would also be dangerous! If a psychopath leader is needed to form a border patrol band, with several sociopathic followers, and if a tribe has no psychopath leader, the tribe would be at risk of losing territory, or not forming a war party when needed. If only one generation were unprotected by psychopaths the entire tribe would eventually be vanquished!

A tribe needs to have several types of whichever individuals are critical to tribal survival. Some individual types are more essential than others. For example, a full-time tool-maker, who makes weapons for the warriors and tools for construction work, is not as essential as the individual who is capable of forming a border patrol band and inter-tribal war party. This is because weapons and tools can last more than one generation, but border skirmishes and the requirement of tribal defense when attacked are roles that can't be neglected for even one generation.

7. Poisson Considerations

We are therefore forced to consider the importance of those that are currently categorized as scoring below the threshold for psychopath on the PCL test, namely, the sociopaths. Whether the PCL score threshold of 27 or 30 is used the number of present-day psychopaths is only ~ 1 or 2 % (according to Hare, 2016). What percentage of "psychopaths" is needed for a robust representation during many generations of tribal history? Let's reconsider the Poisson distribution for N > 4, shown in Fig. 7.3.

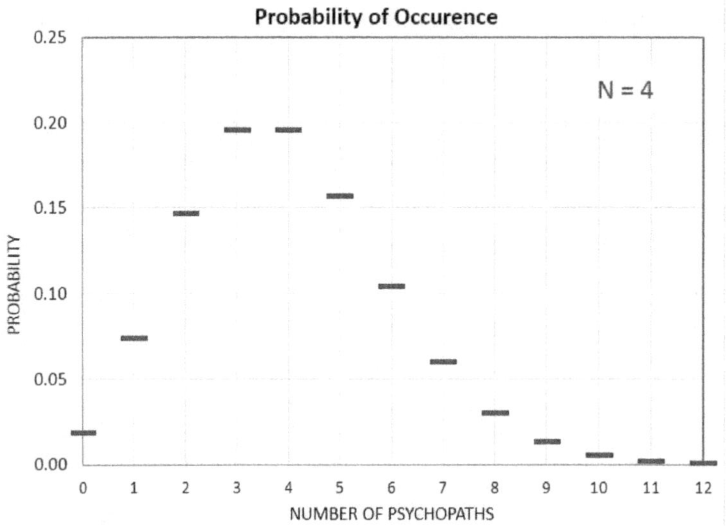

Figure 7.3. *Probability of occurrence of psychopaths when the optimal number is 4, using Poisson statistics.*

This graph shows that when the tribe's optimal number of "essential individuals of a specific type" is 4 there is a negligible probability (2 %) that any single generation will have zero of them. This is a safe strategy, but where on the PCL distribution is there a sufficient number of newly-defined "essential individual types" to provide N = 4?

For a typical tribal size of 150 (~ 50 adult men) 4 of these warrior types corresponds to 8 %. For the smaller tribe of 60 (~ 20 adult men) 4 of these warrior types corresponds to 20 %.

Let's reconsider Fig. 6.2 (repeated on next page) with our quest for an approximate 8 to 20 % of the population with the highest PCL scores.

The combined population of sociopaths and psychopaths is ~ 8 %. This is close to the desired 8 % that assures that tribes with typical population size of 150 will always (98 % of the time) have a sufficient number of high PCL scoring individuals for the existence of border patrol and warrior personality types. Adding the "Unreliables" to the "Sociopaths plus psychopaths" yields 27 %. This would be adequate for providing security to tribes as small as ~ 50.

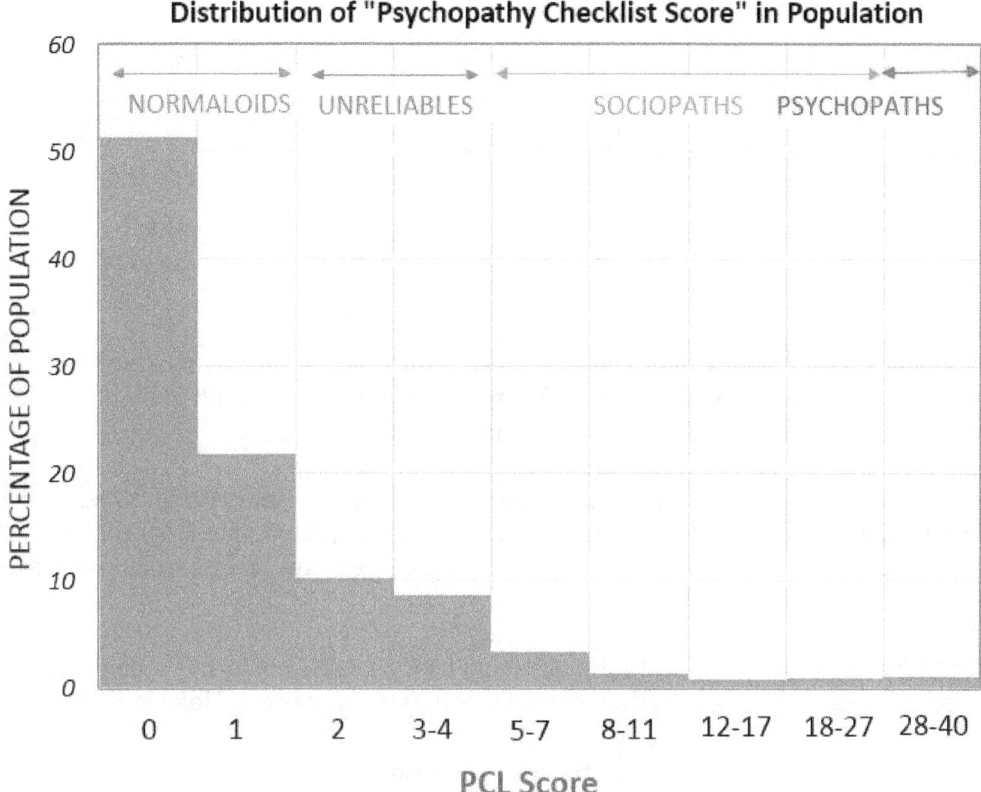

Figure 7.4. *An approximate histogram showing percentages of a present-day population with score in the indicated ranges.*

The consideration of Poisson statistics leads us to consider the possibility that sociopaths (and occasionally "unreliables") have an important role to play in tribal affairs. They, in the absence of psychopaths, could handle border patrol and warrior duties. These individuals will exist for essentially all tribes (~99 %), or the entirety of a single tribe's history.

We should also keep in mind that the incidence of the population with scores distributed along the PCL dimension is uncertain (cf. Fig. 6.1). In addition, when considering AE tribes we may not be able to use the present-day distribution of PCL scores.

7. Poisson Considerations

Sociopaths are the Critical Individual Type

I suggest that sociopaths are the "ruffians" who provide border patrol protection, and who form war parties when they are needed.

If this is the case, then what's the role of the psychopath? Psychopaths have been described as lousy soldiers (Hare, 1993) because they lack discipline, are impulsive and can't form bonds with comrades. They are so socially disruptive that if they can't be recruited by the sociopaths to perform border patrol and warrior duties reliably they are candidates for having no positive role in any tribe!

If psychopaths are the unwanted male type, then why do they exist? Why haven't the forces of evolution removed their numbers, while leaving the sociopaths to protect the tribe?

Multi-gene theory may be the explanation. According to this speculation, evolutionary forces reward sociopath genes, while tolerating a few hyper-sociopath individuals (i.e., the psychopath) who inherit too many sociopath genes.

Tribal culture may be important in channeling sociopaths into useful roles, while controlling psychopaths. This subject is so new, and unexplored, that it is probably too early to take strong positions on any interpretation of how useful sociopaths and psychopaths are to the AE tribe.

We also have plenty of speculating to do about how culture's control of sociopaths and psychopaths has changed from the small-tribe AE to the super-tribe Holocene.

I'm looking forward to future progress in this new field.

Chapter 8. Multi-Gene Considerations

An individual's genotype can be thought of as a random combination of genes from the individual's tribal gene pool, which in turn is a subset of the species gene pool. When a gene location has more than one variant the alternative allele may be rewarded by evolution for its presence in heterozygous individuals in spite of its homozygous expression being mal-adaptive.

Among the 3 billion "base pairs" of human DNA ~ 0.1 % differ from person to person (i.e., 3 million base pair differences). Protein-coding genes comprise ~ 1.5 % of the entire genome, so there are ~ 45,000 base pair differences among the ~ 20,000 protein-coding genes. In other words, a typical gene has ~ 2 base pairs that differ among individuals. An individual with 46 chromosomes in each somatic (body) cell will have the same 40,000 genes in each cell. Most of them will have base-pair differences. However, a base pair difference at an isolated location (SNP, or single-nucleotide polymorphism) usually has no phenotypic effect. Chunks of base pair differences are more likely to influence phenotype. For a hypothetical chunk size of 100, for example, ~ 200 genes (with phenotypic effects) will differ from other individuals. It is possible that individuals differ from each other on the basis of 100 to 500 genes that have two or more alleles.

It has been estimated that ~ 20 % of "human genome" differences are mainly brain related, and another 30 % have lesser influence on the brain. An allele might affect many traits; this is referred to as pleiotropy. For example, the "Ellis-van Creveld syndrome" causes its carrier to have the following traits: 6 fingers, short stature and heart murmurs. These phenotypic effects are seemingly unrelated, yet they are caused by just one allele.

Before continuing I want to state that psychopathy, and probably sociopathy, are strongly determined by genetics. Hare (1993) writes "…the behavior of psychopath is notoriously resistant to change."

Let's begin with the simplest case possible: one gene location having only two alleles. Let's use "a" to refer to the most frequent allele, and "A" to the less frequent allele. The frequency (or incidence) of A is F(A). If F(A) = 0.10, then 10 % of this gene pool's population has the A allele. Since an individual has a paternal and maternal gene allele at each location, there can be individuals with the following allele combinations: aa, aA, Aa and AA. This notation assigns the first letter refers to paternal inheritance and the second letter refers to maternal inheritance; aA and Aa have the same effects on trait profile. The aa and AA individuals are said to be homozygous (one for "a" and the other for "A"), while the aA and Aa individuals are heterozygous. The probability of producing individuals who are homozygous for "a" is P(aa) = 0.89. The probability of producing individuals who are heterozygous is: P(aA) + P(Aa) = 0.10. The probability of producing individuals who are homozygous for "A" is P(AA) = 0.01. Note that these heterozygous

8. Multi-Gene Considerations

aA and Aa individuals, and the homozygous AA individuals, can have many traits that differ from the more common homozygous "aa" individuals.

Now consider the situation with two gene locations, each with two infrequent alleles: A and B. Their frequencies are F(A) and F(B). The possible allele combinations for individuals is: aa, aA, AA, bb, bB, BB, aB and Ab. There's no need to derive probabilities for these combinations because present purposes are served by merely stating that a modest number of gene sites with a small number of alleles are capable of producing individuals with an immense number of trait profiles.

Sickle cell anemia is a "single gene, two allele" situation: the aA individual is protected from malaria while the AA individual suffers from a usually fatal death. It can be said that the A allele is adaptive because the majority of individuals are aA, and are protected against malaria, while a minority (4 % in Africa) "pay the price" for a benefit enjoyed by the majority.

A similar argument might justify the suggestion that "the genes for sociopathy are adaptive, in spite of a minority of carriers who are homozygous for the sociopath gene and are psychopaths." The very simplest multi-gene model that can be imagined for providing an account of sociopathic and psychopathic minorities is a "one gene, two allele" model. According to such a model the "aa" individuals are "normaloids," the "aA" and "Aa" individuals are sociopaths and the "AA" individuals are psychopaths.

Another way to state this is:
    Normaloids are homozygous for "a"
    Sociopaths are heterozygous ("a" and "A")
    Psychopaths are homozygous for "A"

A more realistic model would involve either more alleles for a single gene location or more gene locations that are multi-allelic.

A careful reader will notice that I am arguing for a gene that produces psychopathy, whereas the true situation may be that psychopathy was always the default condition for ancestors prior to the ancestors of chimpanzee and humans first experiments with eusociality. The genetic problem would then be why did some people begin advancing along the eusocial path, eventually leading to most people being somewhat eusocial, while ~ 1 % remained un-eusocialized. Would the arguments of this chapter still apply? Yes, we could then state that A is the new allele with eusocial traits, and simply associate the normaloids with "AA," sociopaths with "aA" and the psychopaths with the original "aa" genome.

Another alternative is that another gene inhibits expression of normaloid "a" gene by "covering" it and preventing it from producing proteins. We would then be dealing with "aa" and "cC" genetics, where the "C" gene covers the "a" gene (via the "methylation" process) and the "c" gene doesn't.

As far as I know the status of research on this matter is insufficient for taking a position on any of these alternative models. For present purposes, it is not necessary to favor one or the other alternative.

This chapter's goal was to present an argument for sociopathy being adaptive in the AE, while characterizing psychopathy as a mal-adaptive consequence of needing sociopathy genes. I think this goal has been met.

For the purposes of this book it is not necessary to take a position on how the genes produce "normaloids," "unreliables," "sociopaths" and psychopaths." We know this happens, and there are genetic mechanisms that can achieve the observed results.

I hope the foregoing does not give the impression that only one or two genes are responsible for causing an individual to be psychopathic. The authors Glenn and Raine (2014) provide a full account of current thinking about the genetic underpinnings of psychopathy, with the usual caution and caveats required of all academics. They write "…we will never be able to use genes to predict which individuals will become psychopathic or persistent criminals. In reality, hundreds and maybe thousands of genes are involved, each of which makes a small contribution…" (pg. 47). It's my impression that these authors are near one end of a spectrum of academic cautiousness, in which every position has some validity. I think it would be fair to state that at this time we don't know whether psychopathy is produced by just 2 or 3 genes, with a few alleles, versus thousands of genes with two or more alleles.

Chapter 9. Dunbar Number

Our ancestors spent most of their millions of years living in tribes with populations of 100 to 200 individuals. Smaller bands of men performed specific tasks, such as hunting, construction projects and border patrol. Human nature evolved for the social setting of small tribes.

A eusocial species form collectives with characteristic numbers of individuals. Humans form tribes, and the most common tribal size is about 150 (less important peaks exist at 50 and 500, as described below). Tribes with a structure that favors a total population peak near 150 may exhibit population variations over time between 100 and 200. When tribal size grows toward that upper limit, tribal fission is likely to occur. A charismatic leader will collect a small following and leave the tribe in search of some promised land. When a tribe goes below the lower limit, there is a strong incentive for the tribe to grow. All tribes have "ownership" of a territory. Hunting and gathering occur within that territory. Somewhere near the center of that territory is a settlement which serves as a home base for most tribesmen.

Border Skirmishes

Tribes are a social collective, and like all social collectives they compete with each other. Consider, again, the most frequent conflict category between tribes: skirmishes between small bands of individuals at territorial borders. E. O. Wilson (2012, Ch. 8) called attention to the similarity of human border skirmishes with those practiced by chimpanzees; he summarized the latter this way: *"Chimpanzees live in groups ... of up to 150 individuals, which defend territories ... Within each of these ... small parties form ... averaging 5 to 10 strong ... The patterns of collective violence in which young chimp males engage are remarkably similar to those of young human males. ... The purpose of the raids on neighboring communities is evidently to kill or drive out its members and acquire new territory."* E. O. Wilson surmises from this similarity that humans have been behaving this way for 6 million years, or since whenever the human and chimp lineages diverged.

Imagine that during the AE human tribes of ~ 150 individuals were organized in a similar way to the chimpanzee bands of ~ 150 individuals. Consider the 5 or 10 individuals within the band of males that spend time near the tribe's territorial border, looking for an opportunity to engage in a skirmish to attack and possibly kill a lone individual, or smaller band, from the neighboring tribe. If those individuals liked picking fights, and if they were uninhibited by empathy for fellow humans of another tribe when they were fighting, that band would have an advantage in prevailing during the skirmish. Border skirmishes not only protect territory, they can enlarge territory by stealing it from neighbor tribes. Every tribe must have had a few such males, which I will refer to as "ruffians" (which the last chapter identified as resembling today's sociopaths). A tribe with ruffians would therefore benefit in competition for territory compared to a tribe without ruffians.

Using round numbers, these tribes of 150 individuals would number about 50 adult men, 50 adult women and 50 babies and children. The men associated with mostly each other; and they traveled throughout the tribal territory. They defended territorial boundaries, hunted, made weapons and tools and built huts. The women mostly associated with each other and did food gathering safely within tribal territory while avoiding territorial boundaries. Their social lives were mostly confined to each other and maternal matters.

If a tribe's population decreased significantly, a neighbor tribe that noticed this might conclude that the smaller tribe was vulnerable. This is how inter-tribal warfare might begin. Successful warfare leads to increasing territorial size and population capacity. The importance of tribal size for inter-tribal warfare outcomes is illustrated by studies of our closest related species, chimpanzees. Michael P. Ghiglieri writes (2000, pg. 175) "... male chimps ... waged war on a neighboring community only when it ... was a lot smaller and weaker than their own community, containing half or fewer adult males."

Because of the importance of being prepared for either initiating inter-tribal warfare, or defending the home tribe from warfare initiated by a neighboring tribe, tribal survival depended on the social cohesiveness of male tribesmen. If there were 50 adult men in a tribe, all 50 men must have been able to trust each other during battle. Trust is built upon a history of interpersonal experience. With lifetimes of maybe 40 years during the AE there are limits to the number of interpersonal relationships that can be assessed for trustworthiness. The Dunbar Number of 150 is usually explained as the maximum tribal population size that provides a sufficient number of interpersonal assessments needed for establishing trustworthiness for the subset of the tribe that must work together. For the tribal social structure given above, in which adult males form a cohesive association, a tribal size of about 150 (total for men, women and children) determines the value for the Dunbar Number.

Within a tribe the adult men form small bands for specific tasks. Hunting parties may be one of the most important and enduring band. Infrastructure construction and maintenance (huts, trails, storage structures, wells, etc.) will have optimum numbers for those tasks. Border patrol is an ever-present need, so those bands may form and remain stable with the same men. How many men would be needed for each band? Of course it would vary with the task, but we can be guided by a propensity for present-day sports teams to number 5 to 10 members. Present-day sports teams consist of this number of players (basketball = 5, baseball = 9, football = 11, Army squad = 4 to 10, etc.). In sports teams every member has a special role, so we can assume that within the AE tribal team

9. Dunbar Number

special roles also existed, and each member was chosen for their role based on ability for that role. Teams of 5 to 10 men may have also been typical during the AE.

When the optimum total tribal size is close to the Dunbar Number we can assume that the social structure involves the trusting cooperation of adult men. Inter-tribal warfare would require the participation of all able adult men. Mutual trust among all warriors is important. Since 50 is approximately the maximum number of people that can have a sufficient history of associations for achieving a reliable reading of trustworthiness for each other, the Dunbar Number of 150 is a natural consequence for total population size.

Other social structures exist, and lead to other optimum "community sizes." Dunbar and Sosis (2017) cite the following peaks in the histogram of tribal sizes: 50, 150, 500. Presumably these less common but still present smaller and larger population size "attractants" correspond to different social structures.

The next chapter is a speculation on the rarity of psychopaths during the AE, and the relationship of psychopathology with brain size.

10. Eusociality, IQ and Conscience

This chapter is devoted to a very simple idea that is almost impossible for most people to understand. The human path along a eusocial transition modifies individuals to behave in ways that preserve group prosperity and dominance over other groups. When humans began evolving higher intelligence during the eusocial transition, possibly 1.8 million years ago, it became possible for individuals to question their instinctive self-sacrificing behavior. The tribes whose gene pools evolved an additional mental module for "checking" this questioning, and preserving patriotism, enhanced their group performance. This new mental module is now called "conscience" and it provides a moral framework for justifying automatic and unquestioning patriotism.

Transition #3, eusociality, requires that most individuals change their allegiance from self (and close kin) to the collective, which for humans is the home tribe. This simple-sounding change in allegiance is somehow nearly impossible for most people to fully understand. The thought is like the visual blind spot in each eye's visual field that is conveniently overlooked. At least it's possible to prove to someone that they have blind spots by asking them to cover one eye and try to see something that moves into the blind spot of the other eye. But thoughts are sometimes more difficult to prove. This chapter is devoted to trying to prove something that is conceptually easy to understand but resistant to the contemporary with a "conscience." I will explain this cryptic statement in due time, starting with a description of the eusocial transition for the AE small tribe.

Examples of Eusociality

Tribal allegiance means that occasionally an individual will sacrifice self-interest for the good of the tribe. An example would be food sharing after a hunt. The hunter and his family may want to gorge themselves, but the tribe is better served by sharing. OK, that was easy – right?

Now consider helping your neighbor build a hut. This labor, and the time it took, could have been spent on improving one's own hut, or merely relaxing and watching the neighbor struggle with tasks needing another pair of hands. Offering to help could accrue future rewards to self, I acknowledge, since "a favor made is a favor returned." This reciprocity was converted to mathematical equations by Hamilton (1964), and now goes by the name "reciprocal altruism." You may therefore object to this as an example of eusociality, but it still could be.

Suppose a fellow tribesman is poor at making his hunting tools, such as a hatchet, or throwing spear. A better craftsman might offer to demonstrate how it's done, or simply make one and give it to the less able tribesman. Again, you may object by pointing out that a craftsman who helps another tribesman strengthens the tribe, which contributes to the helper's prospects for survival. Indeed, and this is what eusocialization is all about.

10. Ancestral Psychopaths

Since tribal survival relies upon hunting and gathering within a territory that can be safely moved within by home tribesmen, tribes need to prevent territorial encroachment by a neighboring tribe. The "ruffians" who patrol the border are ready to attack and kill any individual (or small group of individuals) belonging to the neighbor tribe. Because these border patrollers expose themselves to deadly encounters they must be eusocialized; after all, the main beneficiaries of their behavior are the fellow tribesmen whose hunting and gathering within tribal territory sustains the tribe.

When the tribal patrol "ruffians" attack vulnerable neighbor tribesmen they are not only protecting the home territory, they may also enlarge the home tribe territory by a small amount. The history of skirmishes may reveal the merits of all-out tribal conflicts. When one tribe is attacked by another, all healthy adult males will be expected to join as warriors defending the tribe, according to the eusocial explanation. Again, you might argue that if the home tribe were to be overwhelmed the vanquished would either be killed, enslaved or impoverished – and this would include everyone who was weighing the option of joining the battle – so joining the battle is in one's self-interest. My response to that objection is that just one man out of 50, for example, is unlikely to change the outcome of an inter-tribal conflict. Eusocialization predicts that all adult males will join in all-out inter-tribal conflicts.

My final example will be more difficult to argue with. Change places with the other tribe, the one that initiated the attack. It is a home tribe for its individuals, so when this other home tribe decides to initiate an attack on their neighbor tribe how should the healthy adult men respond? If they have been eusocialized they will readily, and unthinkingly (this is key), join as warriors for attacking their neighbor tribe. When one tribe attacks another we can assume that a calculation has been made, involving an assessment of how many healthy adult men are present in each tribe, allowing the attack decision to be made based on a favorable count. (Among chimpanzees, the rule of thumb is that the other group should have half or fewer healthy adults before the decision to attack is attractive.)

When a home tribe decides to initiate inter-tribal warfare the chances are good that it will either win, obtain a partial victory, or retreat due to stalemate. One of the goals of the Yanomamo (indigenous Indians of the Venezuelan jungle) when they decided to attack a neighbor tribe was to abduct women (Chagnon, 1983). Women were treated as a resource for tribal population growth. I allege that every able-bodied adult male joined in the attack even though a single individual would usually not affect the outcome. This joining is most easily explained by eusociality!

Increasing Intelligence Threatens Eusociality

Human brain size has approximately quadrupled since our lineage separated from the chimpanzee lineage. The increase has been described as exhibiting two growth spurts, the main one starting at ~ 1.8 million years ago (Homo habilis) and the second and less dramatic one starting at ~ 300,000 years ago (Homo sapiens). An increasing brain size is associated with increasing intelligence. It is tempting to assume that the first brain growth spurt was mostly in the posterior lobes, and the second one was mostly in the pre-frontal lobes. This is based on the fact that embryology tends to recapitulate phylogeny, and during embryology the pre-frontal lobes are the last to develop.

Posterior lobes provide "situational understanding" whereas pre-frontal lobes produce "lifestyle behaviors." If the first growth spurt was mainly due to posterior lobe enlargement then it would be correct to state that it produced an increase in IQ (since IQ resides in the posterior lobes). Brain size and IQ estimates are shown in Fig. 10.1. In this figure I have arbitrarily adopted IQ to be proportional to the cube of brain size.

The evolution of increasing IQ had its risks. As "situational understanding" improved, so did the individual's capability for questioning his eusocial enslavement to the tribe. For example, the most intelligent individual in the tribe might ask the following: *"Why should I join my fellow tribesmen as they prepare to invade a smaller neighbor tribe? After all, our territory is secure, and life is stable, so who cares if we increase tribal territory? This will just increase our tribe's population, and when it gets too large there will be a splitting of the tribe and we'll end up with the same population and the need to shrink territory back to what it is now. Oh, I know! This entire process increases my tribal gene pool; so all of these instincts to invade the poor neighbor tribe is just for helping our genes become immortal. To Hell with the genes! They are just using me for their purposes! I'm staying home; let the poor fools who don't understand this, the low IQ ones, risk their lives by invading the neighbor tribe."*

This imaginary soliloquy by a high IQ tribesman illustrates the threat posed by IQ to maintenance of tribal eusociality. Recall, a tribe is strongest when everyone is in unquestioning agreement with the merits of patriotic behavior. Even chimpanzees have an observable level of eusocial development. They are capable of sympathy, maintain inter-personal bonds, they maintain border patrols and engage in occasional inter-tribal warfare. Their commitment to a level of eusociality is not threatened by IQ because their IQ is low. The human commitment may have begun to be threatened during the interval of fast IQ increase that started 1.8 million years ago, indicated in Figure 10.1 by the time interval label "B".

The individuals who posed this threat resemble today's psychopaths because their behavior involves "conscious, calculating thinking." (I use the term "proto-psychopath" for pre-Holocene and "psychopath" for Holocene for reasons to be described later.) Let's try to "game out" this unfolding drama with reasonable speculations.

10. Ancestral Psychopaths

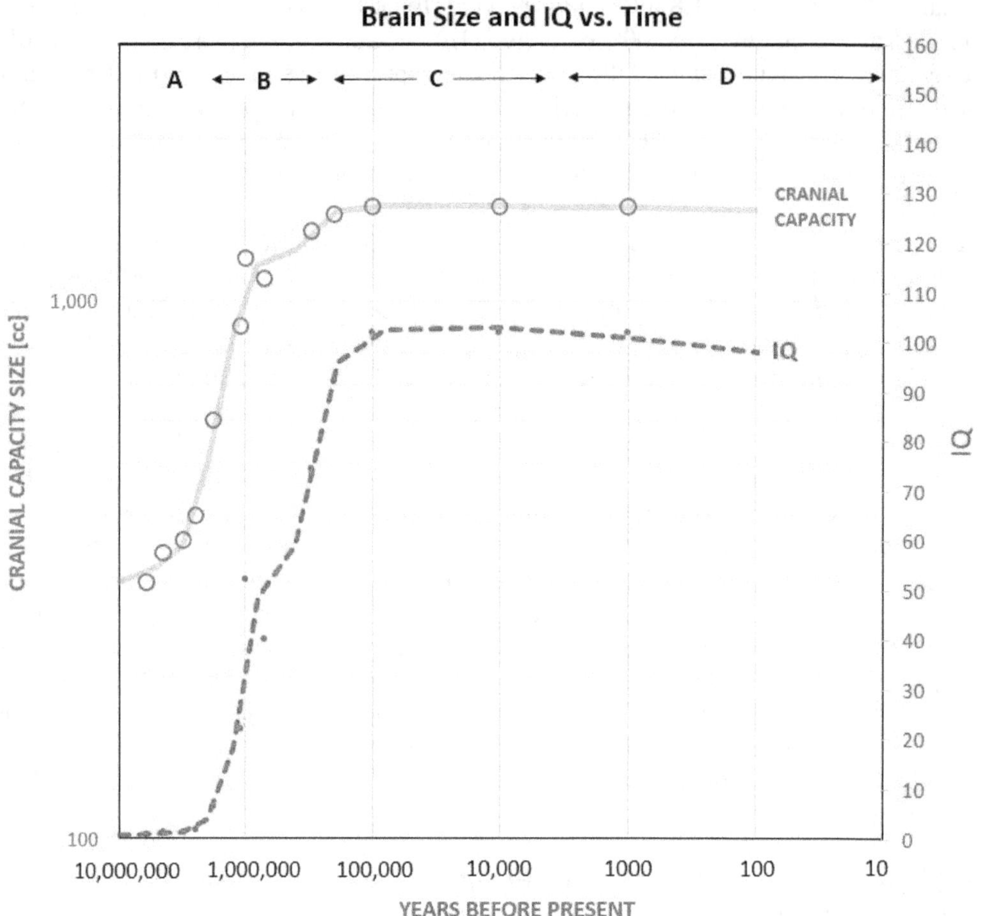

Figure 10.1. *Brain size, based on cranial capacity, versus time. The IQ plot is arbitrarily taken to be proportional to "cube of capacity." (The time intervals are described in the text.)*

Starting sometime late in the IQ rise that began 1.8 million years ago, the B time interval, the numbers of proto-psychopaths was increasing such that their tribal incidence" approached one. In other words, before this critical time few tribes included a proto-psychopath, but afterwards the probability of any given tribe being "infected" by a proto-psychopath was greater than 5 %, or 50 %, etc. Figure 10.2 illustrates a possible scenario of increasing proto-psychopath incidence. During the IQ rise that begins at ~ 1.8 million years ago the incidence rises from zero to the above cited critical levels of 5 % to 50 % presence per tribe. The maximum is at ~ 200,000 years ago.

I assume that proto-psychopathy was zero before the B time interval (time interval A) because psychopathy requires a sophisticated ("street smart") understanding of other people. It also requires a cunning ability for deception. Each of these mental traits was rapidly increasing during the time interval B.

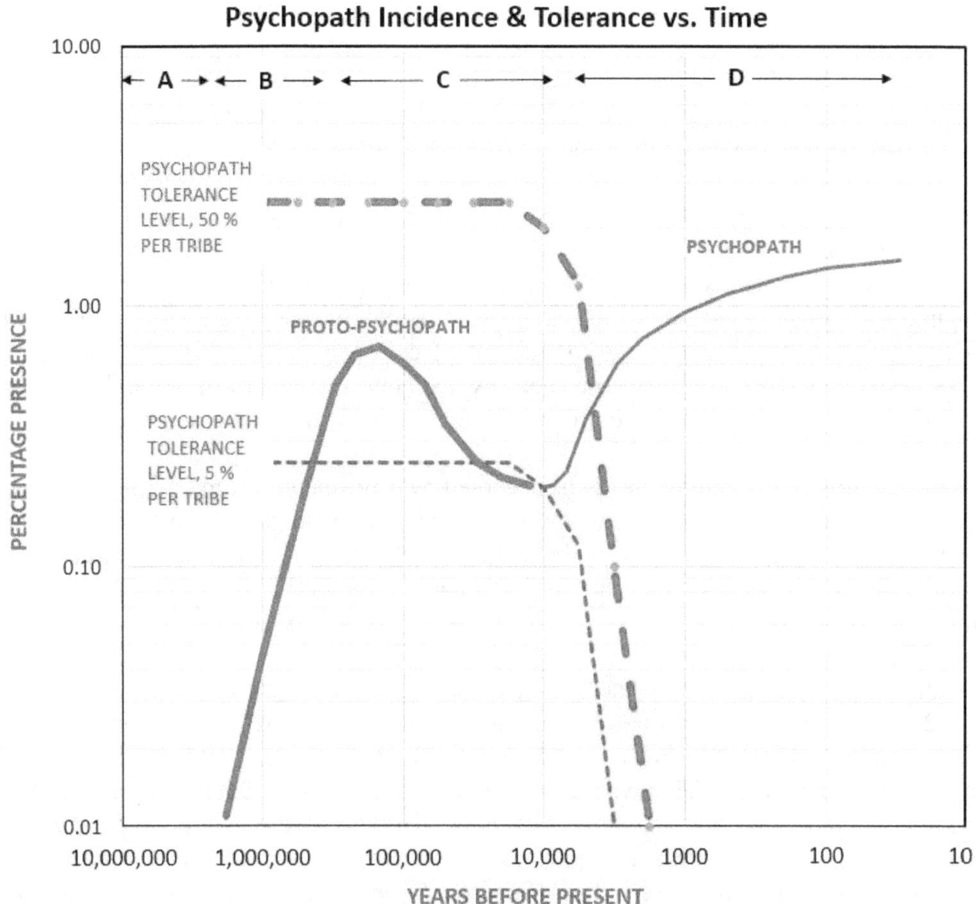

Figure 10.2. *Illustration of possible change in the incidence of the proto-psychopath (before Holocene) and psychopath (during Holocene) in relation to tolerable levels for psychopathy (dashed traces) based on tribal size. During the interval labeled B brain size was growing fast, giving rise to the calculating proto-psychopath. During interval C a "conscience" mental module that imposed "morality" upon behavior was evolving; this reduced the adaptive value of psychopathic behavior, and reduced proto-psychopath incidence. During D tribes were coalescing, allowing psychopaths to roam freely within the super-tribe without detection at each new location. (The proto-psychopath and psychopath traces are not based on data, but are for illustration purposes only.)*

10. Ancestral Psychopaths

Why wouldn't proto-psychopathy simply continue to rise above the critical levels? The answer, I propose, is the cultural evolution of "morality" followed by the mental module evolution of **conscience**!

Evolution of Conscience

If some tribes overlooked the trend of increasing social disruption caused by proto-psychopaths, and the resultant weakening of patriotic fervor, they would be at a competitive disadvantage with neighboring tribes that somehow responded to reduce the penalties of the new psychopath influence. But what could a tribe do?

The first thing tribes could do is undergo the cultural evolution of an invented "morality" for the protection of eusocial behavior. This "morality" would identify individual slackers (lacking patriotism) for punishment by other tribesmen. Cultural evolution is fundamentally random, so some tribes may have adopted the required "culturgen" while others didn't. (A "culturgen" is a component of culture that has a specific purpose.) Tribes that adopted the morality culturgen (by accident, presumably), would have been winners since they would be more prosperous and stronger than their neighbors.

However, every new culturgen has to be accepted by tribesmen for it to be fully effective. We should expect resistance of any new imposed behavior, regardless of how valuable it may be for tribal survival. Even the winning tribe can expect to experience some discomfort with the new culturgen that demands loyalty to this funny new "morality" thing.

Any discomfort among individuals in the winning tribe meant that an evolutionary reward was present for any genetic mutation that relieved this discomfort. In theory, a new mental module in the brain could have evolved that incorporated morality and executed it automatically. This would have reduced discomfort with the culturgen. Any tribe that included individuals with this new mental module, which we now call "conscience," would be rewarded with not only fewer individual slackers but lower levels of discomfort with the execution of moral behavior. This is my suggestion of how a "conscience mental module" evolved.

Where would such a mental module reside? Most likely in the left pre-frontal cortex. This is based on present-day findings from split brain patients whose study reveals differences in left and right pre-frontal cortices. The left is consistently pro-social, and the right is consistently asocial. A fuller description of this was given in Chapter 5.

When might this have occurred? How about 300,000 years ago? That's when the *Homo sapien* brain growth spurt began (in the pre-frontal lobes)!

We can now interpret the Fig. 10.2 time segment labeled C. That's when most tribesmen were evolving a conscience. A conscience secured their unthinking patriotism. Approximately 99 % of tribesmen (i.e., everyone who wasn't a proto-psychopath) eventually evolved a conscience. With a conscience in place, "conformance" could evolve. Conformance is applying "social pressure" on fellow tribesmen with lesser developed consciences. Conscience and conformance are a natural pairing: one constrains personal behavior and the other applies the same constraints on others.

Conformance could provide a check on proto-psychopaths. The adaptive value of psychopathy would be reduced when conformance was applied within the tribe. This brought the incidence of proto-psychopaths to low levels (shown as ~ 0.2 % in Fig. 10.2), which meant that AE tribes at the end of time interval C didn't have to deal with psychopathy's socially disruptive effects (except on rare occasions).

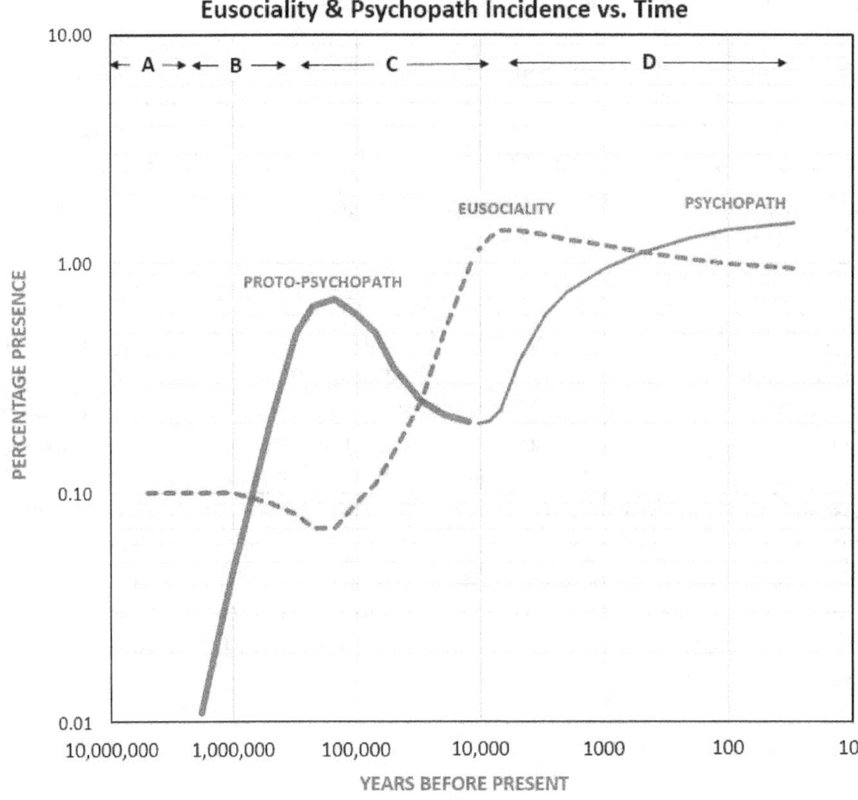

Figure 10.3. *Hypothetical relationship between level of eusociality (arbitrary scale) and psychopathy versus time. (All levels and shapes are for illustration purposes only; they are not based on data.)*

10. Ancestral Psychopaths

The mental module that produced a conscience, and that also commanded conformance to others, had the result of restoring and enhancing eusociality. A hypothetical plot of the level of eusociality (using an arbitrary scale) is shown in Fig. 10.3.

Throughout the time interval labeled "C" tribes could continue to evolve an ever increasing diversity of talent among individuals (improving the value of division of labor), and thereby gain in eusocial strength.

No Logical Basis for Obeying the Conscience

Being good, or doing the right thing, is equivalent to living one's life in accordance with one's conscience. It's difficult to acknowledge that this has no logical basis! The reason for this difficulty is that it suggests that psychopaths are more logical than normaloids, and if we believe that living logically is better than living enslaved to some genetic trick, called conscience, then we end up legitimizing the psychopath.

The flaw in this argument is the allegation that living logically is what we should strive to do, or that we even have "free will" for choosing to do this. Living logically is never what people do because of the way our brains are constructed. Is sexual intercourse logical? It's a trick of the genes. What about wanting children and raising a family? Another trick. Or the immense satisfaction for many old people in having grandchildren? It's a genetic reward for being an obedient slave.

In my book *Genetic Enslavement: A Call to Arms for Individual Liberation,* chapter after chapter illustrates how illogical human nature is. My last chapter in that book addressed a possible reader concern that I was justifying abandonment of good behavior (i.e., justifying psychopathy) by revealing how illogically enslaved people were to the genes that assembled them. So in that chapter I argued that by revealing everyone's enslavement to good behavior, regardless of logic, I would have no effect on anyone's behavior. This position was justified by my assertion that good people couldn't help themselves; our behavior is good because we are born "good." In other words, we behave in ways that our genetically-assembled brains dictate, so gaining insight is just a fun thing to do, and is completely harmless. (Professional psychologists might have a different opinion, and to some extent they are occasionally helpful. I should therefore be prepared to apologize for exaggerating a point.)

The Situation before the Holocene

To the extent that conscience imposes a check on logical thinking, and thus preserves eusocialized behavior (which includes the most important category, "patriotism"), humans have been enslaved to the genes that assembled a conscience ever since that mental module evolved. When this mental check was in place it became acceptable for the genes that assemble humans to evolve greater intelligence. It is amusing to note that the evolution of something in the left pre-frontal lobe ("conscience") allowed for a continuation of the evolution of something in the posterior lobes (IQ). This apparently has been a winning strategy for at least 300,000 years.

Throughout the time intervals A, B and C tribes continued to maintain tribal territories, and they competed with each other for retaining or expanding territory. Border patrolling continued, and a small population of "ruffians" for this duty continued to exist. The population of "ruffians" was maintained at maybe ~ 10 % (as an "evolutionary stable strategy"). A majority of each tribe (~ 90 %) kept the tribe viable through such mundane and daily sustaining activities as hunting and gathering, the building and maintaining of infrastructure, tool and weapon making, etc..

When tribes began to coalesce in response to their shrinking territory during the Holocene warming, a super-tribe could not tolerate the same incidence level of psychopaths that existed before the Holocene. For example, a super-tribe of 3000 total population, with ~ 1000 adult men, would require that the incidence of psychopaths be lower than 0.1 % in order that such tribes had a lower than 50 % probability of being "infected." An incidence higher than that would almost guarantee the presence of at least one psychopath, who would remain in the super-tribe as he moved after each local detection. Therefore, during the time interval indicated by the letter D the incidence of psychopaths is expected to increase. This is just a "taste" of the immense changes that occurred during the Holocene.

At the start of the Holocene warming (~ 11,700 years ago) proto-psychopathy would have been brought to low levels, low enough that few tribes had to deal with the problem. So, when the Holocene began, here's where things stood:
1) almost everyone (99 %) had a "conscience" and understood the "the difference between right and wrong,"
2) these people felt compelled to do "right" and not do "wrong,"
3) they enforced "conformance" on everyone in the tribe, using social pressure, thus maximizing everyone's preference for doing "right,"
4) the strength of "conscience" varied across the tribal population, with ~ 10 % of them (the "ruffians") having a weak enough sense of morality that for them there was no hesitation about killing neighbor tribesmen at territorial borders,
5) the incidence of proto-psychopaths was low enough that most AE tribes had none,
6) the level of eusociality was at an all-time high.

The next few chapters deal with how the Holocene "changed everything"! The groundwork of those chapters will allow a more informed discussion of why I distinguish between proto-psychopaths and psychopaths. In those later chapters I will discuss other aspects of the Holocene traces in the figures of this chapter.

Chapter 11. AE Immune System

Every transition that involves a joining of elements to form a new level of organization requires a change of allegiance from the lower level to the higher one, and this requires some method for assuring that non-compliance is identified and dealt with. Transition #2 is useful in understanding how the human Transition #3 (the "eusociality" transition) has floundered in accomplishing the analogous task. Sociopaths and proto-psychopaths are an essential part of this story.

When single cells came together to form a multi-cellular organism the slow forces of evolution hit upon the immune system as an effective mechanism for identifying cells that weren't cooperating and which threatened the viability of the organism. The three categories of cells that were identified for destruction are cancer cells (or pre-cancerous cells), cells that had mutated in a way that changed their functionality, and aged ("worn out") cells that had slowly lost functionality (i.e., senescence).

I don't know enough about ants, bees, termites and naked mole rats to use them for illustrating how their transition to eusociality was accompanied by the evolution of ways to enforce the transition of loyalty from those individuals to the social collective of their respective colonies by ridding themselves of pre-collective selfishness. Therefore, I will attempt to use human examples of how the Transition #3 process may have worked. I will resort to the immune system analogy as much as possible.

Ancestral Environment Immunity Experiments

This chapter is restricted to what may have happened during pre-history, referred to by sociobiologists as the "ancestral environment" (AE). I will depart slightly from this definition by arbitrarily assigning the AE to times before the Holocene epoch, which began 11,700 years ago (when glaciers began to melt and recede, ushering in our present warm inter-glacial period). The next chapter will consider changes occurring during the Holocene. The reason for this distinction is that during the AE, before the Holocene, all human tribes are thought to have been small (~ 150), whereas during the Holocene some tribes grew in size to very large populations. I will argue that large tribes provide a social environment that is different in significant ways from the small tribe environment, and this difference means that some genetic and cultural adaptations that evolved during the AE were either ineffective or dysfunctional during the Holocene.

The human analog of a senescent cell is an old person. For tribes that are constantly moving, an old person is left behind if they can't keep up. For itinerate tribes the handicap of an old person is more of a challenge. In some of these societies it is customary for an old person to ask to be killed. An extreme solution was developed by the Ache of Paraguay: some young men were given the job of killing old people.

The human analog of a cell with a deleterious mutation is someone who is born disfigured, or retarded. The Spartans threw defective babies over a cliff. The schoolyard bully illustrates how a flawed person who survived to childhood might have been "weeded out" of a tribe. Initiation rituals serve a similar purpose for boys who survive to young adulthood. Those who fail the initiation rite are social outcastes, which is a kind way of removing them from the tribal breeding pool.

Cancer cells and proto-psychopaths resemble each other: both look out for themselves without regard to any other of its kind in a collective. Just as the cancer cell can be thought of as relapsing to cell behavior that existed before cells combined to form an organism, a proto-psychopath could be thought of as a human who behaved like humans may have behaved before they lived in tribes. I now believe that the origin of psychopaths is more complicated. First, during the AE the proto-psychopath must have evolved in response to evolutionary pressures by the majority of tribesmen who had adopted "morality," and who had evolved a "conscience," and who enforced "conformance" upon all tribesmen – including the proto-psychopath. Second, the proto-psychopath and psychopath may have been an unwelcome side-effect of the evolutionary rewards for male sociopaths. The argument for this position will be presented gradually throughout the next few chapters.

When I became interested in this matter I initially thought that the leaders of the border patrol bands would be psychopaths, and the follower males would be sociopaths (those who were slightly less psychopathic than the psychopaths, but were more numerous). However, for two reasons I changed positions, in favor the idea that the border patrol is composed of males in the following three categories: sociopaths, unreliables and maybe even some normaloids (cf. Fig. 7.4 for how these PCL groups are defined). One reason for this change is that present-day psychopaths make lousy soldiers because they lack discipline, and are incapable of caring for their fellow soldier (i.e., are incapable of feeling camaraderie and forming "got your back" bonds). Psychopaths also avoid conflict when it doesn't serve their personal interests (they would say that patriots are suckers). The other reason, as explained in earlier chapters, is that psychopaths comprise too small a fraction of any human population and they may not even be present in some tribes (cf. Poisson statistics, Chapter 7 and the previous chapter). If a tribe couldn't form border patrol bands, for example, they would be vanquished as soon as a neighbor tribe figured out that they couldn't defend their territory.

We should expect that the forces of evolution will assure that a sufficient number of ruffians for border patrol and warrior duty are usually present in a typical tribe (this is an example of what sociobiologists refer to as an "evolutionary stable strategy"). The number of ruffians in these tribes could be about 5 or 10 for border patrol duty, out of 35 to 60 men. The ruffians who patrolled the border allowed the others within tribal territory to engage in the productive labors of hunting and gathering with less concern for attack by neighboring tribesmen.

Whereas border skirmishes were a nearly continuous form of conflict, paleontology evidence suggests that neighboring tribes occasionally engaged in open warfare (e.g., prehistoric mass graves and palisades, Keeley, 1996). It is likely that ruffians played an important role at those times, either as tribal chiefs or warriors. It is reasonable to imagine that whereas the tribal ruffians victimized neighboring tribesmen while on border patrol, they were a core for the formation of a larger force for all-out inter-tribal warfare.

Note that a niche for ruffians is an example of "division of labor." Also note the similar role of "border skirmish ruffians" to the soldier ants or bees whose role is attacking anyone getting too close to the ant colony or bee hive. Finally, note that ruffians are analogous to the creation of protective skin during Transition #2.

Female Sociopaths and Proto-psychopaths

During the outbreak of inter-tribal war all male sociopaths and unreliables, and almost all of the normaloids must have joined the border patrol ruffians in forming a warrior force. The occasional proto-psychopath may have pretended to be a warrior, all the while finding ways to avoid danger. Only the artisan who makes tools and weapons would be allowed to stay home with the women and children when warfare broke out (Gary, 2014, Chapters 10 and 11). In this way all able-bodied males could be viewed as helping the tribe as eusocial members. What about the female sociopaths and proto-psychopaths?

The female sociopaths and psychopaths had no useful border patrol role, and most likely had no useful warrior role. The primary value of females for the tribe was making babies and raising children. In fact, wars were sometimes initiated for the abduction of females, who would be brought back to the home tribe (Chagnon, 1983). They were valued for their baby-making capability. Even chimpanzees sometimes abducted female chimpanzees from another group (they never abducted males from another group). As long as they made babies, and weren't socially disruptive, the female sociopaths and occasional female proto-psychopath were welcome.

A female proto-psychopath probably couldn't control herself enough to avoid being socially disruptive. Within a small tribe they would have been quickly identified. Some toleration of their disruptiveness could have been an acceptable response because the proto-psychopath woman was able to make babies, many of whom would have been sociopath males - a needed commodity. By this reasoning there should have been even more tolerance of sociopathic women.

Proto-psychopathic men, however, had no redeeming value (except for their role in fathering sociopathic babies). They weren't reliable enough for border patrol, and there might not have been any useful roles for them during intra-tribal warfare.

Dealing with Sociopaths and Proto-psychopaths

I'm assuming that during the AE all tribes were small. This allowed for easy identification of the four categories of potentially disruptive individuals: male and female sociopaths, male and female proto-psychopaths. Any "tribal immune system" must have been most concerned with the male and female proto-psychopath categories.

A male proto-psychopath was likely to be more socially disruptive than useful for a tribe. The anthropology literature has evidence for how tribesmen dealt with the outwardly disruptive person. As already mentioned, an African hunter/gatherer man who was disruptive was ambushed and murdered by fellow tribesmen. The prehistoric Hawaiians used a "throttle cord" when their disruptive target was next to a tree.

A female proto-psychopath had more value to the tribe than her male counterpart because she was a good source for the creation of sociopathic male babies. Since the AE tribe was small enough for the other women to identify proto-psychopathic women as untrustworthy, their socially disruptive effect was somewhat limited because avoidance and shunning could be employed to minimize their disruptiveness.

It is unsurprising that a histogram of tribal size exhibits a peak at the Dunbar Number (Dunbar and Sosis, 2017). When tribal size grows much larger the proto-psychopath (both male and female) become more difficult to identify since interpersonal interactions between any two tribal members is reduced. It is ironic that this problem might have been solved by a male proto-psychopath "charismatic leader" collecting a following and marching off to an imagined "promised land." I wonder if the genes, in their infinite wisdom, evolved this trick for preserving the tribes that they created (as means for the genes to achieve immortality).

Morality, Conscience and Conformance

As speculated in the previous chapter proto-psychopaths began to appear, and rise in incidence, during the brain expansion interval that started ~ 1.8 million years ago. The niche for unscrupulous behavior came into existence as IQ, and "situational understanding" improved. By 300,000 years ago the incidence of proto-psychopaths could have become large enough that small tribes had a non-negligible probability of having one or more proto-psychopaths. At that time there might not have been any tribal cultural traditions, or social instincts, that prepared the rest of the tribesmen for dealing with the proto-psychopath's social disruptiveness.

11. AE Immune System

An immune system's first task is to identify the component of the collective that needs to be either sequestered or eradicated. If we use today's understanding of the psychopath as a stand-in for the AE's proto-psychopath we would state that the tribal proto-psychopath would have been identified as the person whose work style was erratic, who didn't follow-through with promises, who stole, lied, and who couldn't be trusted for any tribal duties. But we don't know what the proto-psychopath was like, and how many of today's psychopath traits we can ascribe to him. I will simply state that the proto-psychopath must have been identifiable and that his presence was socially disruptive. Because much of this section's discussion relates to what was treated in generality in the previous chapter, a crucial figure from that chapter will be repeated (next page).

Assuming the proto-psychopath was identifiable, what immune response measure could have been taken to minimize, or remove, his socially disruptive effects? In the last chapter I suggested that cultural innovations were probably the first measures taken. A simple culturgen would have been "avoidance" of the unusual individual. Note: whereas the present-day psychopath is a master at imitating normalcy, this sophisticated capability probably didn't exist for the proto-psychopath. The culturgen of "shunning" is more extreme than avoiding, and it might have been employed. Banishment may have been difficult to accomplish, but it's another possibility. Murder by ambush is a final option, and we know that during the Holocene this was sometimes practiced.

Once a culturgen is adopted by a tribe there are rewards for a genetic accommodation. As explained in detail by Lumsden and Wilson (1981) when a new culturgen is adopted there will be rewards for the incorporation of the associated behavior in the brain's pre-wiring. In other words, when a culturgen has been adopted for a long time there will eventually follow the evolution of a genetic predisposition for the culturgen's behavior.

Consider the concept of "badness" and the placing of another person's behavior into that category: stealing is bad, not sharing food is bad, lying is bad, etc.. If this is accomplished somehow by culture, and if this cultural construct becomes elaborated to include many things as being bad, we have the beginnings of a culture of "morality." The longer this culture of morality endures in tribal history, the greater is the likelihood that brain pre-wiring will include some automatic categorizing of things observed as belonging to "badness." The way someone responds to things observed and categorized, such as badness, becomes part of the "morality" mental module that is evolving.

The value of having a "morality mental module" is that it helps in the automatic recognition of bad people, and provides guidance for our behavior with them. Morality can also include "good" things, and help us identify good people and guide us in our behavior with them.

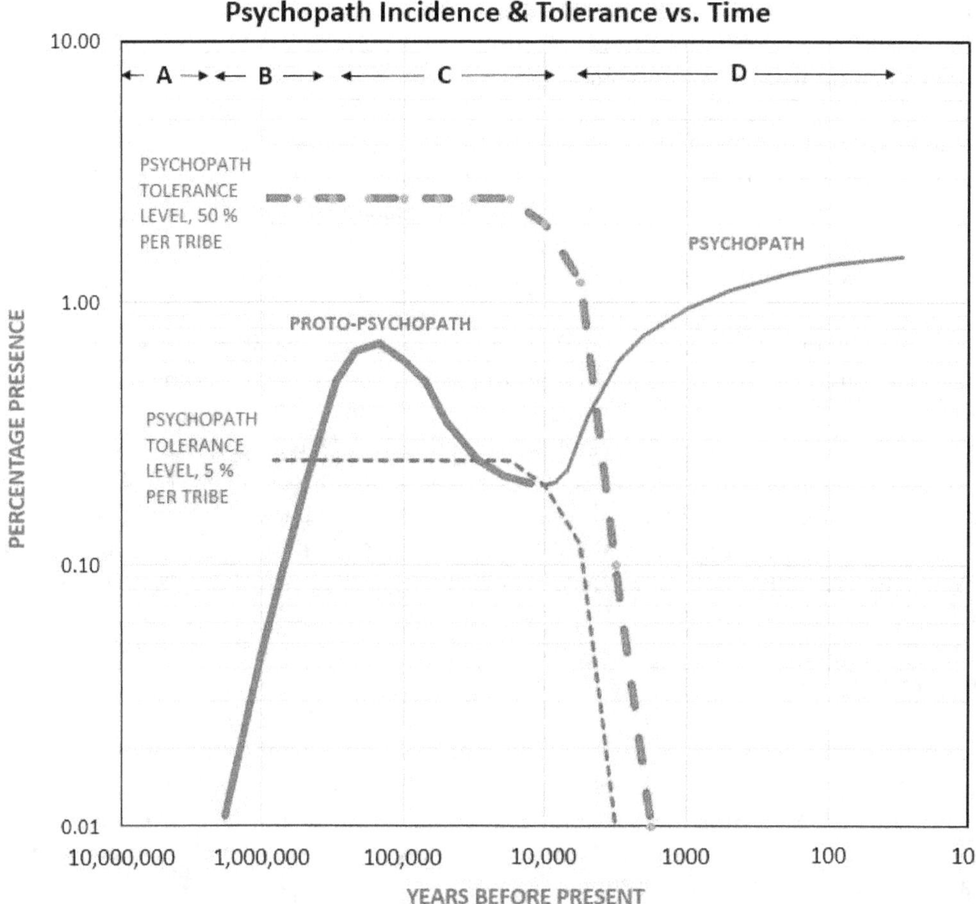

Figure 11.1. *Repeat of Fig. 10.2.*

It's a small step for the morality module to evolve the capability for identifying in one's own behavior things belonging to good and bad categories. The next evolutionary advance is the capability to conform one's own behavior to be compatible with the morality that was initially used to categorize other people's behavior. This entire package of capabilities is what we now refer to as "conscience."

Each step in this evolutionary advance sets the stage for another advancing step. The final step in this process, as I understand it, is to enforce others to behave in conformance with the same morality that we have accepted for ourselves. If nearly everyone in a tribe shares the same morality, then conformance is just a matter of enforcement. Conforming one's own morality to the one widespread in the tribe is part of the process, but somehow it occurs automatically. Conformance of morality and behavior is a major accomplishment along the path to ever greater eusociality.

11. AE Immune System

Such conformance was not needed for the ants, bees, termites and naked mole rat along their transition to eusociality because they lacked a thinking brain capable of thinking thoughts that needed to be reined-in.

[As an aside, one of my principal complaints with civilization is that the collective tells the individual what thoughts are permitted (e.g., "political correct" thoughts). As a farm boy I recall a horse's rejection of having a halter placed over its head; it chafes at the restrictions of the loss of freedom when this is done. As much as I want my tribe to survive, I also want the freedom to think outside my tribe's sanctioned realm.]

When most of our AE ancestors evolved a primitive version of morality, and then a conscience, and when they enforced conformance upon all tribal members, any proto-psychopath in the tribe would have been handicapped. The incidence of proto-psychopaths, who by definition lacked a conscience, must have declined. The reduction of proto-psychopaths must have secured the eusocial transition. By the time of the sudden beginning of the Holocene the incidence of proto-psychopaths must have reached a minimum. By that time all small tribes had "tools" for minimizing the proto-psychopath's socially disruptive effects. As the next chapter will show, these tools were incapable of working during the Holocene.

Chapter Summary

This chapter has been mostly a review of concepts implicit in the previous chapter. I have relied upon much speculation in imagining the effects of sociopaths and proto-psychopaths on AE tribes, and how tribesmen dealt with them. I have tried to imagine how the social collective's "immune system" came into existence and adapted to changing needs in those ancient times.

The male *sociopaths* were tolerated because they played a useful role in preserving or expanding tribal territory by joining small bands that attacked neighboring tribesmen in border skirmishes. They were also useful to the tribe during inter-tribal warfare.

The occasional male proto-psychopath would have had minimal usefulness to tribal welfare. He could not be relied upon for border patrol duty, and he might not have been reliable enough for use during inter-tribal warfare. If he was too disruptive he might have been banished or murdered.

The female sociopath wasn't useful for border patrol duty, nor was she employed as a warrior during inter-tribal warfare. She was, however, useful in making babies, some of whom were male sociopaths. The female sociopath could be tolerated, provided her social disruptiveness was not excessive.

The occasional female proto-psychopath may have fared better than her male counterpart because she could make sociopath babies. Avoidance and shunning might have been a common way of tolerating these women.

The biggest challenge for the small AE tribe, as brain size increased, and IQ rose, was how to constrain the socially disruptive effects of the male proto-psychopath. I speculate that a cultural form of morality was adopted, and it was eventually incorporated as a "morality mental module" for automatic action. This was followed by the evolution of conscience for constraining one's self behavior. Eventually, the constraint by a conscience upon self was extended to other tribesmen, which we refer to as conformance. Only the proto-psychopath escaped the new burdens of morality and conscience; however, he could not escape the social pressures of conformance. This led to the decline of his kind during the last few centuries before the start of the Holocene.

What are the similarities and differences between Transition #2 and #3? They are similar in that the first step for a collective is to identify individuals who are a threat to the collective's survival. Whereas in Transition #2 such individuals were marked for destruction (apoptosis), Transition #3 made a distinction between threat types. Sociopaths performed a useful role of protecting the tribe in the way that skin protects the individual organism. The proto-psychopath was tolerated within limits, with distinctions between male and female proto-psychopaths. If the male proto-psychopath was too disruptive to tribal harmony his murder was an option. If the female proto-psychopath was too disruptive, she could be tolerated by avoidance and shunning.

Before the Holocene began there may have been a stable "steady state" between the forces of good and evil. The normaloids had evolved a "mental module conscience" that relied upon morality for enforcing conformance upon all tribal individuals; this constrained the occasional proto-psychopath and minimized his disruptive threat to tribal eusociality. For as long as tribes were small, and proto-psychopaths were always identifiable, the human experiment with the eusocial transition was preserved.

Chapter 12. Thought Experiments for the A. E.

The Ancestral Environment, AE, is important for understanding human nature, a nature that we're burdened with during our experiment with civilization. Any attempt to understand contemporary dysfunctions should begin with an understanding of the world our natures have prepared us to inhabit. One of these "dysfunctions" is the presence of rape among humans, intra-species war and feeble intellectual curiosity (i.e., a lack of interest in self-discovery). This chapter will attempt to understand the origin of these human traits, as well as the immense diversity of human abilities.

Imagine a region during the AE where a few HG tribes are undergoing the usual and chronic inter-tribal conflict over territory. Each has a few ruffians (sociopaths) who like warfare, or at least feel driven toward it. They are more numerous than their infamous "cousin" the proto-psychopath. The two categories resemble each other, but differ in degree. His lack of empathy allows the male sociopath to perform border patrol duty effectively, but when he isn't patrolling the border, or waging inter-tribal war, he has "free time" and may mingle among normal tribesmen. The ruffian sociopath produces an undertone of a disruptive violation of social norms. His behavior is mostly under control among fellow tribesmen due to "social pressure" and the threat of being ostracized or banished if he can't behave. The sociopath isn't dumb, and he understands that he needs the tribe for his survival, as much as the tribe needs him for their survival.

Rape as an Adaptation

Before considering some thought experiments that may elucidate social life in the AE, I want to speculate about something that may have puzzled the careful reader in the last chapter: If the bands of border patrollers spent most of their time in their assigned role patrolling the border, preventing them from devotion to raising a family, how would their genes for sociopathy be maintained within the tribe? My answer will be speculative, and somewhat resembling a "thought experiment," so this is the right chapter for it.

Many species rape: ducks, birds, snow geese, fish, sheep, orangutans, chimpanzees, gorillas - and especially humans! Rape is a "loser" male's last option for contributing to the species gene pool. It is most instructive to consider strategies employed by Rocky Mountain bighorn sheep, as described in a scientific journal (*Science*, 1984; sorry, but I lost the reference).

This study concluded that rams had three main strategies for reproduction: 1) mate guarding, 2) mate sequestering and 3) opportunistic rape. The rams that "guarded" were relatively dominant. Those that sequestered were less so; which explains why they forcibly moved their mate to the periphery of the herd to prevent his ewe from returning to the center of the herd (where her selection of males would be improved). The most subordinate rams waited on the sidelines for opportunities to rape unguarded ewes.

Thornhill and Palmer (2000) suggested that human males rape for the same reason: namely, that men who cannot gain sexual access to women based on their personal success resort to rape as the next-best option. In other words, rape is adaptive from the gene's perspective. This is not to excuse rape, which the authors make clear when they wrote "...everyone has the same goal regarding rape: to end it." The subject, however, is so clouded by a "political correctness" emotion that some readers have unfairly criticized the authors for even publishing their findings.

Rape by victorious warriors seems to be a human universal. What began as a routine ritual after one tribe succeeded in subjugating another after victorious battle (pillage and general mayhem) continues to the present time when countries battle each other to a decisive ending. The normal penalties for raping within one's own society are not imposed on rapists by an invading army (or marauding party) when they are victorious. This may be due to the fact that there is minimal danger that the husband, or family of the wronged woman, will be able to achieve revenge after their tribe (country) is subjugated by war. During World War II the European women (especially the French) were surprised to discover that the victorious American soldiers did <u>not</u> rape them, which is an exception that supports the generality of the rule.

It can be shown through a series of arguments that the evolution of women's concealed ovulation contributed to the advance of human dominance of the planet. The first step is to argue that concealed ovulation encouraged the evolution of monogamy. Monogamy, in turn, led to an increased paternal investment, and that contributed to an extended childhood, which allowed for more brain development before adulthood, which made humans smarter and the planet's most dominant species. I won't labor you with more detail for this sequence of arguments here, but I need to establish the fact that male investment in raising offspring is an important human evolutionary accomplishment. It's true that men and women "use" each other. I like to say that *"Men like women because they can make babies, women like men because they can contribute resources for raising babies, and the genes like both because this is a possible path to genetic immortality."* Women prefer to be monogamous with men who can be "good providers." (They also cuckold their husbands for ~ 20 % of their children, but that matter isn't relevant for this book.) Men who are losers are, by definition, poor providers. This is why loser men are forced into rape as their only strategy for serving their genes.

This position is apparently "uncomfortable" for hyper-liberal sociologists, psychologists, social activists, and even some evolutionary psychologists (e.g., J.T.). Their argument is that males are obsessed with over-powering females for some reason related to a dysfunctional culture (try that for explaining why ducks rape!). An excellent treatment

12. Thought Experiments for the A.E.

of rape is given by Michael P. Ghiglieri in Chapter 4 of his book *The Dark Side of Man: Tracing the Origins of Male Violence* (2000).

It is easy to imagine that rape served the genes in many ancestral situations, but it surely didn't provide the individual with improved health, greater longevity or an improved general well-being. What rape provided was a desperate vehicle for keeping the loser's genes in the gene pool!

Now we're ready to return to the question of how sociopaths reproduced given that they spent much of their time patrolling the tribe's border with a few other males. They could have, and this is pure speculation, seized opportunities from the periphery of the tribe for raping unattended females – just like the subordinate bighorn sheep. This speculation is compatible with the sociopath personality type, which includes violence, lack of empathy, disinterest in domestic duties and infidelity.

If you're ready for more speculation, let's do some "thought experiments."

Thought Experiment #1: Risks of Cleansing the Tribe of Sociopaths

It is possible that during every tribe's lifetime a normaloid wonders what life would be like if the sociopaths and proto-psychopaths didn't exist. If today's crime statistics applied to the small HG tribe in the AE, then this imaginative normaloid might exclaim "Given that more than half of serious crime is committed by the proto-psychopaths in our tribe, and most of the rest are committed by the ruffian sociopaths, what a wonderful world this would be if we could cleanse our tribe of both the proto-psychopaths and sociopaths!"

So let's try to imagine what would happen if this tribesmen was able to persuade the rest of the normaloids in his tribe to get rid of the proto-psychopaths and sociopaths in their tribe. It's not necessary to speculate on how such a cleansing could be accomplished because this is just a "thought experiment."

Initially, the cleansed tribe would be more efficient and stronger without the distraction of criminal proto-psychopaths and sociopaths, and no crime.

Eventually, however, a neighboring tribe would notice that the cleansed tribe's sociopath border patrol was missing. Territorial incursions would increase, and readings would be made of how the cleansed tribe reacted. Based on these readings a neighbor tribe would initiate inter-tribal warfare, and the cleansed tribe would be asking itself "where are our sociopath warriors when we need them?" Before they could answer this simple question, the tribe of normaloids would be vanquished, and either killed or taken as slaves. The cleansed tribe would therefore be wiped out, and none of them would be our ancestors!

12. Thought Experiments for the A.E.

There must be many examples of this in the historical record. For example, a civilization arose in a Y-shaped valley in southern Mexico, and when the Aztecs to their north learned about it they attacked and destroyed it. Only advanced architecture exists today to challenge paleoanthropologists. Similar destructions of an advanced civilization must have happened often, and there is minimal knowledge about their existence because the victors wrote a history that glorified themselves and belittled the vanquished.

During the Holocene, a super-tribe civilization that arose without sufficient attention to the contributions of sociopath protection could exist for only as long as it remained unknown by other super-tribes. This lesson is an essential one for the consideration of Western Civilization creating colonies for the purpose of preserving the values and stories of accomplishment of the home civilization. It will be treated in more detail in later chapters and also the appendices.

The message for this thought experiment is that AE tribes and Holocene super-tribes need sociopaths, and any tribe or super-tribe that gets rid of them will have a short-lived reward.

Thought Experiment #2: Risks of Asking "Why Be Good?"

Imagine a thoughtful normaloid who learns that proto-psychopath criminals commit half of all serious crime (Hare, 1993). He also notes that sociopaths are often freeloaders. He then asks himself "why am I so conscientiously devoted to tribal welfare?" If he is capable of brave thought he will realize that his behavior amounts to enslavement to the tribe with fewer rewards than the freeloaders and criminals. He may note that his individual welfare is jeopardized as he works to promote tribal strength. Why does he behave this way, or, rather, why should he continue to behave this way after seeing how the tribe is taking advantage of him?

Since he's a normaloid he will discover that he can't change his behavior. He will be good with others because he can't be otherwise. All normaloids are like this, because the genes enforce it. "So much for insight" this normaloid may mutter, as he continues to "do good" and contribute to tribal harmony and cohesive strength, both essential ingredients for preserving society's eusocial strength.

In truth, most normaloids are incapable of these insights! The forces of evolution have placed boundaries on human thought, and crossing these boundaries is so threatening to tribal survival that brain circuits have evolved that forbid these thoughts. At least they're forbidden to normaloids.

The Holocene psychopath, however, has no trouble crossing these boundaries, and the sociopath is also less encumbered. This is because the genes that allow them this freedom are needed for the maintenance of a tribal niche for sociopaths, and the sociopath has to be free of such good behavior restrictions if he is to be an effective border patroller and warrior. This is an aspect of multi-gene theory which I hypothesize accounts for the preservation of a few percentage of a population of sociopaths performing ruffian roles while the cost of doing so is a small population of disruptive and criminal psychopaths.

[Dear reader: if you haven't already figured this out, I'm a "normaloid" with a PCL score of zero. I can't explain how I was able to cross the boundaries of thought that keep normaloids enslaved.]

Thought Experiment #3: Rewards for Diversity

Imagine the following two tribes in chronic competition: Tribe 1 consists of men who are all the same, and Tribe 2 consists of men who differ in many respects. In Tribe 1 all warriors make their own weapons, whereas in Tribe 2 an artisan with special talent for craftsmanship makes weapons that all of his tribe's warriors use. Tribe 2 will have the best weapons.

Assume that there are about 50 adult men in each tribe, and imagine how teams of men for specific tasks are formed (not only for warfare but also hunting, construction, etc.). As explained in Chapter 9, teams of 5 to 10 men must have been as typical during the AE as it has remained throughout the Holocene. In teams every member has a special role. If each member was chosen for their role based on ability for that role, Tribe 2 would have stronger teams than Tribe 1.

This is merely one example of many that could illustrate the merits of diversity of talent among tribal membership. It seems inevitable that whenever groups compete evolution will reward those groups with the greatest diversity. It is therefore unsurprising that humans exhibit an unsurpassed diversity of individual capability.

The presence of diversity is not without risks. One of these is the presence of psychopaths; another is a hyper-tolerance of differences that can undermine resolve to not tolerate psychopaths. This sensitive topic is treated in following chapters.

Thought Experiment #4: Rewards for Adventurousness

Imagine two tribes situated along similar bends of a river. One tribe is comprised of cautious individuals, and the other is comprised of reckless ones. For some reason, possibly related to ancestral mythologies about hidden dangers in the mountains, neither tribe has explored what's on the other side of the mountains that the river flows out of. Whenever someone of the first tribe, the one with cautious individuals, thinks about exploring the fabled dangerous mountains they ask themselves: "Why? My life in the village is fine. I would have everything to lose and nothing to gain by wasting time and energy looking for something better." An individual of the other tribe will ask himself: "Why not? Yes, I have a comfortable life in my village, but I wonder what's on the other side of that beautiful mountain ridge."

One individual from the adventurous tribe sets out to climb the treacherous mountain slope, but he is never heard from again. This confirms the cautious tribesmen that they are right to be satisfied with their comfortable life. But others in the adventurous tribe are undeterred, and another of them sets out to see what the problem could be. He also never returns.

Eventually, someone from the reckless and adventurous tribe returns, and he is filled with stories about the wonderful valley on the other side! He describes the safest way to navigate through treacherous river rapids and narrow ledges. One by one, he leads fellow tribesmen to a wonderful valley where a new "founding" tribe is eventually established.

The "moral" of this story is that *recklessness* is an evolutionary adaptation from the standpoint of the collective. However, from the standpoint of the individual the cautious tribe individuals were making rational decisions and the reckless tribe individuals weren't.

Thought Experiment #5: Rewards for Fascism

Imagine a tribe that is besieged by a stronger tribe. Dire prospects call for an extreme strategy. Imagine that a tribe in this situation adopts, temporarily at least, a belief system calling upon all individuals to become devoted exclusively to tribal welfare. Individuals must place greater importance on serving the tribe than themselves as individuals, or to serving family, friends, truth, ideology, humanity or anything that could compete with tribal goals. If the tribe were a thinking entity, and could invent the perfect tribesman, an unthinking tribal robot, it would be programmed to take orders from a tribal leader whose only purpose was to create an invincible tribe. "Individualism" would be replaced by robotic loyalty to the collective. Such a tribe would be fully eusocial for as long as necessary to survive.

I'm describing fascism! The strongest fascist tribe, or society, would have to intimidate all tribesmen to follow directions, and this could be done with an appropriate number of enforcers of conformance to the fascist dictator's pronouncements. If such a tribe, or society, could be fashioned, it would be formidable.

We should assume that such tribes may have existed in the past, and that some people among us today are prone to becoming unthinking robots ("I was just following orders"), needing only a strong leader capable of giving direction to a following. Hitler was a

12. Thought Experiments for the A.E.

charismatic leader who was able to convert some ordinary people to act as stormtroopers and to convert the rest of Germans to be followers. The Nazi conversion of a society to fascism may have happened on a smaller, tribal scale during the AE. These people, fascist cult leaders and unthinking followers, may be with us today.

Since a fascist dictator can enjoy a prosperous lifestyle, there is an incentive for the unscrupulous psychopath to mislead society into thinking that they are about to be destroyed by some "other" entity. We should be wary of anyone rousing the rabble by claims that the "other" is preparing to invade us. Their apparent goal is to achieve dictatorial control over us for as long as it takes to fend off the invasion by the "other," but their goal is to prosper as dictators for the rest of their lives. The willing follower may have had AE ancestors who in fact survived tribal challenges by replacing individual goals with group survival goals for as long as was necessary for tribal survival. It is possible today for a society to be converted to fascism by a clever cult leader with enough charisma to convert the populace to succumb to fascist rule. His rabble-rousing cry would be to sew fear that we are at risk of being invaded by "others," and only he can save us from this invasion.

Chapter 13. Holocene Opportunities

Interglacial warmings brought tribes closer together, and tribal coalescence led to super-tribes that prevailed in conflicts with neighbor tribes that remained small. Super-tribes offered new opportunities for both sociopaths and psychopaths, the former needed and the latter not needed. Governance was invented, and laws were formulated and enforced for minimizing disruption by the sociopaths and psychopaths. Religion may have been modified to deal with sociopaths, but moral arguments and heavenly rewards are unlikely to have influenced the psychopaths. Whereas the psychopath was a rarity in a small AE tribe, in a super-tribe there must have been many of them simply due to the larger population of the super-tribe. Small tribe methods for dealing with the psychopath would not work in a super-tribe because the misfit could simply relocate to a new location in the super-tribe. This is civilization's big challenge, and there may be no solution!

Holocene Climate Changes

To understand how civilizations arose, which led to discontents, and how sociopaths lost some of their value to the social collective, and how new opportunities opened up for proto-psychopaths to prosper, and evolve into psychopaths, we must understand early Holocene climate change and how they permitted small tribes to coalesce into super-tribes.

For the last ½ million years, approximately, the climate has undergone warming events lasting ~ 10,000 years at intervals of approximately 100,000 years. The warmings are called "interglacials" because they led to partial melting of glaciers. Each interglacial would have improved conditions for fauna and flora. During an interglacial each acre of land could support a greater number of animals, vegetation and therefore humans. Human hunter/gatherers would have roamed over new territory, and tribal populations could have expanded. Since tribal size tends to be limited to the Dunbar Number (~ 150) we can imagine that tribal territory size for those at the Dunbar limit for population size were motivated to shrink territory size. If tribes reduced territory to match requirements for their population, tribal separations would have decreased.

Tribal Coalescence

A mechanism for tribal coalescence must have existed during the AE because tribes that were "too small" (for defending themselves) would have benefitted by coalescing with another "too small" tribe – thus achieving a population size closer to the Dunbar Number. During the AE there must have been a mechanism for tribes that were already near the Dunbar Number to avoid coalescing because they would have created a problem of

13. Holocene Opportunities

having proto-psychopaths living among them without being identified as such by the normaloids.

But such coalescences must have occasionally occurred, at least during the early Holocene. We know this happened because today we have societies of millions of people. During the Holocene such coalescences would have been more feasible because tribes would have been living closer together, due to the feasibility of each tribe shrinking its territory in response to a more verdant landscape. The first such coalescence events might have met with resounding success in inter-tribal conflict, due merely to an outnumbering of warriors on one side.

The importance of tribal size for inter-tribal warfare outcomes is illustrated by studies of our closest related species, chimpanzees. Michael P. Ghiglieri writes (2000, pg. 175) "… male chimps … waged war on a neighboring community only when it … was a lot smaller and weaker than their own community, containing half or fewer adult males."

However, among humans there are challenges that would have to be overcome after the coalescence of tribes, even when the resulting population did not exceed the Dunbar Number. The two tribes would have had differences in any number of things, such as language, dress, beliefs and rituals, and there would have been resentment in both directions. For probably the entirety of the AE, lasting millions of years, our human ancestors were selected by evolution to dislike anyone who didn't resemble them in all these matters. For this reason it is likely that the first coalescences were between tribes that had recently fissioned because of prior population growth, since they would have had fewer differences than other tribal match-ups.

The successful presence of one large tribe creates an evolutionary pressure for others to do the same. I will refer to any tribe with a population exceeding ~ 200 as a "super-tribe." Any super-tribe comprised of members that came together from tribes with different customs would face the challenge of achieving mutual toleration. Ingrained instincts worked against such toleration. These super-tribes, as well as those that came together with similar cultures, would have to overcome the suspicion that naturally occurs for strangers. By the definition of a super-tribe some fellow tribesmen will be strangers whose trust cannot be assumed.

This aspect of super-tribe society is, in essence, the birth of "discontent with civilization" that Sigmund Freud wrote about. It started with a resentment of required tolerance of fellow tribesmen strangers that was imposed on all super-tribe members by super-tribe leaders, and as super-tribes grew in size to form a society the same discontent became targeted at the society, and collection of societies that constituted a civilization. As future chapters will argue, the "discontent with civilization" was added to by the occasional hijacking of governance by the new psychopath and his tyrannical rule.

13. Holocene Opportunities

Sociopath and Psychopath Opportunities in Super-Tribes

Sometimes I consider the present-day psychopaths, plus the sociopaths (e.g., PCL > 5), as a group; after all, they both like to "game the system." This group comprises ~ 8 % of the present-day population. Some social requirements are resisted (or ignored) by all of the sociopaths (as well as the psychopaths). Whereas about half of serious crime is committed by psychopaths, some of the rest must be committed by sociopaths, especially the high-scoring sociopaths. Most serious crime is therefore committed by the 8 % of people who are either sociopaths or psychopaths.

The super-tribe presents a social environment that is favorable for both proto-psychopaths and sociopaths. A super-tribe with a population several times the Dunbar Number should be more favorable to them than a tribe whose population is close to the Dunbar Number. The larger the super-tribe, the more likely it is for the proto-psychopaths and sociopaths to thrive. After a cheater cheats, he or she can simply move residence to a new part of the super-tribe where their bad reputation is unknown. (The term "grifter" is used to describe this lifestyle.) Evolutionary pressures will tend to reward proto-psychopath and sociopath genes, and therefore increase the incidence of sociopaths and proto-psychopaths during the Holocene. Indeed, the wonderful environment for proto-psychopaths in super-tribes led to the evolution of the proto-psychopath into a more effective *psychopath*!

After the First Edition of this book was published I learned that others have speculated about the opportunities for psychopathy presented by large population societies. The concept described resembles mine, but their descriptions appear to apply to sociopaths more than psychopaths (the distinctions are unfortunately muddled in the literature). The articles for these speculations are Figueredo et al., 2006 and Figueredo et al., 2008 ("Psychopaths Flourish in Mega-Cities."). A brief review of this work is given by Geher, 2018. It was even suggested that the incidence of psychopathy is currently rising because the proportion of the human population living in cities is increasing. The psychopath guru, Dr. Hare, acknowledges this by writing (1993): *"Sociobiologists take the view that behavior development is influenced by genetic factors, and they might argue that the number of psychopaths must be increasing simply because they are very promiscuous and produce large numbers of children, some of whom may inherit a predisposition for psychopathy."* [Notice the use of "might" and "may" – this is typical writing style for anyone concerned about reviewer comments and criticism by academics.]

Governance

Early in the Holocene the hunter/gatherer lifestyle was gradually being replaced by the more settled lifestyles of herding and agriculture. Agriculture is evident by 9500 BC, and evidence of herding is present at least 10,000 years ago. Both forms of agriculture

13. Holocene Opportunities

involve the storage of food. Food storage sites would have attracted wandering marauder tribes. Farmers, and those who relied upon the farmers for food, would have been motivated to protect these storage sites from the marauders. This provided an opportunity for the ruffian sociopaths! They could be "employed" to protect food storage sites, or to fend off the alien tribe marauders whenever they were known to be nearby. (Notice that I didn't include the home tribe's psychopaths as employable for protecting food stores; they are simply too unreliable for this duty.)

Sociopaths might also be needed for their traditional role of guarding territorial borders, which was what they were good for before the Holocene. More than one roving band of border protectors may have been employed since super-tribes had larger territories and therefore longer territorial borders to patrol. The term "employed" is apt, because the farmer's food would have been exchanged for the protective service sociopaths provided.

Whenever tribal size persisted in exceeding the Dunbar Number a form of "governance" would be needed. The old system of interpersonal relationships, based on trust (which is based on experiences from repeated interactions), couldn't provide the necessary trust of every person with all others in the tribe. A tribal chief could play a newly important role for addressing these new needs.

Tribal rules needed to be explicitly specified, and since lifestyles were changing (with the adoption of new ways of herding and farming) some mechanism for establishing and changing those rules had to be created. The chief needed a "council" to give advice. A rudimentary form of our familiar three branches of government may have been created 8000 years ago: 1) a council, answerable to the chief, that advises on new rules (congressional), 2) a group of men whose job is to "enforce" those rules (executive) and 3) the chief who hears plaintiffs argue their cases for the chief to rule on (judicial).

The chief and his council would have needed to form an army of sociopath warriors for the tasks of fending off marauding bands and waging war with other tribes (defensive and offensive). A standing army would have to be "supported" by the others (herders, farmers, merchants, builders, etc.). This meant that a system of taxation would need to be created. It's possible that a subset of the warriors were used for the enforcement of tax collection. These "policemen" could also be used for the enforcement of other tribal "rules."

All of this governance was new and we have to imagine that the populace was resentful, or "discontent." The most unnerving part of living in a super-tribe would be the requirement of accepting strangers as fellow-tribesmen. Imagine, for possibly millions of years the forces of evolution had rewarded humans who couldn't tolerate strangers, and suddenly a generation of humans was being forced to tolerate them.

13. Holocene Opportunities

Some super-tribes would have been composed of individuals who had a slightly greater inherited trait for tolerance of strangers than found in other super-tribes. These super-tribes would have achieved a semblance of internal harmony slightly more easily than the others. If all other things about super-tribes were equal, then the super-tribes composed of individuals with a greater readiness for tolerance would eventually prevail. Given that the most tolerant societies today are found in Scandinavia I visualize this gradual evolution of tolerant super-tribes as occurring more rapidly at northern latitudes.

A super-tribe society consists of a high population density central area surrounded by a low population density area where farmers and herders reside. A tribesman who was unable to tolerate strangers would feel more comfortable being a farmer, where he wasn't forced on a daily basis to be with people of differing backgrounds (e.g., tribesmen who had recently joined the super-tribe). A tribesman who on the other hand was more tolerant of strangers would feel comfortable living in the higher-density town, or city. Such city dwellers could be described as "progressive" (or "liberal"), while the farmer could be described as "conservative." This pattern of political inclination must have existed for possibly 8000 years, for it is found to exist today (Geher, 2018 and Murphy, 2018).

Warfare

During the early Holocene we may assume that super-tribes occasionally engaged in open warfare with neighboring super-tribes. This is a safe assumption because we know such warfare occurred when the historical record began, in the late-Holocene, and there is paleontological evidence for inter-tribal warfare during the pre-historic mid-Holocene (Keeley, 1996). It is "human nature" for humans to wage wars, so the impulse to fulfill this need during the early Holocene can be safely assumed.

The sociopaths would have been the obvious recruits for governance-supervised warfare. Any super-tribe that overlooked the opportunities for war-making would be evolutionarily disadvantaged. Also, any tribe that neglected to prepare for such warfare would be evolutionarily disadvantaged. It is safe to assume that any super-tribe that lost a war would suffer serious losses in their genetic contribution to future generations. This could be accomplished through death, of course, but also by being enslaved, or simply being exploited by over-taxation.

Our default assumption should be that inter-super-tribal warfare occurred on occasion, and that all super-tribes needed to remain war-ready. This, in turn, meant that every super-tribe had to rely upon a standing army with plenty of warrior sociopaths and desperate normaloids.

13. Holocene Opportunities

What about the psychopaths, who can't be overlooked when a population of sociopaths have to be maintained? The psychopaths would be useless. If they were recruited for warrior service they would be the first ones to desert, and somehow escape notice for their desertion. Within the heartland, psychopaths would weaken societal strength because they only care about themselves. Psychopaths are almost always "social parasites" with no redeeming value. They are usually the consummate "social parasite." (Chapter 19 lists some exceptions - examples of how psychopaths can actually contribute to society.)

Holocene Immune System

A tribe of 100 to 200 individuals (35 to 60 adult males) would typically have no more than one male psychopath, assuming present-day incidence (1.5 % of 35 to 60 is ~ 1). Members of the AE small tribe would have been able to identify these misfits, and were able to deal with them in order to preserve tribal harmony. I've suggested that avoiding, shunning, banishment and murder were employed. In a super-tribe, with a population 100 times larger, for example, there could have been many more male and female psychopaths (10,000 * 2/3 * 1.5 % = 100). It's possible that most of them could escape detection, because whenever one was detected he, or she, could simply relocate to a part of the super-tribe where their reputation was unknown! We should ask: Were the AE tribal tools for detecting and dealing with psychopaths useful in the super-tribe setting? The same question should be asked about the high-scoring sociopaths.

Psychopaths today are fully aware of what behaviors are sanctioned by society, and the high functioning ones are expert in exhibiting compliance when others are present. The low functioning psychopaths have trouble with compliance, and they are therefore often frustrated by pretending to be good. There must be a blending of traits from low-scoring sociopaths to high-scoring sociopaths, and from them to psychopaths. High-scoring sociopaths (11 < PCL < 30, for example) may have been viewed by others as occasionally psychopathic. There are twice as many high-scoring sociopaths than psychopaths, so the high-scoring sociopath population can't be ignored when considering the feasibility of super-tribe members identifying the high-scoring sociopaths and controlling their behavior. Any super-tribe that failed to identify and control high-scoring sociopaths would be at risk for a weakening of tribal strength and a compromise of tribal harmony.

How did super-tribes deal with disruptive sociopaths who were high-scoring but low-functioning? They were more likely to be influenced by social pressure than the psychopaths. It is possible that religion was made use of to deal with the sociopath. Religion promises eventual punishment for misdeeds, even when they are undiscovered. By invoking a God who sees all, and who punishes much later, the evil-doer who believes in such a god would be left wondering if their evil deed, which may not have been noticed by fellow super-tribesmen, may in fact be punished at some distant future time. This would produce hesitation before future selfish acts. If this preposterous culturgen ever got a foothold in a super-tribe, that super-tribe could reap immense benefits! How can such a preposterous belief system be invented? I don't know, but we know it happened because religion is widespread today. This theory for the modification of AE religions to Holocene versions is described in the next chapter.

Another way that a super-tribe could reduce the parasitic behavior of sociopaths, and the criminal behavior of psychopaths, is to enforce compliance with tribal rules. In small tribes, social pressure (e.g., gossip and subsequent avoidance) must have been effective. But for super-tribes, the tools of governance would have to be employed. The "police" and "judicial" powers of the chief would be available. Super-tribe laws could then be tailored for the control of psychopaths and the discouragement of sociopath cheating.

Super-tribes that accidentally experimented with religion and the creation of a governance that formulated and enforced laws would have an advantage over super-tribes that didn't. The forces of evolution need only small differences in things that matter, plus time, and amazing results can be achieved.

Chapter Summary

This chapter has dealt with changes during the early Holocene, when tribes began to coalesce into super-tribes. The success of super-tribes over small tribes meant that eventually all tribes were super-tribes (except in remote and relatively barren areas, which had little to entice the interest of super-tribes).

New challenges appeared with super-tribe life: whenever tribal size exceeded the Dunbar Number significantly (~ 200) there were too many tribesmen for everyone to know everyone, so distrust of strangers within the tribe became more common. This is the birth of what has come to be referred to as a "discontent with civilization."

Super-tribes unintentionally provided new and previously unknown opportunities for sociopaths and psychopaths. They could cheat in one part of a super-tribe, and upon discovery, move on to some other part of the super-tribe, where they could repeat and refine their cheating tricks on new and unsuspecting victims. Small tribe methods for dealing with sociopaths could not be relied upon, so governance, and maybe religion, provided new tools for controlling the sociopath. The psychopaths posed a greater challenge because they are unlikely to be influenced by either social pressure or religion. The small changes in how society dealt with the psychopath began a slow evolutionary change of the AE proto-psychopath to a Holocene psychopath.

13. Holocene Opportunities

The super-tribe sociopath remained useful for warrior duty, as well as internal enforcement of laws. His appetite for violence was an asset for border patrol duty as well as inter-tribal warfare, but he was somewhat disruptive in the heartland.

Chapter 14. Mid-Holocene Discontents

The latest interglacial warming <u>changed everything</u> for humanity! The new requirements imposed on human nature for super-tribe living were too extreme for a smooth transition. We therefore should not be surprised to find that during the Holocene, as super-tribes and their governments developed, most people harbored an underlying and persistent "discontent" with the new social setting. The closer to "civilization" we came, the greater the discontent! The problem of minimizing the disrupting influence of psychopaths remained unaddressed.

This chapter presents new perspectives on the major themes described so far. They may seem like miscellaneous ideas for the beginnings of discontents with the "civility" requirements of super-tribes, and their fullest expression, civilization, but they will be needed for following chapters.

Sociopaths form a Protective Tribal Skin

The sociopath was needed by small tribes to defend territory, and to defend attack from neighboring tribes. Consider this analogy: sociopaths are to the tribe, as skin is to an organism!

If sociopaths formed a protective "tribal skin" for small tribes, and if chimpanzees achieved the same "border patrol" protection, then we are justified in suggesting that this mechanism has been relied upon by our ancestors for 7 to 10 million years.

A traditional way to describe tribalism is to recall the old saying: amity for same tribesmen, enmity for others. This is the so-called "tribal mentality." The notion of a protective "tribal skin" for defending borders is a new element that might be useful in understanding the essential nature of a tribe. It also represents a "division of labor" which is a defining characteristic of eusocial species.

The role I'm suggesting for sociopaths implies that during the millions of years of sociopath evolution they were intended to spend most of their time near the borders of tribal territory. Not only would this maximize their usefulness to the tribe, but it would minimize their disruptive influence upon tribal internal social relationships.

I suggest that during tribal coalescence this basic deployment of sociopaths was preserved. They were needed to defend the super-tribe's territory, which meant spending most of their time away from the center of tribal social life.

14. Mid-Holocene Discontents

The niche size for sociopaths guarding super-tribe territory may have been a smaller percentage of the population than existed for the small tribe. This is because territorial boundary is proportional to the size, or diameter, of the territory while the area enclosed (and population to be protected) is proportional to the square of size. In other words, as territory area increases in response to population growth, territorial border length increases at a slower percentage rate than territory area.

There is evidence for the suggested relationship of decreasing percentage of sociopaths needed as population increases. Estimates of Holocene standing army size have been found to not scale with population size; the larger the population the smaller is the percentage of the population devoted to a standing army.

What could be the implications for super-tribe society if the greater the population the smaller percentage of sociopaths is needed for border protection? Super-tribes may have a problem of an excess of sociopaths wandering within social center settings, causing social disruption from criminal activity. Thus, as super-tribe population increases so may the need for dealing with unwanted sociopaths within society.

As an aside, there is an incentive for every tribe, or super-tribe, to minimize the numbers of sociopaths it must support, which favors tribal territories that are as circular in shape as possible.

Psychopath Burdens

For every six sociopaths there will be one psychopath. This may be because sociopaths are a multi-gene creation and it's possible for too many sociopath genes to be found in one person, the psychopath. (I acknowledge that alternative explanations for the genetics of sociopaths and psychopaths is possible.)

Since psychopaths had no redeeming value to a society (until the late-Holocene) anything that increased their numbers would have incurred an evolutionary penalty. And since psychopaths are an unavoidable byproduct of the production of sociopaths, anything that creates more sociopaths than needed is penalized by evolutionary forces. (That statement is probably true even for alternative theories for the genetics of sociopaths and psychopaths.)

However, just because psychopaths are a burden to tribes and super-tribes, doesn't mean that genes that produce both sociopaths and psychopaths are kept to a minimum by evolutionary forces. This would only be true if group selection was 100% determinative of gene frequency. Game theorists have developed a theory called "parochial altruism" (Choi and Bowles, 2007) showing that when episodes of inter-tribal conflict occur at widely-spaced time intervals there are fluctuating changes in which *different* genes are rewarded by evolutionary forces. Two categories of genes are identified in making this argument: 1) genes coding for behaviors that benefit group strength (during inter-group conflict) and 2) genes that undergo an increase in gene frequency in the tribal gene pool (during peaceful interludes) that favor individual carriers while reducing group strength. The longer the peaceful interlude, the greater are the rewards to the second gene category. The people who are plentiful carriers of this second gene category have been described as social parasites. They steal from others while shirking productive labor. The other names for "social parasite" is "psychopath" (and to some extent "sociopath")!

Parochial altruism theory has been used in speculation about the "need" for occasional inter-tribal warfare in order to keep the tribal gene pool "cleansed" of the parasite genes. Thus, a super-tribe can be "too successful" if it creates an empire that is unchallenged for many generations. It would become weak from within due to the rise of parasite gene frequency, which would weaken the empire sufficiently for surprise challenge by a neighboring tribe that had continued to cleanse itself of parasite genes by continual conflict with nearby tribes of comparable "significance." The fall of the Roman Empire to barbarian tribes is used to illustrate this theory (Turchin, 2007, Wilson and Wilson, 2007).

Psychopaths were social parasites with negligible redeeming value to the tribe during most of the Holocene. They weakened the tribe by stealing resources and eroding trust while avoiding productive contributions to the societal economy. If a super-tribe was at peace too long, psychopaths would exploit parasitic opportunities. Genes for sociopathy and psychopathy would then be expected to become more frequent, and culturgens for controlling psychopathic behaviors might not have strengthened at the same pace. Peaceful episodes might also have reduced the perceived importance of maintaining a sociopath-based army of defenders.

How can a super-tribe that has achieved success with its competition simultaneously reduce genes for psychopathology while not changing the incidence of genes for sociopathy? If it can't, then maybe the increasing opportunities for psychopathy genes will produce more sociopaths than are needed.

This is a recipe for disastrous consequences for any successful super-tribe. Psychopaths are tolerated at higher levels than before super-tribes, and sociopaths are more numerous than are needed for territorial defense. Sociopaths are therefore more often found within the heart of tribal life, and psychopaths would always be found there, and both would form a criminal class! One result could be the collapse of the once successful super-tribe.

14. Mid-Holocene Discontents

A New Religion Emerges

The previously chapter's suggested origin theory for new styles of religion is worth repeating. It is one of humanity's most "spectacular stupidities" (cf. Ch. 17), so the origin of religion deserves special treatment.

When super-tribes formed, the old religion was mal-adapted to new needs. The old religion dealt with ancestors (or their "souls") rising up in the sky from funeral pyres and ending-up somewhere among the stars. It also gave meaning to dreams about those ancestors. The old religions tried to give an account for the origin of the Earth, animals and humans.

Super-tribes created new challenges for controlling the disrupting and freeloading problems produced by psychopaths and sociopaths. Anything that reduced these problems would be rewarded by evolutionary forces. I suggest that small changes to religion were (accidentally) introduced that described consequences for bad behavior. According to the new religion: cheating and criminality are supposed to be noted by an all-seeing God, who keeps track of "who's naughty or nice" and at the end of a person's life sends them to either an eternal heavenly home or a hellish purgatory! A sociopath or psychopath may know that they can escape detection by fellow tribesman for a bad act, but if there's a possibility that an all-seeing God is watching them, and keeping track of all their behaviors, they might hesitate with what they were considering doing.

The religions that we know today include a morality that is in approximate alignment with what we can imagine were the needs for controlling sociopaths and psychopaths. These moralities resemble that of a normaloid's conscience! Martha Stout (2005, Ch. 12) agrees, and writes *"... conscience is also the place where psychology and spirituality meet, an issue on which the recommendations of psychology and the teachings of the major religions and spiritual traditions of the world completely concur."* This is indirect confirmation of my speculation that religion was molded during the Holocene in an attempt to control sociopaths and psychopaths.

For such a religion to have credibility it would be necessary for most of the super-tribe to believe in it. As preposterous as this belief system is to any thinking person, our human ancestors were apparently gullible enough to believe it. The belief might have been provisional at first, but when tribal strength improved for those who were provisional believers it was evolution's turn to take over. Since a super-tribe that was lucky enough to create such a religion had a reduced level of social cheating and criminality, it would have been rewarded with more victorious outcomes in competition with tribes that had the old religion. Eventually, no super-tribe remained that had not adopted the essentials of the new religion. The new religion could be viewed as a super-tribe's replacement of small tribe "social pressure" for being good.

Oceanic Oneness with the Universe

This may be an aside, but religions celebrate something that goes by many names: oneness, unity, inter-being, and an overwhelming and oceanic feeling of connectedness with the universe (everyone and everything)! People who report experiencing this oceanic oneness are grateful for the experience, and portray it as positive, or rewarding; it is not just some neutral, other-worldly experience. This oceanic connectedness feeling is associated with spirituality, and may be generated by the conscience. Sociobiologists might interpret the capacity for this feeling as an emotional reward for accepting one's place as simply *one individual of a eusocial collective!*

The emotions have been described as a genetic reward for being properly enslaved to those genes (Gary, 2014, Ch. 6). For example, sexual union is pleasurable in spite of the risks to individual well-being (a dozen diseases, discovery by a spouse, etc.) because it accomplishes something the genes anthropomorphically want – their immortality in the species gene pool. The genes appear to pursue this goal at our individual expense, whenever necessary, and they trick us into a blind acceptance, or eager appreciation, by creating a genetic reward that is great enough to overcome logical hesitation.

Dancing Bears

Just as a domesticated dancing bear isn't really happy, and would prefer to be living free in the wild, so is the man who has to pretend to be comfortable being polite and accepting of strangers. I will repeat this thought over and over, because it is key to understanding so much of our present predicament: **Humans have recently had to become civil with strangers, and since this is a requirement of every society with a population larger than the Dunbar Number we should expect members of populace societies to harbor a measure of discontent about this recent requirement imposed on them by society.**

If humans resent the requirement of civility that large tribes have to impose on them, then the amount of resentment within a super-tribe must affect the super-tribe's success in competition with other super-tribes. All other things being equal, the super-tribe that has the least amount of resentment of strangers among its membership will be stronger and will prevail. This means that "the forces of evolution" will favor genes, and tribal culturgens, that enhance civil behavior for harmonious intra-tribal relationships.

Rejection of strangers within one's tribe because of differences in appearance or beliefs can be described as "intolerant" while acceptance of them is "tolerant." Intolerance and tolerance can also be equated with the terms conservative and liberal. A conservative longs for a return to the old small-tribe lifestyle, where no strangers are present, while the liberal is OK with, and may actually prefer, the presence of strangers and different

14. Mid-Holocene Discontents

people in his tribe. A tribe that welcomes differences may even benefit from the enhanced "diversity of labor" that they welcome.

I suggest that conservatives and liberals began their disagreements 10,000 years ago, when tribes had to coalesce into super-tribes for tribal survival. Every society has a history of trying to persuade tribesmen to be more liberal. A society that failed to persuade a significant number of its membership would be at a disadvantage, all other things being equal, in inter-tribal competition.

Both tolerance and intolerance can be extreme. Hyper-intolerance is when differences in people are noticed, and they are harassed. This can be good, such as noticing when someone cheats, so that they can be dealt with by gossiping. Psychopaths *should* be noticed and dealt with by avoidance, shunning or banishment. The problem is that some of them are adept at appearing normal, and are able to escape detection until it is too late.

Some societies today are hyper-tolerant. For example, an excess of tolerance in Sweden has recently led to an excess of migrants who aren't assimilating, and are abusing welfare privileges, which is producing a backlash of "intolerance" that undermines societal harmony. I will explore this problem in later chapters.

Chapter 15. Psychopath Hijackings

Whereas the small tribe usually did not have any psychopath to worry about, when they did he was rendered harmless through either avoidance, shunning, banishment or murder. Super-tribes lost the ability to deal with psychopaths because detected psychopaths could simply relocate and continue to parasitize the super-tribe. The psychopath was never meant to lead a tribe, or super-tribe. By Mid-Holocene the societal structure had changed enough to open an opportunity for psychopaths to take control of societies. This would lead to societies comprising a civilization to be dominated by psychopaths, which produced an additional feeling of discomfort among normaloids.

So far I have portrayed the psychopath as having no useful role for the tribe (in the AE), or the super-tribe (in the Holocene). The psychopath was a liability of the small tribe whether he was just another tribesman or somehow became leader of the tribe. A small AE tribe that tolerated a psychopath in either role would be weakened and at increased risk of defeat by a neighbor tribe. The Holocene super-tribe was more vulnerable; this is because the psychopath was able to move in response to detection. In addition, some psychopaths were masters of imitating normalcy and could present a charming persona in order to gain trust. We should ask: "Can a psychopath achieve some role within the super-tribe that others can't dislodge him from, and thereby ruin the lives of the helpless normaloids in that tribe?"

During the Holocene there was a proliferation of "division of labor." Artisans invented irrigation, farmers sent their pigs for slaughter and their apples to the cider mill. All of this activity needed protection from marauding tribes. In response to this desperate need a standing army was created, and taxes were collected to pay for the army. Psychopaths and sociopaths are on a spectrum of personality traits. A charming personality could be found among both groups. Some standing armies might have been led by sociopaths, but probably not psychopaths.

Inventing Feudalism

How long would it be before one of the psychopathic leaders of an army gained control over civilian leadership, and invented feudalism? I can imagine the situation of a psychopath inventing the word "king," as if it had a heavenly-granted entitlement, and proceeding to rule as a beneficent protector of the farmer and the others needed for a farming society.

The king could have declared "ownership" of the farmland, and allowed the farmer to work the land in exchange for protection. A small tax was needed to maintain the king's

15. Psychopath Hijackings

army. What could be done by "the man with a hoe"? He needed protection, and the protection the king provided was "a deal too good to refuse."

Whereas feudalism was the main form of societal governance in medieval Europe (from about 800 AD to 1600 AD), it must have had beginnings in pre-historical times during the Holocene. Every farm-based society must have attracted marauders, so the need for protection was immediate. Initially, farmers may have informally agreed to come to each other's aid, as if an attack on one was an attack on all. Farmers under this informal agreement would constitute a partially effective deterrence because they would likely be no match for marauding tribes.

Eventually, this situation must have been viewed as an opportunity for "unemployed" sociopaths, and they may have entered into an agreement to protect the farmers who would allow themselves to be taxed to pay for the sociopath "gangs." A psychopath, noticing the payoffs for power, might wonder if he could imitate a sociopath and outwit the leader of the sociopath gang.

Psychopathic Tyrants

Feudalism, in some of its many forms, must have been present during the entirety of the Holocene. The opportunity for achieving more power over society must have been recognized by the feudal kings on many occasions. Leaders with psychopathic behavior have been recorded innumerable times by historians. For example, an Assyrian general who was victorious over a city ordered his men to gouge out the eyes of the losing population in order to secure their servitude as slaves.

Genghis Khan united tribes to form an empire that was safe from external marauders (the Mongol Empire); he then became the world's most infamous marauder by victimizing Eurasia. It has been estimated that one in 200 of the world's men have genes from Genghis Kahn; obviously, one of the goals for marauding is raping. Genghis Khan was a psychopath!

Other opportunities for psychopaths existed during the late Holocene. The Roman emperor Caligula (1ˢᵗ Century AD) was described as an insane tyrant, known for extravagant cruelty and insatiable lust.

England's King Henry VIII (16ᵗʰ Century) executed two of his eight wives and an estimated 70,000 others who opposed his rule. Another psychopath!

Russia's "Ivan the Terrible" (same century) "showed signs of cruelty, deviousness and vengefulness since childhood." As a ruler "… he ordered the brutal killing of people without proving their guilt – often just for fun – sometimes together with their kin and familiars. Ivan the Terrible showed great imagination in sentencing people to the most painful kinds of death, including burning people at the stake, impaling and boiling to death. In addition, he was married at least seven times and is believed to have killed at least two of his wives, as well as his eldest son." (Wikipedia).

Adolf Hitler, possibly the most famous psychopath of modern times, won an election in 1933 and schemed his way to becoming Chancellor of Germany. He is responsible for the death of 1/3 of the Jewish population of Europe, as well as a total of possibly 70 million people during World War II, which he started.

Joseph Stalin may have defeated an invasion by Nazi Germany, and lifted the Russian economy during his 31-year rule, but he feared the Jews, persecuted them, banished them to gulags, and is responsible for the death of possibly 7 million Russians during his rule.

The evidence is abundant that during the Late Holocene psychopaths have been able to rise to the top of societies and impose horrendous suffering upon a victimized population. This suggests that whatever "tools" were developed by AE small tribes for dealing with the occasional psychopath were useless during the Holocene when all tribes were super-tribes. Somehow, that occasional psychopath of the AE was able to escape detection in the Holocene and maneuver himself into positions of power.

The mid-Holocene invention of religion was supposed to keep the psychopaths afraid of after-death consequences for bad behavior, but religion has failed Holocene societies. Instead of curtailing psychopaths, religion has kept normaloids meek, and powerless in protecting themselves from the ascendant psychopath.

What's wrong with the normaloids?

Present-day Occupational Hijackings

Today, whereas about half of psychopaths spend some time incarcerated (the "low-functioning" psychopaths), the other half don't (the "high-functioning" psychopaths). Since psychopathy is determined by pre-frontal lobe function and IQ is determined by the function of posterior lobes, a safe default assumption is that psychopathy and IQ are uncorrelated. I speculate that it's the below 100 IQ psychopaths who end up in prison while the above 100 IQ psychopaths are successful in society and avoid prison.

As documented by several authors there are clear patterns of the incidence of psychopaths by occupation category (see Murphy, 2018, for an overview). For example, the highest incidence is for CEOs and lawyers (Dutton, 2012). Even "police officer" and

15. Psychopath Hijackings

"clergyperson" have a disproportionally higher incidence of psychopaths. Unsurprisingly, the occupations with low levels of psychopathy include nurse, caregiver and therapist. One interesting finding is that whereas doctors are on the low psychopathy list surgeons are on the high psychopathy list. (Warning: be nice with your surgeon!)

Regional correlations of psychopathy incidence reveal that Washington, D.C. is at the top of the list. In fact, it's so far above all other regions that it has to be treated as an "outlier" in order to proceed with standard statistical analyses of other regions. This finding could be explained in part by the fact that their population includes people seeking power (i.e., politicians resemble CEOs in this respect). Many lawyers and lobbyists are also present in Washington, D.C., and lawyers (and probably lobbyists) tend to be shameless psychopaths. Another factor is that most of the population of Washington, D. C. is urban, and there's a strong correlation of psychopath incidence with urban vs. rural.

Demogogues

Perhaps I have given too much importance to the role of demagogues rousing the rabble. Could it be that the masses of rabble have an insatiable appetite for violence and mayhem, due to genetic influences, and the only role of a demagogue leader is to organize the masses in order to maximize their effectiveness?

Can we find evidence from field studies of our closest related species, the chimpanzee? Michael P. Ghiglieri has written extensively (1988, 2000) about chimpanzee violence. He describes many similarities of chimpanzee and human violence. In addition to border patrolling by small bands (2 to 6 males), and their routine murder of smaller groups of chimpanzee belonging to neighboring "tribes," open warfare occurs at less frequent intervals. Their version of inter-tribal warfare can lead to total decimation of the males and youngsters of the vanquished tribe (the fertile females often join the winning tribe). Ghiglieri makes the important point (2000, pg. 176) that "Also significant is the fact that none of these apes learned these violent behaviors by watching TV or by being victims of socioeconomic handicaps … Nor were these apes spurred to war by any political, religious or economic ideology, or by the rhetoric of an insane demagogue."

Allow me to suggest that human demagogues should be thought of more as opportunists, seizing upon societal unrest, than as ideological persuaders, or originators of social movements. This provides a more nuanced view of psychopath hijackings. The masses want to be hijacked!

When a society is influenced by psychopaths in many job categories, and if in addition the governance of that society is rendered less responsive to societal needs by corrupted people in the government, a recognition of impotence by the ordinary person will have an undermining effect. Optimism about one's future ("social mobility") will be undermined. The belief in fairness in all aspects of life will be undermined. The will to work hard will be undermined.

These interpretations of the opportunities for a good life in such a society will produce its own type of discontent. The same person, living in a small AE tribe, would have experienced a more "democratic" relationship with the tribe. Small tribe life is without a chief most of the time, and tribal decisions are arrived at by consensus. The Holocene brain is no different from the AE brain in its expectation of control over one's life, and being an important tribal member. The immensity of a super-tribe can make an individual feel relatively unimportant.

There are several reasons the individual who lives in a super-tribe can feel "out of place," or "discontent." I want to emphasize two of them:

> **Discontent with civilization is produced by 1) having to encounter and politely tolerate strangers on a daily basis, and 2) feeling the frustration of living in a society dominated by psychopaths.**

Chapter 16. Too Much Tolerance

Psychopaths achieved too much control over societies during the Holocene. Why did the measures that kept psychopaths under control before the Holocene stop working? Tolerance is something invented by super-tribes for preserving harmony among strangers. Psychopaths took advantage of hyper-tolerance, and now it's too late to undo our over-eagerness to be nice.

Tolerance! That's what was needed when the early Holocene tribes coalesced into super-tribes. After a joining of tribes there must have been widespread suspicion and resentment of those strangers who the tribal leader decreed had to be trusted. They dressed differently, spoke with a different accent, used different sayings, practiced different rituals, and believed in different mythologies. Yet, this large and cumbersome tribe was victorious over all smaller tribes. So all tribesmen had to keep their instinctive intolerance in check, and feign tolerance.

Super-tribes that made the transition more smoothly were presumably rewarded with more victories. In this awkward manner the Holocene was evolving tolerance, or at least a reluctance to be publicly intolerant of those who could reasonably be considered to be a threat to society (e.g., a "slippery" psychopath).

Still, within each society that was successful there was a spectrum of tolerance. At one end were those who remained fundamentally intolerant, which we now recognize as political "conservatives." At the other end of the spectrum were those who made the coalescence work by overlooking differences, which we now recognize as political "liberals." (During the Holocene the conservatives lived in a farming and herding countryside surrounding a more populous super-tribal center that was dominated by liberals.)

Before the Holocene, during the AE, everyone lived in small HG tribes. I can imagine that psychopaths weren't tolerated when they became noticeably disruptive. Nor was the sociopath tolerated who was off-duty patrolling the tribe's territorial border and spent time in the tribal heartland with occasional disruptive behavior.

During the early Holocene social adjustments were required, and this involved allowing fellow tribesmen to have roles that didn't exist in the small HG tribes. For example, someone who dug irrigation ditches would dress differently to match digging needs, and his different dress would have to be tolerated by everyone else. It may have become common to simply notice that someone was different and assume that they had a useful role to play for the super-tribe. It must have become habitual to assume that someone who looked different, or acted differently, was nevertheless a welcome member of the super-tribe.

Is Tolerance the Problem?

Automatic tolerance can be both good and bad, just as a "double-edged sword" can cut both ways. Sure, it's good to automatically tolerate the ditch-digger with his unusual clothing and work style, but it's bad to tolerate a psychopath who is pretending to be an innocent shop keeper.

In a tolerant super-tribe it is possible to maintain the attitude that "Yes, he's quick to anger, but he's good at what he does, so let him be." That's what a liberal might say about a fellow worker who is a psychopath. Or, as one psychologist recently wrote: "…knowing more about disorders makes us less likely to stigmatize those who think or act differently." (Draaisma, 2018).

It's possible that unjustified tolerance for criminals is based on a belief that the criminal was rejected by his mother in childhood, or discipline was inconsistent, or frontal lobe development was arrested at the 10-year old stage – none of which was the future criminal's fault. As Hare wrote (1993, Ch. 12): "The term *treatment* implies that there is something to treat: illness, subjective distress, maladaptive behaviors and so forth. But, as far as we can determine, psychopaths are perfectly happy with themselves, and they see no need for treatment." Imagine the following conversation with a psychopath: "I was in the bar last night, and the guy next to me had a really cool watch. I asked him for it, and he didn't want to give it to me, so I beat him senseless. I ended up getting what I wanted, plus everyone's respect in the bar. It was his fault for not giving me his watch. I did what I had to do, and everything turned out fine. So what's the problem?" What good would it do to wag your finger at someone like that? Or try to appeal to "being nice"?

Remember that in a super-tribe when someone is found out to be a cheater, they can move to a new location where they are unknown and repeat their scam. This illustrates the importance of the Dunbar Number, a maximum tribal size for which it is possible for an adult to achieve and maintain assessments of trustworthiness of all other adults with whom they must maintain a knowledgeable relationship. Small tribes were usually smaller than the Dunbar Number, so everyone knew everyone well enough to know who the cheaters were. In a super-tribe, with thousands or hundreds of thousands of people, it is not possible for every cheating psychopath to be known by everyone else.

A psychopath is therefore able to thrive in a super-tribe for two reasons: 1) his faults are "overlooked" in the interest of being tolerant, which is a super-tribe culturgen, and 2)

16. Too Much Tolerance

when he is discovered to be a no-good cheater he can move to a new location where his reputation is unknown.

Religions superficially appear to nurture tolerance. According to one translation the Christian bible states "You have heard that it was said 'Eye for eye, and tooth for tooth.' But I tell you, do not resist an evil person! If someone slaps you on the right cheek, offer the other cheek also." (Mathew 5:39). This excess of tolerance is just one illustration of how culturgens were evolving during the mid-Holocene, making people behave differently from their nature that had evolved to serve small-tribe living situations.

The spectrum of attitudes about how to understand psychopaths is instructive. At the hyper-liberal end we have the expression of those who object to research into the biological basis of the psychopath. Here's an excerpt from the book *Psychopathy: An Introduction to Biological Findings and Their Implications* (Glenn and Raine, 2014): *"... some [suggest] that biological research on crime may open the door to discrimination based on genes ... Some have even alleged that research examining the genetic factors that may contribute to crime is similar to 'the kind of racist behavior we saw on the part of Nazi Germany' (Palca, 1992)."* Does Palca realize that Nazi Germany was created and led by psychopaths, and if the world wants to avoid a repeat of the Nazi nightmare we should understand psychopathy better, in order to be quicker in recognizing it, with a hope to avoid being gripped by the clutches of future psychopaths? With scientific cheerleaders like Palca and those who in effect become "apologists" for psychopaths, stifling research into the enemy of all stable societies, we may remain clueless throughout the entire process of a disintegrating civilization caused by the dominance of psychopaths in society and the rise of psychopathic tyrants.

We need a *greater* understanding of the genetics of psychopathy, not polite excuses for them that defaults to the assumption that they're the product of impoverished childhoods. We also need an increased <u>in</u>tolerance for psychopaths and sociopaths. The fact that just the opposite has evolved during the Holocene illustrates how dysfunctional our slow-evolving "civilization" culture has become. It also illustrates how broad a base there is for discontent among well-meaning normaloids. For as long as hyper-tolerance is central to super-tribe culture we can expect discontent to exist and grow.

Global Distribution of Hyper-Tolerance

We cannot be sure of the relative importance of cultural influences versus genetic ones in understanding the origins and maintenance of today's hyper-tolerance. Genetic evolution is much slower than culturgen evolution, but the former keeps a flexible "leash" on the latter (Lumsden and Wilson, 1981).

16. Too Much Tolerance

Maybe there's a clue in the global distribution of tolerance, which peaks in Scandinavia and is rare in the Middle East. There are many theories for why this global pattern exists (Gary, 2014, Ch. 19), but there is a more important question: Does an intolerant society protect itself from tyranny? The answer is "no," and the evidence is that the Middle East is also the historical center for tyrannies while Scandinavia is the antipode for tyranny.

Does this mean that intolerance is not an antidote to the proliferation of psychopaths (and sociopaths)? No, it just means that human history is too complicated for drawing simple conclusions about what works and what doesn't for something as complicated as psychopaths hijacking societies.

Perhaps it is misleading to attribute the tolerance of sociopaths and psychopaths on such an overall concept as "tolerance." Maybe human behavior can be better understood as resulting from a "Hodge podge" of mental activity in a brain that lacks the architecture for maintaining internal consistency. The next chapter explores this idea, and it also prepares us for an understanding of why some normaloid people can actually embrace psychopathy while others are abhorred by it.

Chapter 17. Spectacular Stupidity, or the Modularity of Mentality

Humans are "multiple mental module" automatons! Mental modules are, by definition, mostly disconnected from other mental modules. This allows a human to believe in incompatible things, and to behave in ways that are starkly incompatible with each other. We need to understand this in order to fathom how an otherwise intelligent person can support an aspiring psychopath dictator.

My Personal Experience with Spectacular Stupidity

My tax preparer is a Flat Earther! When I learned this I was simultaneously shocked, saddened and ecstatic for encountering my best personal example yet of "uneven intelligence." My tax preparer is a smart guy, overall, but like everyone else he has "blind spots." He is talented in a realm of man-made laws, but he is spectacularly stupid in the realm of natural laws. I am the opposite, being baffled by man-made laws while being instinctively comfortable in the realm of natural laws. My tax preparer might be amused by my puzzlement about "depreciated income." When I find "uneven intelligence" in people I *don't* know, I use the term "spectacular stupidity."

Probably everybody has "blind spots" in their mental capabilities. Whereas I am unaware of my literal blind spots (unless I cover one eye and prove that it's there) I am somewhat aware of my mental ability blind spots. I am sometimes baffled by the TV remote and iPhone. Based on this someone might say that I lack "tech savvy" – but I've invented an avionics instrument for "clear air turbulence" avoidance and have written more than a thousand computer programs using FORTRAN and QuickBasic.

Thankfully, everyone has different talents. This is especially true for humans since we are partially eusocialized and our species exhibits an impressive division of labor. For example, Mozart and Beethoven had perfect pitch, in addition to genius-level musical ability. There is little doubt that these abilities are genetic! The only person I have personally known who had perfect pitch (as well as the calendar ability: naming the day of the week for any date in his life) was an idiot savant! This person could be described as having "spectacular stupidity" – but I state this with empathy for his handicap and no animosity.

It's difficult to view people as having different levels of intelligence in different areas; we instead tend to view people as uniformly smart or dumb. The difficult truth to accept is that any given person can be simultaneously intelligent about some things and spectacularly stupid about others.

At a young age I learned that human nature had two stark flaws: 1) some people were horribly mean in specific situations, and 2) some people could be spectacularly stupid on specific things. The first of these revelations was natural for someone born the year World War II started, for there were picture books of the war on the family bookshelf. The second of these flaws became apparent when I learned that some people believed in prayer, angels, heaven and Hell and the biggest one of all: God. "How could people be so stupid?" I wondered, at the age of 8.

Societal Evidence for Spectacular Stupidity

When I feel especially discouraged by national trends I shrug and say to myself: "America deserves what's happening to it!" I may then re-state this sentiment by the following: "75 % of Americans deserve what Trump is bringing about!" This clarification is based on a 2016 presidential election voter turnout of 50 %, half of whom voted for Trump.

I may then recall my favorite list of American idiocies:

1) More Americans know the names of The Three Stooges than the three branches of government (74 % vs. 42 %, Zogby poll),
2) 20 % of Americans can't find the USA on a map,
3) 20 % of Americans believe the sun revolves around the Earth.

If about half of Americans are this dumb, then maybe they're the ones who didn't vote. Good, we don't need those votes.

Even if the Russians hadn't meddled, and James Comey had behaved better just before the election, which probably would have led to Hillary Clinton winning, my dismay would still be warranted; a slim victory in either direction doesn't erase the fact that about 75 % of the electorate are to blame for the combined sins of lazy neglect and tolerating evil!

How Can This Be?

Who are those 25 % of Americans who voted for Trump? There's no easy answer, because several reasons are given for their vote. Some noticed that the bankers who caused the 2008 Great Recession went unpunished (by the Obama administration). Some were in desperate financial straits, and they were willing to risk anything for change. Some were profoundly gullible, and were vulnerable to a carnival barker's pitch. Some said "We need a strong leader" (yes, but Hitler was a strong leader, as was Stalin, Genghis Khan and others). Many noted that "He talks like me, he's one of us!" This last group of pathetic people did not hesitate in their embrace of Trump. However, according

17. Spectacular Stupidity

to the theme of this book I must present the following as a final candidate explanation for the amazingly widespread support of Trump.

For thousands of years people in populous societies have had to feign tolerance of "other" people who are technically part of the home society. Finally, during the 21st Century, there has been a loosening of social pressures that allow the resentments of those "others" to be expressed. The Roobification of America, and Europe (cf. Appendix B), has emboldened a growing segment of these populations to express their real feelings. And these feelings are of hunter-gatherer people forced to live in civilization where their natural intolerance of strangers has been suppressed for thousands of years.

In every modern society people form a spectrum spanning conservative to liberal (i.e., country folk to city dweller). The rural conservatives are instinctively resentful of civilization's requirement that they pretend to embrace strangers, and finally the time has arrived that allows these intolerant people to express their true feelings openly. When this happens the instinctively liberal urban liberals are surprised, because they have been clueless for thousands of years about the true feelings of the conservatives. Sure, there have been episodes of breakdown of outward societal tranquility, but the optimists among liberals instinctively believe that such outbreaks are just brief reversals of the civilized state and that since humans are basically good they will always return to civilized behavior.

The thing that's unique about our present breakdown of civilized behavior is that the Roobification process has empowered a majority of the *hoi poloi* to become brazen in their shamelessness. Trump is therefore a welcome champion of their complaints about the elites forcing them to pretend to be civilized. Since civilized societies have never been as Roobified as now, there is little reason for believing that civilized behavior will bounce back. So many norms are being broken in America, on an almost daily basis, that there may be no return to the old norms. Timothy Snyder has warned about the dangers of not learning from past experiences that "norm breaking" is a path for weakening democracy so that it can be replaced by tyranny. His book *On Tyranny: Twenty Lessons from the Twentieth Century* (2018) is one of the scariest books on my recommend list.

Katy Tur describes in her book *Unbelieable* (2018) a memorable encounter at a Trump rally. Before the rally started she was in a bathroom trying to curl her hair with a curling iron when a woman entered and offered to help. Katy hesitated, wondering if it would be safe to hand a hot curling iron to a Trump supporter. The woman explained that she was a hairdresser, and this was good enough assurance that the offer was genuine. Indeed, the woman did a good job, and they both left to join the rally with their opposite outlooks. At this rally Trump attacked the press viciously, almost suggesting violence against them. There was thunderous applause, presumably agreeing with the accusation about how unpatriotic and dangerous the press corps was. Katy wondered if the woman who had helped her with the curling iron was one of those cheering.

While in a checkout line I sometimes find myself wondering if the person next to me is the same kind of person who Hitler mesmerized. Human nature doesn't evolve in a mere 8 decades, so people like those who were exuberant supporters of Hitler, and the Nazi agenda, are with us still. Hitler got ~ 33 % of the vote in March, 1933 (in a field of 6 candidates), and his popularity increased afterward.

A non-Jewish German woman who lived through part of the Nazi era wrote that the scariest part of her ordeal was worrying about friends or neighbors reporting her for suspicion of having unpatriotic thoughts (Arendt, 1966). If Trump succeeds in becoming America's first fascist dictator, and considering the devotion of Trump supporters, we should not discount this possibility; we should be mindful of the same suspicions and apparatus for reporting wrong thinking friends and neighbors to the Thought Police in our near future.

What is it about "human nature" that allows a civilized society to make the transition to such reprehensible behavior so quickly? How can neighbors betray neighbors, and friends betray friends, on behalf of a corrupt version of patriotism?

Dissociation Allows Compartmentalization of Mentality

Here's a similar question that's already appropriate to ask, regardless of Trump succeeding in his aspiration for becoming a dictator: "How can an otherwise intelligent and reasonable person become a Trump supporter?"

My best approach to answering such a question is to recall that humans are "multiple-module mentality automatons." About 20 % of the human genome has effects upon the brain's "wiring" (i.e., inter-neuronal connections and synapse strengths). Human evolution has selected whatever genes led to success in producing grand-children (a shorthand way to measure genetic success). For millions of years this evolutionary selection was made for humans living in tribes with a hunter-gatherer lifestyle. If genetic success required being good with fellow-tribesmen, then a gene (or genes) for a mental module that produces intra-tribal cooperation would be rewarded. If genetic success also required being cruel to neighbor tribesmen, then a gene (or genes) for creating a mental module for such cruelty would be rewarded. Both mental modules should then co-exist, regardless of any theoretical incompatibility. Presumably they are not connected with each other.

The "modularity of mentality" theory is a good perspective for understanding human nature. Psychiatry coined the word "dissociation" over a century ago in order to refer to

17. Spectacular Stupidity

an observed "compartmentalization" of thought processes. Any given person is thus capable of believing two incompatible things. For example, Isaac Newton's Newtonian physics is a very reductionist way of understanding how everything in nature moves, yet throughout his life Newton pursued a study of the bible for revealing religious meaning and predictions of future events. Because religion and science are incompatible it is noteworthy whenever an accomplished scientist is religious. Contemporary examples include Freeman Dyson and Charles Townes.

A naïve view of brain function would have trouble accounting for the coexistence of incompatible beliefs, or behaviors, in the same individual. But because different genes assemble different mental modules to meet different needs, it is apparently useful to maintain a lack of interconnection between modules. A sociobiologist who needs to account for the tribal amity/enmity phenomenon would understand the need for evolution to create a compartmentalization of mentality as a way for individuals within a tribe to out-compete other tribes.

Neuropsychology Insights

I am now going to burden you with a tutorial on one of my favorite subjects. Some of this material was presented in Chapter 5. Have patience, for the matter is relevant to understanding how people can exhibit spectacular stupidity.

Neuropsychologists have found many examples of "modularity of mentality." The most salient of these is the allocation of tasks between the frontal and posterior lobes. Two frontal lobes exist, one in the left hemisphere and one in the right. An overall perspective is that they act together to control the body (the right controls the left half of the body, and the left controls the right side of the body).

The parts of the frontal lobes that command body movement are located next to the posterior lobes (called the "motor strip"). The front parts of the frontal lobes are called "pre-frontal." Planning (or "executive function") occurs in both pre-frontal regions. Consciousness is most likely found in the left pre-frontal. The right brain pre-frontal has more connections with the "limbic system" (located at a lower level, both physically and phylogenetically), and it is therefore more "emotional" and is prone to negative moods and anti-social behavior (swearing, fighting, sex, etc.). Left pre-frontal is somewhat detached from the limbic system's primitive constraints, and it is prone to being more optimistic, or cheerful, and is sociable in a positive way.

There are three posterior lobes in each cerebral hemisphere. Vision is processed in the "occipital" lobes at the back of the brain, where the optic nerves send the eye's visual signals. On each side are the "temporal" lobes, where the ears send their signals for the processing of sound. These two lobes process information coming from outside the body;

they are therefore "remote sensor" processors. Near the top and middle are the parietal lobes; they receive signals from sensors located within the body, such as touch, temperature and joint position. This lobe is an "in situ sensor" processor. The locations of the three posterior lobes and the frontal lobe are shown in Fig. 17.1 (which is a repeat of Fig. 5.1).

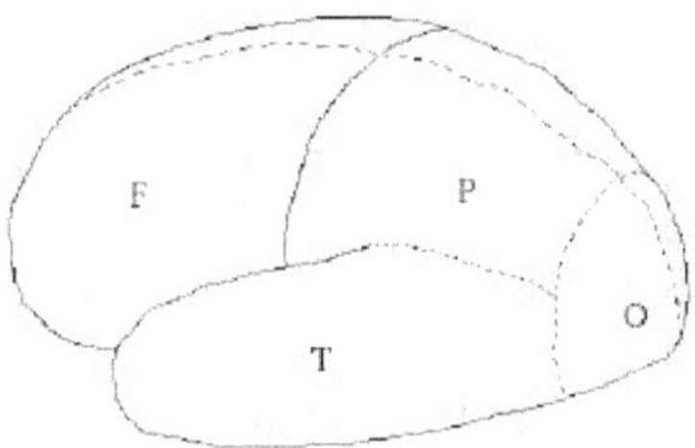

Figure 17.1. *Brain lobes: Frontal, Parietal, Temporal and Occipital. The view is of the left side, front is toward the left.*

The left and right cerebral hemispheres are close to anatomical mirror images of each other. However, they have some functional differences. For example, as described in Chapter 5 language (reception and production) is located in the left hemisphere and spatial recognition is located in the right hemisphere (cf, Fig. 5.2).

Again, as described in Chapter 5, performance on an IQ test is completely determined by the posterior lobes and "personality" resides in the frontal lobes.

I hope the foregoing helps the reader to understand that the brain is "compartmentalized" into modules with specific processing capabilities, and the modules are not connected with all others. The human evolutionary history has determined which modules need to be interconnected.

It is important to recognize that the brain is just another organ, like the heart or kidney. Each organ exists to promote survival of the genes within the species gene pool that assemble that organ. To be more specific, each part of an organ is assembled by genes whose job is almost exclusively devoted to assembling that organ part, which has for its ultimate "objective" genetic survival. It should not be surprising, therefore, for one of the brain's mental modules to perform a function that differs from another in ways that defy over-arching logic of theoretical consistency.

Accepting Unexpected Differences in People

These understandings of brain activity, reducing it to a collection of physical mechanisms, helps us understand how someone could be both intelligent and believe in

17. Spectacular Stupidity

the following hair-brained things: astrology, angels, prayer, God, life after death, flat earth, ancient aliens, alien abductions, intelligent design, global warming is a hoax, Apollo moon walks were a hoax and Trump is a great leader who will make America great again.

What are we to think when some of our favorite celebrates are discovered to have a fatal personality flaw? Consider Charlie Rose, Morgan Freeman, Harvey Weinstein and Bill Cosby: they are very talented men who took advantage of their "power" to seduce or rape women. Rape is an evolutionary adaptation, at least for those who are desperate enough or powerful enough to get away with it. The mental module for rape is able to coexist with mental modules for doing the right thing in other circumstances.

The question I've tried to answer is "How come some intelligent and otherwise nice people are horrible in other respects or spectacularly stupid in some of their beliefs?" One of these horrible beliefs is support of Trump and thus enabling him to convert one of the world's most effective democracies to a dictatorship. Can't good people see that Trump is a horrible human? Can't people recognize a psychopath when they see one?

I think about these things when I'm in a crowd. If the person next to me is friendly I am still able to imagine them reporting me to Trump's Thought Police at some future date.

It's easier to be brave during my 80th year on this wonderful Earth than when I was 30, and starting to raise a family. But it's also true that when I was 30 America was a different place. America has never been as close to dictatorship as it is now!

I hope this chapter has helped answer the question "How can an otherwise intelligent person be a Trump supporter." Maybe human stupidity isn't infinite, as Einstein jokingly suggested, but it sure is spectacular!

Chapter 18. Psychopathy Examples

In previous chapters I've alleged things about psychopaths (e.g., "too unreliable for warrior duty because they are only concerned with Number One!"), and the reader might have assumed that this was based on my familiarity with psychopaths. Wrong! I am aware of encountering only one likely psychopath, though I must have encountered more since I've either known or dealt with several hundred people in my life. Whereas recognizing a low-functioning psychopath is probably easy, because they're unable to mimic normalcy, recognizing a "high-functioning" psychopath is definitely difficult. Before the use of the *Hare Psychopathy Checklist* became common input for parole hearings many prison psychologists and psychiatrists were duped by the psychopath being considered for parole. Even the world's expert on psychopaths, Robert D. Hare, was unaware that he was having dinner with a psychopath who was the organizer of a conference where Hare was to give a talk the next day.

In retrospect, I probably had one encounter with a psychopath while working at Caltech/JPL. He was at a high level of JPL management, recruited from a major oil company, and his dismissive treatment of me concerning a proposed spacecraft mission (with a scientific goal about which I was a world expert) was classic psychopathic. With sociopaths I have a more personal experience, and I will briefly describe examples of sociopathic behaviors at the end of this chapter.

Reviewing a list of 20 items in the Psychopathy Checklist (cf. Fig. 6.3) can produce an "intellectual" understanding of psychopathy. However, real-world encounters with them can provide a more emotionally-balanced understanding. This chapter's purpose is to present examples of psychopath behaviors, taken from a classic book by Dr. Robert D. Hare, *Without Conscience: The Disturbing World of the Psychopaths Among Us* (1993). After each entry in the next section I'll give a chapter location for the quote from this book – which I highly recommend.

In the next section some of the traits are starkly evocative of what most people have noticed about Donald J. Trump, who at the time of this writing (2018 October) is currently president of the U.S., I will append trait descriptions that Trump exhibits with the notation "(DJT)."

Psychopath Samplings

A psychopath was relaxing at a harbor and noticed a couple showing interest in a boat for sale. He walked up to them and introduced himself as the owner. He invited them in to inspect the boat, and before long he had a down payment check for $1500 – and promptly disappeared.

18. Psychopathy Examples

Before the Hare Psychopathy Checklist was in common use at parole hearings prisoners tried their best to appear normal in order to fake results of traditional psychology testing. The psychopaths were best at this. During one prisoner interview a psychopath stated that "… psychologists and psychiatrists were air heads who believed anything he told them." (Ch. 2)

Psychopaths frequently lie about their past, and they have a "smooth lack of concern at being found out." (Ch. 3, DJT)

A prisoner who was the typical "mile-a-minute" fast talker "… with the psychopath's characteristic ability to contradict himself from one sentence to the next." (Ch. 3, DJT)

"Psychopaths view … the weak and the vulnerable – whom they mock, rather than pity - [as] favorite targets." (Ch. 3)

"Their statements often reveal their belief that the world is made up of 'givers and takers,' predators and prey, and that it would be very foolish not to exploit the weaknesses of others. In addition, they can be very astute at determining what those weaknesses are …" (Ch. 3)

A woman with a long history of frauds and petty thefts explained her belief that "money grows on trees": "They say it doesn't, but it does. I don't *want* to do it to people, it's just so *easy*." (Ch 3)

Psychopaths lack <u>fear</u>! A prisoner stated that "… he did not really understand what others meant by 'fear.' … When I rob a bank I notice that the teller shakes or becomes tongue-tied. One barfed all over the money." (Ch. 3)

A disconnection from feelings is common for psychopaths. "'He is truly one of the most dangerous sociopaths I have ever seen' said the Superior Court Judge after sentencing 37-year old San Jose attorney Norman Russell Sjonbourg for the brutal slaying of one of his clients from whom he had embezzled money. His third wife … [stated] that when she first met him 'He seemed like a nice guy, soft spoken and exceedingly charming.' But she also note 'From the start Russell spoke about this emotional void, an inability to feel things like everyone else; to know when to cry, when to feel joy.' … he 'led a kind of paint-by-numbers emotional life,' and that 'he read self-help psychology books to learn the appropriate emotional responses to everyday events.'" (Ch. 3)

"… a chronically unstable and aimless lifestyle marked by casual and flagrant violations of social norms…" (Ch. 4, DLT)

"... are highly reactive to perceived insults or slights. ... the slightest provocation is sufficient to overcome them. ... They take offense easily and become angry and aggressive over trivialities... Their outbursts ... are generally short-lived, and they quickly resume acting as if nothing out of the ordinary has happened." (Ch. 4, DJT)

"An inmate in line for dinner was accidentally bumped by another inmate, whom he proceeded to beat senseless. The attacker then stepped back into his place in line as if nothing had happened. Despite the fact that he faced solitary confinement ... his only comment when asked to explain himself was "I was pissed off. He stepped into my space. I did what I had to do." (Ch. 4)

"Are psychopaths particularly well suited for dangerous professions? ... a former student of mine ... doesn't think so. ... He studied British bomb-disposal experts ... [and] found that the soldiers who performed the exacting and dangerous task of defusing or dismantling IRA bombs referred to psychopaths as 'cowboys,' unreliable and impulsive individuals who lacked the perfectionism and attention to detail needed to stay alive on the job. ... It is just as unlikely that psychopaths would make good spies, terrorists, or mobsters, simply because their impulsiveness, concern only for the moment, and lack of allegiance to people or causes make them unpredictable, careless, and undependable – likely to be 'loose cannons.'" (Ch. 4, DJT)

"Obligations and commitments mean nothing to psychopaths. ... Their performance on the job is erratic, with frequent absences, misuse of company resources, violations of company policy, and general untrustworthiness. They do not honor formal or implied commitments to people, organizations or principles." (Ch. 4, DJT)

"Sociobiologists take the view that behavior development is influenced by genetic factors, and they might argue that the number of psychopaths must be increasing simply because they are very promiscuous and produce large numbers of children, some of whom may inherit a predisposition for psychopathy." (Ch. 4)

"Unlike most other criminals, psychopaths show no loyalty to groups, codes, or principles, other than to 'look out for number one.'" (Ch. 6, DJT)

"On average, about 20 percent of male and female prison inmates are psychopaths. Psychopaths are responsible for more than 50 percent of the serious crimes committed." (Ch. 6)

"Perhaps half of the repeat or serial rapists are psychopaths." (Ch. 6)

"We found that 25 percent of the men in the sample [of wife beaters were psychopaths]." (Ch. 6)

18. Psychopathy Examples

"… the behavior of psychopaths is notoriously resistant to change." (Ch. 6)

"The violent recidivism rate of psychopaths is about triple that of other offenders." (Ch. 6)

"… the maximum possible score on the *Psychopathy Checklist* [40, is] … given to fewer than one in two hundred serious offenders. [I think this should be interpreted to mean that the incidence of a PCL score = 40 is ~ 0.5 / 200 = ¼ %]. (Ch. 6)

"He values people only insofar as they bend to his will or can be coerced or manipulated into doing what he wants." (Ch. 6. DJT)

"… a characteristic typically found in psychopaths: facile distortions of reality even when they know that others are aware of the facts." (Ch. 7. DJT)

"… his wish to be 'liked by everyone,' his euphemistic view of himself as [accomplished], and his 'fear of losing face,' he considered his crimes logical responses to frustration and pressure, or more the victim's fault than his own. … anyone who is stupid enough to trust or believe him deserves the consequences…" (Ch. 7. DJT)

"Their job is made a lot easier simply because a lot of people are surprisingly gullible, with an unshakable belief in the inherent goodness of man." (Ch. 7)

"Most of us would be devastated and humiliated by public exposure as a liar and a cheat, but not the psychopath. He or she can still look the community straight in the eye and give impassioned assurances …" (Ch. 7. DJT)

"… many psychopaths never go to prison or any other facility. They appear to function reasonably well – as lawyers, doctors, psychiatrists, academics, mercenaries, police officers, cult leaders, military personnel, business people, writers, artists, entertainers, and so forth – without breaking the law, or at least without being caught and convicted. These individuals are every bit as egocentric, callous and manipulative as the average criminal psychopath; however, their intelligence, family background, social skills, and circumstances permit them to construct a façade of normalcy and to get what they want with relative impunity. Some commentators refer to them as 'successful psychopaths.' … Rather than refer to these individuals a successful psychopaths - after all, their success is often illusory and always at someone else's expense – I prefer to call them *subcriminal* psychopaths. … I am certain that if the families and friends of such individuals were willing to discuss their experiences without fear of retribution, we would uncover a rat's nest of emotional abuse, philandering, double-dealing, and generally shoddy behavior." (Ch. 7. DJT)

When a psychopath talks his hand gestures tend to be exaggerated, chaotic and somewhat unrelated to what is being said. Because of the inappropriate and forceful nature of these hand gestures they are called "beats" by those who interview people suspected of being psychopathic. In addition to confusing hand gestures "...their speech is full of inconsistent or contradictory statements." (Hare, 1993, Ch. 8). This resembles the split-brain patient who was buttoning his shirt with one hand and unbuttoning it with the other. One neuropsychology theory for explaining this comes from evidence that psychopaths have language production in both cerebral hemispheres (instead of only the left), and neither is connected with the limbic system (the source of emotions). The speculation is that both cerebral hemispheres are competing for language production, and the gestures which normally are produced by the right hemisphere in coordination with the speaking left hemisphere (also in coordination with the limbic system) is confused about which language generation region to coordinate with. (Ch. 8, DJT)

I now want to illustrate psychopathy with a stark example from recent history. In 1989 Lyle and Erik Menendez murdered their parents with a shotgun, and lived lavishly on an inheritance during the months between the murders and their arrests. (The father was a successful executive, and it is noteworthy that there is a preponderance of psychopaths among successful executives.) The Menendez brothers were eventually convicted of the murders and are serving life sentences. I would have liked them to have testified at the penalty phase of their trial with the following:

"We are psychopaths, just like our parents. We didn't ask to be born with psychopath genes. It's not fair to anyone that our parents brought us into the world. It's not fair to us and it's not fair to others, because we can't help ourselves from behaving psychopathically. It's not our parents fault either for giving birth to us; it's the fault of society for allowing our parents to have babies. Worse, it's society's fault for not acknowledging that psychopaths are born, and can't control their psychopathy. It's society's fault for not dealing wisely with us psychopaths, and looking the other way whenever we psychopaths are identified as a problem. Society should thank us for killing two of our kind. We did what society is too wimpish to do. You non-psychopaths who run society are guilty of neglect, and because of that neglect we psychopath brothers were allowed to come into the world. Our actions are therefore your fault. Shame on you!"

What a dramatic defense this would have been! Still, it would have been ignored, because normaloids are wimps. Especially the clueless and shameless hyper-tolerant (i.e., hyper-liberal) normaloids, who prefer to blame bad behavior in adulthood on scars from childhood, that are somehow caused by society. As long as these apologists for criminals influence societal beliefs, and their influence will always be with us, genetically-created psychopaths will continue to be born and flourish at the expense of us normaloids.

As an aside, both of the Mendez brothers have been pursued by women wanting to marry them, and several marriages and divorces by them have occurred. Fortunately, California

18. Psychopathy Examples

doesn't permit conjugal visits for those convicted of murder, so no more Menendez psychopath genes are flowing in our species gene pool. But why would any woman be attracted to a psychopath murderer? Charles Manson, one of the most infamous psychopaths in American history, also attracted women while in prison, and he also had a marriage proposal.

The uncomfortable truth is that some women are attracted to psychopaths because they will not hesitate to kill any other man who is perceived to be flirting with his wife. Why does this matter? Because another man might be a "takeover male," and such men are prone to killing the woman's offspring after the "take over" (this is found among many species besides humans, such as monkeys and especially lions.) We must confront the possibility that some people welcome the psychopath in their lives. This welcome may include marriage, but also leadership of a company or country.

Advice by Ruth Westheimer (1986, pg. 21), a woman's advisor for female sexual fulfillment, is relevant here. She suggested that "Most married women want pirates, or something like pirates..." and "Here is a good marriage fantasy - to imagine that your nice steady husband, who never inconveniences you by being arrested or a fugitive (*sic*), is really a dangerous criminal..." (You can substitute "psychopath" for "dangerous criminal" in this advice.)

Sociopathic Samplings (from one person)

The person I'll describe was diagnosed with "borderline personality disorder" (which I translate to mean "sociopathy") by two clinical psychologists. Her PCL was approximately 13, but this is just an estimate by a non-professional. She died about 20 years ago (from cancer).

Her over-arching character trait is a focus of concern for herself, and an imperfect imitation of concern for others. This was difficult to detect upon casual acquaintance.

She was cheerful and generally charismatic. She made friends easily, and everyone liked her from the beginning. For example, when dancing at a party once, her wig fell to the floor, and without hesitation she picked it up, put it on, and continued dancing. Everyone laughed; the nonchalance about something that would embarrass most women turned into something delightful that was entertaining for all.

She smoothed life's path with lies that served the moment. Occasionally she would be caught, but was never chastened. Indeed, some of her responses to embarrassing questions were disarmingly humorous for their unexpected candor.

She had a "personal boundary" problem, and with no hesitation would sneak looks at other people's mail or other private material.

She would ignore normal child-rearing chores, and attend to her needs instead. Everything was about her, and the needs of anyone else, including her children, were secondary.

She once took the family dog in the car to the mountains, abandoned it there, and drove home. All because she didn't want to be bothered by the obligations of pet ownership (which she inherited after divorce).

A couple decades after she died I learned that she had a long history (~ 20 years) of "shop lifting" at department stores. The excuse given was "They owe it to me because of all the purchases I've made in the past."

In short, this person lacked that most human trait: conscience!

Chapter 19. A Paean to Psychopaths

I'm a "normaloid" with a self-administered PCL score of zero. It would be easy for me to take the position that all psychopaths should undergo a frontal lobotomy, or that they should be either banished or executed. However, the "high-functioning" psychopath (i.e., high IQ, with emotions under control) can have redeeming value in society.

Paean to Psychopaths

For example, I suspect that most trial lawyers are psychopaths (e.g., Thomas, 2013). They like the challenge of maneuvering their opposing lawyer into (humiliating) defeat. If I ever needed to defend myself from an unjust lawsuit I'd want the services of a "tiger" lawyer. As long as lawyers adhere to established laws they can serve society.

Even the surgeon, who is uninhibited about cutting living flesh and organs with a sharp scalpel can be useful. My main concern with them as a group is that I suspect they lobby for surgery as a preferred treatment when non-invasive treatments are more effective. Also, if I ever need a surgeon I have to remember to not offend him before the operation!

I have the same appreciation for people who can work at a humane society facility, surrounded by once abandoned dogs, moaning in pain and loneliness, with marginally empathic veterinarians performing surgery regularly.

I suspect that psychopaths sometimes make good entrepreneurs. They can be creative, and fearless with risky new ventures, and they can also be good salesmen for acquiring financial backing for risky start-up companies.

Some CEOs have what's needed to run a large company efficiently. For example, they don't allow friendships to get in the way of firing non-performing people, under-performing divisions and dead-end projects. They also are less emotional and more calculating in their thinking. Imagine the following business meeting at the Fitbit Company: The CEO starts with "What should we do about the new Apple watch with both pulse and now EKG capability. Should we add EKG to our fitbit?" One argues "Yes, because we had pulse first, and it's not fair that they crowd us out of a market niche." After a few others express themselves the psychopath in the meeting says "EKG capability is expensive, and the Apple watches with it will always cost more than our standard fitbits. It's too late for us to climb the curve to compete for the wealthy Apple customers. Let's settle for our reliable market share of those who either can only afford pulse or who are a stepping stone to EKG." These two styles of thinking illustrate the difference between emotional thinking and cold calculating and unemotional strategizing. The latter is better suited for business decisions, so CEO's may be better in the role of guiding company decisions.

A high performing psychopath has a penetrating insight that places him, or her, on an intellectual terrain with a perspective that allows him to see bullshit more clearly than a timid academic, for example. Academics don't want to displease any of their peers by departing from what's politically correct (because "you never know" when a peer will be the reviewer of a proposal). I suspect that most high functioning psychopaths understand clearly that morality, conscience and patriotism are genetic tricks for enslaving the meek, uncritical *hoi poloi* for the "purpose" of strengthening the eusocial performance of tribes, and now societies. These genetic predispositions are a gene's tricky path to *their* immortality, showing no regard for individual welfare beyond what's needed for their clueless slave to perform on their behalf.

My most important paean to psychopaths is their non-judgmental tolerance of other people's beliefs. If I were to create of list of my favorite "human rights" I'd start with "the right to be left alone." In 21st Century America we tend to forget the past centuries and millennia of small-community religious zealots who kept track of who neglected to attend church last Sunday or who stated an opinion that might be taken as slightly blasphemous. Villages are famous for nosy neighbors gossiping about suspiciously selfish (or unpatriotic) neighbors. Enforcers of conformance are the enemy of the intellectually curious. It's my understanding that psychopaths don't care about another person's religion, or lack of religion. They just don't want another person to stand in their way and frustrate them. I think I could remain friends with a psychopath (and maybe I have such friends and don't know it), provided I didn't tell them what to do or get in their way of doing something that didn't concern me.

I'll admit that whenever I'm driving past a church with a full parking lot I mutter to myself "F... idiots!" My anger is motivated by an awareness that most of these people are intolerant hypocrites whose mentality resembles the ones who burned open-minded questioners at the stake (e.g., Giordano Bruno). The same intolerance and impulse to proselytize produced the Crusades. The same people were behind the Catholic Inquisitions. The same kind of people proclaimed Socrates guilty of "corrupting the youth" because he urged them to ask questions. Nazi book-burnings were passively tolerated by the same people, two millennia later. As I mutter my epithet I know that my moral character is better than probably all of those hypocrites in the church.

Preferring Normaloids

In spite of some laudable aspects that at least some high-functioning psychopaths exhibit there are downsides to living in a world with sociopaths and psychopaths (S&P). I prefer to live among normaloids.

For example, I don't like crime. Cheating shop lifters just increase the price of things for non-cheaters. Telemarketing robocalls are done by white collar (sociopath) criminals

19. Paean to Psychopaths

who have no concern about who is annoyed by the way they conduct business. House break-ins, whether by drug addicts who can't function as wage earners or criminals who are too lazy to work, force everyone to lock doors, pay for surveillance systems and undermine social harmony.

I sometimes think of psychopaths as "robots without emotions." They can think, and they can learn to imitate us normaloids, but beginning a friendship with a robot must eventually become unsatisfactory for the void of shared emotional experience.

Probably my most important gripe with having to share the world with psychopaths is about their corrupting influence over governance. Almost every failing that gets a consensus of complaint has straightforward solutions. The reasons they're not discussed is often because a solution would interfere with a business run by a psychopath who has ways to lobby or argue against the solution.

I prefer to live in a world with a high standard of living, based on the labors of devoted and conscientious workers. As long as conscientious workers ply their trade unquestioningly, and hopeful that just rewards will happen, that the world is a fair place, the community will prosper. I am willing to be one of those conscientious workers for as long as I believe in the return of just rewards.

None of these concerns is worth dwelling upon, because psychopaths and sociopaths are going to be with us forever! By "forever" I mean for the next few centuries. Their threat to civilization is insidious and unstoppable. Utopias are only for imagining.

Are Sociopaths and Psychopaths Really the Victim?

It is sometimes suggested that sociopaths and psychopaths (S&P) have worse lives, overall, than normaloids - especially considering the S&P premature and pathetic endings (Stout, 2005, Ch. 10). According to Stout their threshold for boredom causes an excessive need for stimulation, and this leads many of them to suffer from addictions (alcohol, drugs, HIV). It occurs to me that S&Ps are the product of a mutation that benefits the gene while sacrificing welfare of the individual S&P. The reason the gene mutation for S&P spreads is from the higher than normal fecundity associated with the S&P lifestyle. Whereas expanded paternal investment is one strategy for genetic payoff, another strategy could be expanded fecundity accompanied by minimal S&P paternal investment (but greater maternal investment by the victim). This life strategy resembles that of cuckoo birds: the female cuckoo bird lays eggs in the nests of other, unsuspecting birds, and thereby avoids parental work while potentially leading to the production of large numbers of offspring.

19. Paean to Psychopaths

How ironic it would be if through some scientific process it could be shown that S&P males are the true victims of their victimizing personality, who pay the price of their lifestyle by having bad life outcomes and endings. Such a theory would have to address the fact that there are as many female S&P as male.

In addition to most psychopaths coming to a ruinous and premature ending of their lives their combined effect on societal strength may also lead to a premature ruinous ending of civilization. This is one of the topics of future chapters.

Chapter 20. A Paean to Conservatives

Conservatives aren't "bad," they just have a different experience with life, or possibly different genetics, and liberals should understand this.

It is human nature to cast others as either "all good" or "all bad." My experience earning a living in the physical sciences involved the ability to maintain several incompatible theories as possibilities until mounting evidence favors one of them. The same mental approach is useful in understanding why people adhere to their political beliefs.

I may be better qualified than most for explaining liberals to conservatives, and conservatives to liberals – because I have been both and am now neither.

Six decades ago (the 1950s) conservatives emphasized "personal responsibility." This meant accepting responsibility for oneself instead of expecting others to provide help. When a person was demonstrably incapable of taking care of themselves it was their family's responsibility to help, not a government agency. This may seem harsh, considering that America had recently spent more than a decade in an economic depression that inflicted suffering upon people who had no role in creating it. But part of the explanation could be that people living in the country were able to grow their own crops and maintain a level of self-sufficiency that was impossible for city dwellers; in this way conservatism may have retained a foothold in American rural regions. My father grew up on a farm, and so did I. We were therefore somewhat insulated from the urban plight of economic helplessness.

Every country boy will admit to feeling superior to city boys. We had chores and did work outdoors that made us strong, we felt important for the responsibilities that supported our family, we had guns and could hunt rabbits, we knew the outdoors and weren't afraid to explore, we trapped muskrats, we knew when it was safe to walk on river ice, when we swam in the river we knew how to avoid dangerous whirlpools, we camped out, sometimes in abandoned shacks that were said to be haunted, we walked miles to school, we conquered our fear of the dark, we learned to assess which dogs merely barked and which would attack, we could walk in a field of cows and know when a bull's aggression was real – in short, our maturity was years ahead of our sissy city cousins.

Being self-reliant seemed natural because all the wild animals were also self-reliant. Rabbits figured out how to survive cold winters, squirrels provisioned nuts for the winter, racoons figured out how to build tree nests and sneak into chicken coops. The phrase "A wounded eagle, eying the sky" has extra meaning for a country boy: if the eagle doesn't heal in time it will die. There's no "Association of Eagle Assistance," just as there's no

"Association for Farm Chores" to help the wounded farmer. Farmers, like wild animals, must be self-sufficient.

It's normal for country boys to become young men who value self-reliance. It is also understandable that we viewed reliance on others as a weakness, a failure to mature. Farm families were usually large, and when a boy was unable to handle country challenges, he was considered unworthy – if he died, that was nature's way. One of my cousins died at a young age when he foolishly drove a tractor on a hillside in the wrong way. There was no coddling of boys on a farm! We knew that city boys were coddled, and they were cowardly afraid of the dangers we had mastered.

I don't know if city boys understood how we country boys viewed them. Being shielded from work, responsibility, danger and all the challenges of country living meant that they didn't understand the value of maturing in the manner that country boys had to. They may have had other challenges, such as learning the rewards of helplessness. (Sorry, I'm getting carried away with my disdain for coddled child-rearing.)

Conservatism is a natural outlook for country folk. Liberalism, to the extent that it preaches helping each other, is a natural outlook for city people. This dichotomy must have existed for the entirety of the Holocene epoch, when urban life first appeared.

As a 79-year old adult I am both conservative and liberal. I now want to try to explain to my liberal readers a way to understand contemporary conservatives. I will continue to use my life experience for illustrating this.

During all my school years I never saw a foreigner, and only one Negro (using a term of the times, the 1950s, but referred to today as an African American). Our country was made safe from Nazi and Japanese fascism by our fathers (mine served in the Army, as did uncles and most other able-bodied men). The privations of World War II affected all Americans: our mothers who stayed home to maintain the farm, and the children who missed our fathers at an important age. These patriotic sacrifices were unremarkable, given the knowledge of our family ancestry: a great uncle who served as an aviator during World War I, a great-great grandfather who founded a city (bearing my name) in Indiana, distant ancestors in the Civil War, and 7 generations of my ancestors who arrived in America a few years after the Mayflower. My family and relatives have invested in the proud growth of America through civic and professional accomplishments. A parent wants a better life for their children, and grand-children, and they will sacrifice in order to achieve that result. Perhaps this is why we feel entitled to the enjoyment of what our parents and grand-parents sacrificed to create. Why, then, should we welcome illegal immigrants to our land who are seeking better opportunities than were provided by *their* ancestors in *their* home country?

20. Paean to Conservatives

Today when I shop in a supermarket, I am sometimes struck by my minority appearance: firstly, I'm not fat, I dress properly, I speak English well, my race is the one that has been creating America since my ancestors arrived in 1630. I'm also one of those "old white males" that contemporary liberals like to mock.

It is telling that the ones who are most prone to mock "old white males" are the new arrivals to America, who are unsure of how they fit in! There might be an underlying insecurity prompting coddled liberals to fear everything, and to blame the self-sufficient conservatives for creating a world in which they are not sufficiently protected! The coddled liberal has the fragility of a "snowflake," hence this derogatory term for them. The snowflake liberal never learned how to walk on river ice, or swim among dangerous river whirlpools, or hunt rabbits and squirrels, or conquer the fear of camping overnight in a haunted house, or walk miles in all weather conditions to a country school, or have pissing contests in the country school's stinking outhouse. For my first 5 years of school I walked 4 miles of country roads every school day, in rain, snow, icy conditions as well as warm and clear sky weather. The snowflake liberal senses their weakness, their vulnerability, and they feebly blame their betters for their fears. The snowflake liberal fears new ideas because they are aware, perhaps at a subconscious level, about the precariousness of their argument. They shout down speakers with different views without realizing that, as the old Chinese proverb states: "The person whose argument descends to shouting thereby reveals that his ideas have given out."

A person who goes into nature alone is engaging in a "veridical experience" – to use a favorite phrase of child developmental psychologist Jean Piaget's protégé Newell Kephart. Nature can't be negotiated with; it is predictable and has no interest in either helping or hurting a person. For example, if you fall out of a tree, it's not the tree's fault; it's the fault of the climber. If a tree climber hears a limb start to crack, the person can't negotiate with the tree limb to not crack further.

A person who spends a lot of time in the outdoors learns to accept responsibility for their decisions. They also learn how to disregard wishful thinking about a situation and to face it objectively. Anyone who simply prays when they have found themselves in a dangerous situation is less likely to survive than the person who honestly comprehends the situation and formulates a plan of action.

A city person has fewer of these "veridical" experiences. Many of the dangerous situations faced by a city person are more likely to involve social conflicts, and these can often be survived by clever talk.

I claim that a country boy's bravery, developed by outdoor veridical experiences, is good preparation for bravely exploring the world of ideas with a proper disregard for conventional wisdom. I will forever remember a lecture by an explorer who survived on Antarctica alone by learning which pre-trip advice was good, and which was bad, by relying upon honest assessments of what worked. For example, in a very cold climate fat foods were good and sweet ones were bad (as I recall). One "takeaway" from his talk was that I too was an explorer; I explored the realm of ideas instead of the realm of a cold and unforgiving Antarctic landscape. In one case the rewards are personal survival, a feeling of accomplishment and possibly a contribution to general knowledge, and in the other case the rewards are usually limited to a feeling of personal accomplishment.

The same self-reliance developed for assessing the strength of river ice for walking upon could also be used for assessing a philosophical argument. My attitude toward ancient philosophers changed from awe to disappointment as I matured. I have no fear of contradicting the most esteemed philosopher, and I bring the same attitude in my approach to the academic baloney coming from sociologists, or any other academic argument. I have self-confidence in assessing where the ice is thin, on both a frozen river and in an academic argument.

Maybe it could be argued that my ability to extend self-assurance from experience in the outdoors to academic matters is due to intelligence. If my IQ were 3-sigma lower than average I might know where the ice is thin but fail to know where an academic argument is thin. Nevertheless, such a person could still be able to sense when to distrust an academic without understanding the points of the argument. A person can have a low IQ and still sense that another person is cheating them. This ability may come from experiences in which the person was in fact taken advantage of by a more intelligent person. This happens! It's human nature.

Now I can bring my argument to the task at hand for this chapter. Most country folk have a healthy distrust of "city slickers." The country bumpkin may hear the salesman's pitch for a life insurance policy when there are no dependents, and intuitively sense that there's something wrong with the salesman's pitch. That's a capability of the posterior lobes of the right brain.

I try to put myself in the shoes of my old high school friends, most of whom were also farm boys, and I ask myself how they might view America today, as "old white men." Whereas when I was a farm boy a living could be made on a farm by knowing how to mix "slop" and pour it into a pig trough, today a few factory farms have replaced the many family farms. Even the factory farm is computer-dependent, with spreadsheets for everything and computer-driven tractors. My farm boy friends must have first worked in factories after leaving the farm. But slowly the factories were bought by large, international corporations, and the jobs moved overseas where there were fewer to no safety and environmental laws and labor was cheap. The factory workers knew where their jobs had moved to and they must have sensed that worker livelihoods didn't matter to the city slickers running the corporations – which was an accurate surmise.

My old farm boy friends must then have been forced into working at city jobs, probably retail related. As small shops closed in response to super-store openings, they would then have worked at places like Walmart. They would possibly be selling things that they used to produce in the long-closed factories, which were now made by cheap foreign labor; that must have hurt. Other alternatives would have existed, but some of them

20. Paean to Conservatives

would have involved learning MS Word and Excel, or special-purpose programs resembling Excel. These new jobs made them feel like "cogs in a wheel" with minimal control over their lives.

At least on the old family farm there was more control over life; you could gather eggs before feeding the pigs, and you could decide when a pig was ready to be slaughtered. The family garden was subject to even more personal control, such as which vegetables to plant and how many of each, and how the tomato planting could be staggered in time for a lengthened ripening season.

Then there are cultural changes that happen at an ever-quickening pace. The old land-line phone was replaced by a smart phone, but the smart phone had so many new features that it became difficult to do what the old land-line phone had done. The home computer was nice, but it soon became necessary to install virus protection software, and danger was lurking when browsing the internet. Identity theft began, and credit bureau accounts, which no one asked for, had to be frozen between big credit purchases. Cars evolved, and they didn't just drive from place A to B, but they had entertainment centers, and the radio push-buttons disappeared for something mysterious taking their place.

In short, life became more complicated, and there was a sense that you had to keep learning new things in order to keep danger at bay. And whose fault was it, for making life ever more complicated, and keeping wages from growing, causing a stagnation of living standard. It was some unseen entity in the city, some coddled city-slickers who never learned how to walk on river ice!

For my old farm boy friends, who are now old white men, there must have developed a secret wish for a return to simpler times. The motto "Make America Great Again" is meant to bring to consciousness this secret wish for the past. It also causes the nostalgic person to wonder who has been changing America, causing it to become a more frustrating place to live in. The MAGA motto is aimed at conservatives. It's the liberal city slickers who are victimizing us, taking away our old self-reliant selves and delivering us into servitude to some secret city collective.

There is some truth in the suspicions of middle-of-America conservatives. After all, who created the 2008 recession? And was any banker punished for that?

I have been a beneficiary of the changes during the past half century, so I have no personal experience to complain about. However, a little understanding about this, especially by liberal politicians, would be helpful. It would not be too difficult to acknowledge the experience of the disheartened, former rural people. Job retraining legislation would be a small first step. Tariffs are needed for imports from countries without worker safety legislation, or environmental protections, or very low wages.

I'm still conservative on some things, and liberal on others. The only things I'll never embrace are the snowflake liberal positions that are a result of sissy, coddled upbringing (Lukianoff and Haidt, 2018).

Chapter 21. Hyper-Eusociality (Fascism)

It may be evolutionarily advantageous to alternate between a low-level of eusociality, for the purpose of developing diversity and thus strengthening the tribe, and reverting to a high-level of eusociality when the tribe feels vulnerable, in order to survive an expected attack. This instinct may still be present today.

Parochial altruism is a speculation that when a tribe, or society, is enjoying prolonged peace, presumably after vanquishing nearby rivals, the individuals within the victorious tribe are freed from the exigencies of war and they are therefore prone to undergo a transition to greater concern for self. Individualism becomes fashionable as duty to the collective recedes. Behaviors that benefit self, and family or friends, become more common than devotion to self-sacrificing behaviors that strengthen the collective. In short, patriotism is replaced by self-absorbed individualism.

Parochial altruism also specifies that there will be a behavioral flip when the same tribe, or society, is provoked by a stronger rival and must defend itself. The growing feeling of vulnerability evokes an abandonment of individualism, a concern for self, family and friends, as every person hears and answers the patriotic "call to arms." The farmer sets aside his hoe and picks up a spear. The city shopkeeper closes business and he also picks up a spear. Everyone leaves what they had been doing, they set aside the enjoyment of peaceful lifestyles, and they join an army to defend the homeland.

This speculation is both reasonable and inevitable. During the AE any tribe that neglected to defend itself with total resolve when seriously challenged would be vanquished and disappear from evolutionary relevance. Also, any tribe that squandered interludes of peace by neglecting the exploration of diversity for improving tribal prosperity and strength would eventually find itself weaker and more vulnerable than nearby tribes.

I would like to enlarge upon the parochial altruism theory. In anticipation of this I expanded the previous paragraphs to convey more than was given in published accounts of parochial altruism. Whereas these published accounts emphasize the rise and fall of "altruism" during the alternations between warfare and peaceful interludes, my enlarged version states that more things than altruism change during these war and peace alternations. Eusociality provides a larger context for understanding all aspects of individual and social behavior during these two states. Altruism is just one such aspect.

As the next figure illustrates a person's behavior can be focused on different levels of the social realm. A psychopath is always focused on "self." A normaloid is usually focused on mainly "self, family, friends and neighbors." The novel condition that this chapter is about is how normaloids can be changed by tribal necessity, or the belief that there is a tribal necessity, on devotion to "tribe or country" *exclusively*! There are times

21. Fascism

in the AE when tribal survival required that essentially everyone in the tribe reduce their concern for self, family and friends in order to be fully devoted to helping the tribe survive. When this transition is accomplished all tribesmen are "fascist disciples."

Psychopath	Normaloid	Fascist Disciple
SELF	SELF	SELF
FAMILY	FAMILY	FAMILY
FRIENDS & NEIGHBORS	FRIENDS & NEIGHBORS	FRIENDS & NEIGHBORS
TRIBE OR COUNTRY	TRIBE OR COUNTRY	TRIBE OR COUNTRY
HUMANITY	HUMANITY	HUMANITY

Figure 21.1 *Where concern is focused by different people at different times.*

When a tribe in the AE began to feel vulnerable it would have been adaptive for tribesmen to suspend their experimenting with diversity, and the elaboration of division of labor, and instead prepare for defensive warfare. Any tribe that failed to do this would likely soon disappear. The required transition involves the following steps: detecting danger, persuading the entire tribe that danger exists, enforcing conformance with a transition to a patriotic stance, and abandoning all caution when warfare erupts.

How all these things are accomplished to successfully achieve a transition to fascism may have been written about by many scholars. I am only familiar with the following two books on the subject of how democracies transition to tyrannies, which I recommend: *On Tyranny: Twenty Lessons from the Twentieth Century* (2018) by Snyder and *How Democracies Die* (2018) by Livitsky & Ziblatt.

My purpose in presenting a brief discussion of the fascism transition is to call attention to the possibility that the super-tribe is vulnerable to abuse of the instinct to respond to a "call to arms" for the transition to a fascist stance. The abuser I have in mind is a psychopath who has learned to "game society" for personal gain. Recall that in the AE tribes were small enough that most of them did not have a psychopath among their adult male membership, so there was little danger of tribal hijackings by psychopaths. It is therefore not a part of human nature to identify these psychopath hijackings. The super-tribe will have many psychopaths among the adult male population.

Germany was unprepared for Hitler, who railed against vengeance by the rest of Europe after the Treaty of Versailles left Germany weak and vulnerable. Hitler scapegoated the Jews, the communists and all elites – blaming them for conspiring to destroy Germany. It is possible that Hitler believed his rabble-rousing speeches. But it is also possible that he was aware that he was tapping-in to a paranoid vulnerability of the German populace, and that by leading the German people to a new social order, what we refer to as fascism, he could lead a lavish lifestyle. Stalin also lived lavishly, in spite of him being the leader of a country supposedly founded on the communist idea that "everyone receives equal shares of the benefits of societal wealth." Mussolini, the "fascist Casanova," enjoyed a lavish lifestyle. Clearly, the rewards for living lavishly, based on whatever ideology would lead to it, was something that would appeal to any ambitious psychopath.

Every society that is stressed should be wary of the danger that an ambitious psychopath will try to exaggerate the level of existential danger in order to become a leader who will protect the people. America: pay attention!

Chapter 22. Present Predicament

Given today's abundant opportunities for psychopath prosperity, which has a parasitic weakening of society, and their more frequent hijacking of societies, is there a winning path to some stable utopian form of society that rewards honest "normaloids" by either ridding itself of psychopaths and sociopaths or constraining their participation in leadership roles? The answer is "no"!

Millions of years ago, when our ancestors began the eusocial transition, the genes that dictated the assembly of brain circuit pre-wiring could not achieve the eusocial goal in the same way as was done for ants, bees, termites and naked mole rats. These eusocial species could be programmed to act on behalf of the collective, their colony, in a robotic fashion. Pre-humans, however, were more difficult for the genes to adjust to fit into a eusocial mold. This is because pre-humans had thinking brains, and a thinking brain is theoretically capable of asking "why?" Insects can't think, so they can't wonder about "why" something must be done! Apparently naked mole rats are also restricted in their ability to think about their individual welfare.

When pre-humans began the eusocial journey a new brain circuit was needed to curb the ability to ask "why." This pre-wired mental module was probably located in the (left) pre-frontal cerebral cortex, and we now have a name for it: **conscience**! A functioning conscience must have evolved slowly in pre-humans, and today it is present in ~ 93 % of humans (100 % minus 6 % sociopaths and minus 1 % psychopaths). This number assumes that all normaloids have a conscience, sociopaths have a weak conscience and all psychopaths are totally lacking a conscience.

The reasons for a conscience module not being present in 100 % of present-day humans should challenge sociobiologists this century. I have presented a theoretical argument for this, involving the need for border patrol of tribal territory, but this is just a suggestion for critical consideration. The border patrol idea might account for a weak conscience for 6 % of the AE population, and it might account for the total absence of a conscience in ~ 1 or 1.5 % of the present-day population. More investigations of my suggestion and other ones are needed.

What is Our Present Predicament?

What is our present predicament, especially in America and Europe?

A modern society has job opportunities that seem tailor-made for sociopaths and psychopaths: trial lawyers, business executives, politicians, lobbyists, surgeons, police, etc. None of these jobs existed before the Holocene, when the social unit was small H-G tribes. There is a growing suspicion that the incidence of sociopaths and psychopaths is increasing on generational timescales.

Reading the newspaper, or watching the TV news, provides a seemingly endless list of examples of sociopathy and psychopathy at work. Essentially every criminal act is by a sociopath or psychopath. Every white collar criminal act, including political scandals, is due to sociopaths and psychopaths. If all of them could by some magic disappear, what a wonderful world this would be! Crime would essentially disappear and society could be run much more efficiently.

At some level of conscious thinking, this is the goal that has inspired utopias. The universal failure of all utopias may be rooted in their cluelessness of the root cause of failures of traditional societies: unchecked sociopathy and hijacking of their utopias by psychopaths.

Idealists, or at least the progressive idealists, are really aspiring for transforming their American or European society into a utopia. They preach an old sermon, that the road to "a more perfect society" is more tolerance. How ironic that this is, in fact, the opposite of a path to a winning place. More tolerance just widens opportunities for rule by psychopaths.

Consider the possibility that there is no path to a winning place!

The normaloids will never unite to rid society of sociopaths and psychopaths. One reason for this is that the psychopaths and sociopaths rule society! Another reason is that normaloids are intimidated by psychopaths, like meek children avoiding the schoolyard bully. Finally, another is that most normaloids are too stupid to understand their situation.

Political Realities in the United States

I should start by stating that I voted for Republicans for 20 years, and in 1982, during Reagan's re-election campaign, I began voting for Democrats in response to my sense that the Republican Party was undergoing a shift toward mean-spiritedness. Decades later it was found that after about 1988 a small group of Republicans created a project to increase Republican representation in state congresses for the purpose of gerrymandering districts to favor Republicans in their bids for winning seats in the U.S. House of Representatives. A few years later, in the mid-1990's, Speaker of the U.S. House of Representatives Newt Gingrich demonstrated the value of "dirty politics" in winning U.S. congressional races (he had exhorted young Republicans to adopt "dirty politics" starting in 1978.) Consider the following description of Gingrich: "…he pioneered a style of partisan combat – replete with name-calling, conspiracy theories and strategic obstructionism – that poisoned America's political culture and plunged Washington into permanent dysfunction." (Coppins, 2018). The 2000 Bush/Gore presidential election was close, and the Supreme Court decided it in a partisan manner that is still controversial.

22. Present Predicament

After Barack Obama won the presidential election in 2008 the "Tea Party" arose in defiance of the rising influence of liberalism – such as a Negro being president (sorry, is the PC term "black man," or is it "African American"? I can't keep up with the many PC changes).

It was obvious by 2010 that a "tribalization" trend in American politics was worsening. I recalled my writings, starting about 20 years earlier, about "the Roobification of America" (cf. Appendix B). The signs of a coarsening of public behavior could be seen, in hindsight, to have been underway for more than a half century. My *Genetic Enslavement* book, for several editions, anticipated the day that as politicians increased their appeal to the Roobs the day would come that one of them, an actual Roob, would become president. So, during the campaign of 2016 I could see my prophesy being realized as Trump, the consummate "rabble rouser," rose to become the Republican nominee, and surprisingly (to most) was elected president.

Donald Trump, America's most prominent psychopath, is acting as if his ambition is to become a tyrannical dictator. He has many models for how this might be accomplished: Putin of Russia, Erdogan of Turkey, Maduro of Venezuela and Duterte of the Philippines. These dictators have elections, and proclaim to be democracies, but the elections are shams. This may be Trump's plan. He uses every opportunity to discredit the FBI, presumably in anticipation of the Special Prosecutor Robert Mueller's investigation report on cooperation with Russian interference in the 2016 election, and with obstruction of the FBI investigation. Trump disregards information from U.S. government intelligence agencies, and complains about them in a way that appears also meant to prepare for a defense of his relationship with Russia's Putin.

Can the U.S. Congress protect us from Trump's ambitions for tyrannical control? The Republicans in the House of Representatives won their elections by appealing to only Republican voters, thanks to gerrymandering. Primary elections in these gerrymandered districts favor the most extreme display of conservatism, so at the time of the general elections there is usually no contest. What kind of people for entering politics does this situation attract? Psychopaths. It is my impression that almost all Republicans in the House of Representatives are mean-spirited sociopaths or psychopaths. Some of the Democrats are from the same mold, but many are not.

What about the U.S. Senate?

The "founding fathers" created a monster when they provided two senators for each state, regardless of the state's population. California has a population of 39 million, while Wyoming has a population of 0.58 million. The per capita representation for these two states is 67 to 1. The unfairness is compounded by the fact that California is mostly urban while Wyoming is mostly rural. Because there is a strong correlation between liberalism and urbanism, and conservatism and rural, the states with the lowest populations send conservatives to the Senate while the most populous states send liberals to the Senate. Therefore, there is a built-in advantage for conservatism to dominate the Senate.

Another factor to consider here is the difference in public service style by conservatives versus liberals. When a conservative is accused of misconduct (such as sexual), they fight the charge vigorously. When a liberal is accused, he tends to apologize and resign (e.g., Al Franken). Election styles also differ. Conservatives are nasty, while liberals try to be polite.

I have arrived at the conclusion that the U.S. Senate will be dominated by conservatives forever, regardless of the fact that the U.S. population is mostly liberal. Since Trump has adopted the conservative agenda he has their support. We therefore should not expect effective pushback from liberals as Trump navigates to positions of tyrannical dictatorship.

Psychopaths as Leaders

As I write, Donald Trump is president of the USA. He has a hard core support of about 35 % of Americans (or 89 % of Republicans, at the time of this writing: 2018 October). Like Trump, I allege, his supporters "have no shame!" They will allow him any transgression of normal decency, of informal norms that have held the American democracy together for 242 years. Civility seems like some quaint custom from the past. Dr. Robert Hare is emphatic in his warning about "distant diagnoses" – especially about psychopathy. Because of this I hesitate in suggesting that Donald Trump is a psychopath.

OK, that's enough hesitation. I now suggest, dear reader, that Trump is a psychopath! Just review Hare's *Psychopathy Checklist* (Fig. 6.3), and recall my psychopathy traits samplings (Ch. 18, with DLT notations), and check a scoring for Trump performed by Keith Olbermann (Appendix B); the similarities are remarkable!

About 16 years ago I predicted the "rise of the Roob" (Gary, 1992; also described in Chapter 26 of the 5th Edition, 2014). A Roob is someone who thinks his opinion is worth as much as his wealth. This is a cryptic summary of what Jose Ortega y Gasset warned about in his 1930 book *The Revolt of the Masses*. He wrote that an academic in a bar could be humiliated by a louder talking idiot who was full of himself because he earned as much money as the academic. Roger Price wrote *The Great Roob Revolution* in 1970, which can be viewed as an update of *The Revolt of the Masses*. He distinguished between the "rube" and Roob with an understanding that a rural rube could be excused for lacking city manners, but the new Roob lacked manners for a completely different reason: he was courted by merchants who wanted to sell him things, and his uncultured tastes were celebrated in the interest of making the sale.

The Roob is proud to lack manners; he flouts his poor taste knowing that not only do merchants celebrate him, but he remains un-criticized by those with so-called taste, the elites.

Not only does the Roob purchase things with his money, he also votes. Politicians have figured this out, and they join the merchants, and elites, in not criticizing the Roob. Indeed, some Roobs run for office, and win! Trump is the culminating example.

22. Present Predicament

Psychopaths are, by definition, unpatriotic: they behave in ways that serve themselves, as individuals, and secretly flaunt the needs of the group, whether it is society or civilization. The psychopath gains strength by stealing from the group, just as a real life "blood sucker" sustains itself by extracting nutritious blood from a victim. Psychopaths and sociopaths are the consummate parasites of civilization. Ironically, they will accuse true patriots of being "enemies of the people." Trump frequently repeats what Stalin is famous for saying, that "the press is the enemy of the people." Given the "spectacular stupidity" of Trump's followers, this ironic complaint just increases the challenge of true patriots for taking back control of society from the destroyer of it.

The elites are not without blame. Their hyper-tolerance means that they take silly positions, such as "when people behave badly, the fault lies with society," i.e., societal corruption is to blame, not the criminal's nature. This was the position taken in the early days of anthropology, as argued by Margaret Mead, Ruth Benedict and other disciples of Franz Boas. Elites are aghast at the thought that the genes assemble humans for enslaving them into the service of genetic immortality!

It is the liberal elites who prevent us from viewing sociopaths and psychopaths as "evil" and for acknowledging the small good and vast bad that the sociopaths and psychopaths inflict upon society. These hyper-liberals would never consider legislation restricting the liberty of evil people who manage to escape arrest and conviction for law breaking. For example, there will never be a law requiring that politicians pass Hare's *Psychopathy Checklist* in order to assume the position that they won from voters.

The Appeal of Fascism

I suggested in Chapter 21 that during the AE some tribes may have become temporarily fascist in order to survive the challenge by a stronger tribe. I defined fascism as an enforcement upon all tribesmen the primary devotion to tribal survival. This would involve a suspension of consideration for oneself, one's family, friends and personal beliefs. This would make sense whenever tribal defeat would lead to either tribal extermination or the loss of any prospect for genetic legacy for the defeated tribe.

To the extent that some of our ancestors adopted the fascist option for survival, and did so in response to a genetic predisposition for reacting this way to a dire tribal challenge, we should expect some of our contemporaries to have the same predispositions. Since fascism requires a certain type of leader, a charismatic rabble-rousing dictatorial leader, we can also expect to find some of that type among our contemporaries.

But we should also expect to find among our contemporaries a faux fascist leader, an opportunist, in the form of a psychopath. That person will imitate a genuine fascist leader, and appeal to the emotional susceptibilities of fascist followers. Donald Trump invents threats of invasion by "others" – Muslims, Mexicans, elites, liberals and the "fake news press" ("enemies of the people" – as Stalin liked to say).

Much hand-wringing has gone into trying to understand why 1/3 of Americans respond to these absurd appeals. I am somewhat qualified to explain, given my origins as a white male raised on a farm in rural Michigan – a bastion of Trump support. The traditional small family farm is no longer "competitive." Only the large "factory farms" can produce grains, or pigs, or chickens for a prevailing price. These farms are so expensive to set-up that financing comes from international corporations. The local environment is damaged by these factory farms, and this is allowed because the decisions for their operation are made by corporate leaders at distant locations. The small farmer, who long ago gave up competing with the factory farms, has a legitimate complaint – but no one is available to hear it.

Prospects for a Winning Place

The only path to a winning place for humanity will require, as a central component, the exclusion of psychopaths and sociopaths from key positions in society. I keep thinking of a Mars colony as the most likely site for an experiment with such a society. One reason is that applicants for joining such a colony will undergo screening for a variety of qualifications, and excluding psychopaths and sociopaths in a screening would not be objectionable.

Another reason for holding out hope for a Mars colony is that it won't be easily invaded by marauders. This concern was illustrated by Olaf Stapledon in his science fiction book *Odd John* (1935). The main character is a genius who founds a utopian society on a South Pacific island. It is later noticed by the British Navy and destroyed by them because of an unfounded fear and ignorance of what the community was about. Like Stapledon, I regretfully accept that no society can be established beyond the notice of the rest of our fellow humans, and hence no such society will ever endure even if it could be created – unless it was in a remote location, such as Mars or an asteroid.

But what about the matter of requiring that no psychopaths or sociopaths be allowed to exist in a utopian community on Earth? How acceptable would such a requirement be, even among those already residing in the community? Acceptance of this requirement would only be possible if it was understood that psychopathy and sociopathy were genetically determined. Most liberals tend to blame criminality on societal conditions, so I anticipate considerable resistance to accepting the need for excluding these two categories of people.

Even worse, most liberals cannot comprehend the notion that personality is strongly influenced by genetics. When I state that the genes assemble every human for purposes of genetic prosperity in the gene pool, with no regard for individual welfare beyond what the genes need, almost everyone objects with arguments that don't make sense. There's something about the human brain that doesn't want to believe, or is incapable of understanding, this humiliating concept.

22. Present Predicament

Blind Spots in the Brain's Thinking

When I wonder why nearly everyone seems incapable of noticing that we are enslaved by our makers, the genes, I'm reminded of the two blind spots in our vision, which the brain is completely unaware of when both eyes are open. It's adaptive to overlook these two blind spots, and fill-in our perception using information from the other eye, so evolution, with its infinite wisdom, prevents us from seeing what isn't useful to see.

It's such a simple concept that when one thing makes another the relationship between the two is that the "made thing" usually serves its "maker." When I write a computer program the program is meant to serve my goals. When a person creates a robot, we should expect that the robot is constructed for service to the robot maker.

So why can't people see that we are designed to serve those tiny DNA molecules that assembled us? Yes, it's a humiliating notion, but only to people who are enslaved to the genes and whose illusions permit them to nevertheless believe that they are free.

Could the explanation for the inability to comprehend our enslavement reside with tribal viability? For example, consider two tribes, the first one a traditional tribe consisting of fanatical patriots, itching for a fight with a weaker neighbor tribe (in order to enlarge tribal territory). The other tribe consists of people like me, who are thoughtful and who question every traditional tribal wisdom as a possible trick by the genes for self-sacrificial service to preserving the tribal gene pool. It's obvious which tribe will be victorious when the inevitable inter-tribal conflict happens. This illustrates why there must be genetic blinders preventing individuals from being thoughtful and questioning. Compartmentalization of thinking is useful in achieving the required cluelessness of how we're "being used" (by the genes). No wonder essentially all humans are so stupid, and can't see how they are enslaved to their genes!

Given that almost all humans are incapable of understanding that we are enslaved to our genes, and that psychopaths and sociopaths are the way they are due to strong genetic influence, almost all people will reject the notion that the only winning path requires exclusion of psychopaths and sociopaths from any society that hopes to be on a winning path. Consequently, no society will ever be on a winning path, regardless of how conscientious it is about other matters.

Automatons

T. H. Huxley ("Darwin's Bulldog") championed the notion that humans, as well as all creatures, were "automatons." An automaton is like a robot, except that it is assembled by genes instead of people and during individual development, as well as the rest of life, the brain is slowly changed in response to life experiences. In today's parlance, the brain synapses, both excitatory and inhibitory, are enlarged by usage and shrink with disuse. (As an aside, Darwin closed his last letter to Huxley, in 1874, with the words: 'Once again, accept my cordial thanks, my dear old friend. I wish to God there were more automata in the world like you.'" Sagan and Druyan, 1992, pg. 70).

During the 20th Century, sociobiologists added to this picture the idea that the automatons were enslaved to the genes that assembled them, and the genes were the real "winners" since they assembled individuals for competition in the Arena of Life where measurements were made for winner and loser genes. Winner genes lasted in the species gene pool for millions of years, while the individual combatants lasted for merely decades (e.g., "A chicken is an egg's way of making another egg.")

I find this way of understanding "human nature" useful. How else can the absurdity of the pathetic Human Drama be understood?

Que sera, sera

It was a few decades ago when I must have learned good news, such as a JPL proposal being approved, that I pondered the origins of my successes. I was good at imagining new projects that were relevant to society's values and willingness to fund, and I was blessed with good writing skills. These are traits that might result from good frontal lobe "executive function," which is usually attributed to something created by good genes. If my genes were responsible, then I couldn't take credit for them because I didn't choose them; they were the result of blind fate at the time of my conception. If I couldn't take credit for the so-called "nature" of who I am, what about the possibility that my successes were due to good nurturing in childhood. If so, I still couldn't take credit for my successes since nurture is something provided by good parenting, or good schooling, or a good society. Whatever the relative importance of nature or nurture I couldn't take credit for either! My achievements were therefore the result of Luck! I was just lucky, the beneficiary of more good luck than bad, and none of this was of my own doing. I was a spectator of what I was doing; or – to use Huxley's terminology – an automaton! Que sera, sera!

If this is an accurate characterization of who I am, and my successes, then the same characterization would have to be applied to others who were successful. Even more surprising, as I continued to think about the matter, people whose endeavors were frustrated and unsuccessful could not be blamed for their failures. They, too, were automatons, or spectators of lives that just happened to have bad luck.

I now realize that this thought can be extended to the successes and failures of societies, and even civilizations. Yes, a specific cause can be identified, such as the hijacking of a society by a psychopath, producing the society's inevitable weakening and death. A

22. Present Predicament

cancer cell can grow and kill an individual, and no one would blame the individual for the appearance of a cancer cell that grows and threatens life. By the same reasoning the appearance of a psychopath who hijacks a society does not necessarily justify blaming the society. Que sera, sera!

Endings

All present societies, like all past ones, are doomed! Among the hundreds of civilizations in recorded history, a median lifetime is approximately 5 centuries. That's how long it takes for the psychopaths to seize control of a society, and for their cousins the sociopaths to flourish and milk civilization to death. In the case of America, it has taken half this long because of the faster pace of everything, thanks to travel improvements and the internet.

We can't count on political leadership to save us. After all, the region of the United States with the highest incidence of psychopaths is Washington, D.C. (Murphy, 2018).

I've achieved control over my worrying about these matters. It's not because I'm 79 years old, and near my end. It's because the human species is near <u>its</u> end. Things that used to matter will soon not matter – to anyone.

I am one of the first people to have presented a conjecture (Gary, 1992, Ch. 7) on how to estimate the time of humanity's end using Sampling Theory. It has become known by the misleading name: the Anthropic Principle. It goes like this:

Suppose you're asked to guess the length of a finite sequence, and are allowed to fetch a sample at random. Suppose the sequence consists of 100 elements, with each number tagged #1 to #100. There's a 50% chance that an element drawn at random will have a number tag between 1 and 50. The same applies to drawing an element with a number tag between 51 and 100. By a similar reasoning there's a 25 % chance that an element drawn will have a number tag between 1 and 25, etc. Because of this, it is possible to infer the likelihood of the length of the sequence from a random drawing of an element. The rule for estimating the most likely total sequence length is to simply double the number tag and state that there's a 50% chance that the sequence length is below that number, and another 50% chance that it is above that number. Similar statements can be made about the chance that the total sequence has other lengths; e.g., there's a 25 % probability that the total sequence length exceeds 3 times the random number tag, etc.

Now, consider the notion that the total number of humans who will ever exist is a finite sequence. (This relies upon the belief that the universe is "rigid", like a gigantic pinball machine, governed by the laws of physics, i.e., $F = ma$, so that all past and future configurations are inherent in any one configuration.) Consider that we are now at a random location in this sequence. Everybody has a number tag, which we can use birth dates to assign. Whether we start assigning humans a number tag at 50,000 years ago, or

22. Present Predicament

150,000 years ago, human populations were always so small before about 50,000 year ago that we arrive at the same approximate conclusion that humans now being born have a number tag of about 62 billion. (This calculation was performed for the date 1992, when I "discovered" the concept; reasons for sticking with that date are given in my book *Genetic Enslavement*, 2014.) I conclude that when plausible future world population scenarios are used there's a 25 % probability that humanity will begin to undergo a population crash before about 2100 AD! Similarly, there's a 25 % probability that the population crash will occur after 2500 AD. Perhaps the most useful number is that there's a 50 % probability that the population crash will commence before about 2250 AD. The following figure shows shapes for the world's population corresponding to the three scenarios.

To the extent that the above sampling theory analysis is valid we can use it to support the assertion that humanity will NOT adopt a winning path to longevity, and that the psychopaths and sociopaths will milk civilization of all its strength to survive on timescales compatible with Fig. 22.

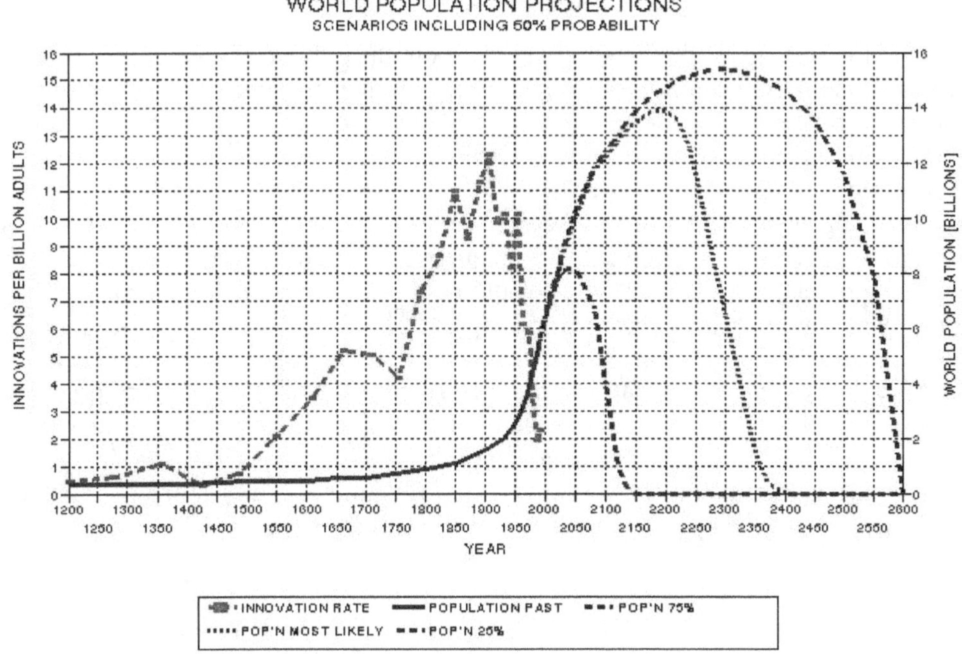

Figure 22. *Three scenarios for future world population, corresponding to the probabilities of 25, 50 and 75 %. (You may disregard the "Innovation Rate" trace; it was used to illustrate a relationship between a culture's promotion of innovation and subsequent population increase, which was a subject of the 1992 analysis.*

20. Present Predicament

Psychopaths resemble cancer cells in having no prevision of the endings they bring about, including theirs.

The prospect of humanity's demise is sort of sad, regardless of when it happens! We have so much potential. H. G. Wells shared this sentiment when he wrote (in 1896):

"In the future, it is at least conceivable, that men with a trained reason and a sounder science, ... may conduct this operation far more intelligently, unanimously, and effectively, and work towards, and at last attain and preserve, a social organization so cunningly balanced against exterior necessities on the one hand, and the artificial factor in the individual on the other, that the life of every human being ... may be generally happy., this is no dream, but a possibility to be lost or won by men, as they may have or may not have the greatness of heart to consciously shape their moral conceptions and their lives to such an end."

The possibility of human improvement, achieved over long stretches of time, is something "...to be lost or won by men, as they may have or not the greatness of heart to consciously shape..."

I have a long-standing interest in speculations about the presence in our galaxy of other intelligent beings. On several occasions my professional career in astronomy has connected with the search for extraterrestrial intelligence, SETI. The latest, and best estimate of the probability for the existence of ETI in our galaxy concludes that we are probably alone (Sandberg, Drexler and Ord, 2018). Another compelling case for humanity being the only intelligent species in the galaxy is made by Ward and Brownlee (2000). If it is true that we humans are uniquely privileged to be the only intelligent species in our galaxy, what a shame it would be for us to so casually and shamelessly ruin the planet, and kill each other in wars, and live life without an appropriate gratitude.

We have a greater "moral obligation" to not squander something so rare and precious? Any answer to this question would be hopelessly subjective, as is the question itself. Why, anyway, should an individual care about the fate of his species? In a few years I will surely die, and eventually so will my species. Regardless of any noonday brightness that humanity may, or may not, achieve, I nevertheless care!

Things aren't all bad, however. As the conservationist Robinson Jeffers mused (ca. 1925): "Good news, oh beautiful planet, the accursed race of man is not immortal."

Appendix A: Individualism vs. Collectivism

The eusocial transition for humans is inevitably different from all previous transitions due to the "intelligence" of the elements coming together to form a new collective. The lack of smoothness, and the inability to complete the transition, is usually referred to as a conflict between Individualism and Collectivism. In this appendix I explore how I view the matter, which I think illustrates why a complete transition will never happen.

During my entire life I have wagged a finger at (or maybe I was "giving" the finger to) society. I disapproved of the way society told everyone what to think, what to believe and what to not question. Gradually I sensed that society assigns everyone the job of contributing to society, and to never mind what might be good for oneself. In other words, I was to become enslaved to a "collective." The collective defines this enslavement to be "good," and it defines dwelling on individual welfare as "bad."

Eventually I realized that I was assembled by genes that were rewarded by the forces of evolution that produced groups of individuals (tribes) that competed with each other. In other words, "group selection" shaped human nature, and therefore my character. This struck me as an "abuse of power" by the genes. This motivated me to write the book *Essays From Another Paradigm* (1992) and *Genetic Enslavement: A Call to Arms for Individual Liberation"* (2004, 2014).

One of my long-standing complaints is the way religion "inhibits questioning." Religions pretend to describe the way the world works, and they then lecture on how to behave. Every religion seems to have a pathetically stupid description of how the world came into being and how it works, and this doesn't provide much confidence in the merits of how they try to dictate behavior. However, religions are a form of "glue" that holds tribes together, and encourages patriotism for competition with other tribes. From an individual's perspective religion is also guilty of an "abuse of power."

I have speculated that religion might have played a role in constraining the behavior of sociopaths and psychopaths, S&P, but it is questionable that they would be as prone to believe in God, Heaven and Hell as the normaloids, who were less in need of constraining. In fact, it is possible that religion rendered normaloids meek, allowing S&P to more freely victimize them. One of the few attributes of S&P that I respect is their tendency to reject a stupid story for why individuals should be enslaved to a collective. Nevertheless, I would prefer to live in a world without S&P.

I think it is possible to live well in a world of mostly normaloids who comprise the "collective," in spite of their stupidity, their nosy intrusiveness and their penchant for dictating how everyone else should think and live. It just requires occasionally having to pretend to be like them, and avoiding serious conversation and personal social relationships with them. This somewhat resembles what S&P have to do: pretending to be like others with full awareness that the others are clueless. The key difference,

20. Present Predicament

however, is that I have no intention or desire to harm anyone; I just want to minimize my contact with the irredeemable and pathetic others with the hope that they will also leave me alone. It is always necessary for the cognoscenti to conceal their understanding of things from the *hoi poloi.*

Here's a trick question: what manipulates individuals for their own purposes and is stealthy enough to deceive the clueless individual without him ever figuring out that he's been manipulated? You're probably thinking that I'm describing what psychopaths do. However, I'm thinking about what the genes do! They create a conscience in each individual (the exceptions being psychopaths) which manipulates behavior to serve the collective, and almost 100 % of individuals never figure this out. The genes and psychopaths have this in common! Even if the cognoscenti successfully avoid psychopaths there is the parallel challenge of dealing with one's own conscience, as well as dealing with busybody normaloids who are predisposed to enforce conformance with the version of morality that prevails in the society in question. Life is a funny proposition, indeed!

I have met a few others who share my view of how an "individual" must navigate life among those in the "collective." The last thing on our minds is to enlighten them, or persuade them to change any of their beliefs. We are non-proselytizers. I think most of us are grateful for living at a time, and in a place, where individualism is tolerated. America's founding, 242 years ago, was forged by strong individuals who hated Great Briton's corrupt exploitation of wealth produced by the colonies. I am lucky to have lived in a country that encouraged individualism, and especially during a century when individualism was most valued and tolerated (the 20th). So far it is possible to publish a book like this, and be left alone. Of course, my bravery in "publishing" this book is based on an expectation that no one will read it. (Some books are meant to be read, others are just meant to be written.)

I sometimes laugh at the loud proclamations of a person who proudly defends individualism, knowing that a real individual refrains from broadcasting who he is; *faux* individuals are actually enslaved to their genes in ways which for them never reveals the meaning of individualism. I also laugh at the loud and patriotic defense of "freedom" by those who also are the most clueless about their genetic enslavement. Patriots are the least free among men, for their battle cries reveal them to be unthinking tools for preserving the collective. The patriot is the most enslaved member of the collective; his goal is to contribute to the collective's unchallenged strength, which in turn leads to even more enslavement of clueless patriots.

According to my dystopian view of the future, the various human "collectives" are now hell-bent on destroying the nest provided by Mother Earth! As the nest is destroyed, the Earth's carrying capacity for humans will shrink. This will exacerbate everything needed for human survival. Humanity will become further dominated by psychopaths, condemning normaloids to despair and death. The *cognoscenti* may fare slightly better, but our basic goodness will condemn us to the same ending as the normaloids. After the psychopaths kill all sociopaths, they will enter into combat with each other. There is small consolation that they will deserve each other!

The eusocial Transition #3 will therefore be short-lived. How fortunate we are, those of us *cognoscenti* alive today, to be at the cusp of human achievement and potential insight. We will be spared the horrors of the human demise. The real winners will be whatever life is left after the psychopaths kill each other and bring the human drama to an end!

Appendix B: The Roobification of America

Bruce L. Gary, 2017.06.27

It is understandable that the triumph of stupidity should occur in America first. After all, it's natural for a person to believe that their ideas on everything have merit because they've succeeded in improving their standard of living. Americans have achieved individual wealth ahead of the rest of the world, and the rise of the Roob, a materialistic version of a rube, is therefore most prominent in America. This explains the coarsening of American culture that has occurred since World War II. It's not only our music, movies, TV, public discourse and interpersonal manners that have declined, it's also our politics. The Republican Party, with which I used to associate, has suffered the most. It is time to wonder if fascism is on our horizon.

From Rube to Roob

Jose Ortega y Gasset wrote *Revolt of the Masses* in 1930. In it he described something that puzzled him: scholars were beginning to have trouble being heard above the noise of uninformed men who brazenly presented their opinions as if they were fact. Gasset struggled to explain this, speculating at length about the appeal for believing that Truth should come from within instead of from an objective, open-minded exploration of ideas based on observations of an external reality. The common man was searching for an explanation of the corruption of society that was ruled by educated people, and the commoner noticed that education involves observation of external reality followed by disciplined thinking. Gasset finally hinted at the possibility that commoners were getting "too smart for their britches" because they were becoming successful in earning a living, and in some instances becoming wealthier than educated noblemen and scholars. The commoner's new-found wealth emboldened him to believe that his opinions therefore deserved the same respect as that of generations of nobility. Opinions that command respect help define a society's culture, and this was the beginning of the commoner's takeover of culture.

Half a century later Roger Price wrote *The Great Roob Revolution* (1970), which finally gave this phenomenon a name. He invented the name Roob in order to make an important distinction: the country bumpkin was a "rube" out of innocent ignorance of good manners from lack of exposure to the customs of urban living, whereas the Roob was obnoxious for insisting that his stupid ideas should not be questioned. Both the rube and Roob were insufferable, but for different reasons. Price clarified the argument that it was the Roob's growing wealth that was the principal force that gave his opinions power. After all, he argued, the shopkeeper who wanted to sell was not going to question the taste of someone with money in his pocket. If the person who comes to town for a carnival has money in his pocket, and if he wants to hear a certain kind of music, then that's the music that the townspeople will perform. If he wants to see a certain kind of movie, then that's the movie that will be made. It's when a rube has money in his pocket that he becomes a Roob!

When scholars and noblemen became less numerous than Roobs, the new imbalance of buying power translated to an ascendance of the Roob. This, Price explained, was why culture was becoming Roobified. Ideas that came from within oneself, as Gasset had argued, were more valid to the Roob than ideas that others arrived at from disciplined argument based on observation of things outside oneself. This would have predictable consequences on a society's culture.

Politicians took notice of the Roob, since his type was numerous and could vote. If the Roob distrusted "pointy-headed" intellectuals, then politicians would mock the puzzled scholars. Adlai Stevenson was the first politician to be mocked as an "egg-head" by a political opponent (in 1956). I remember this well, because I was in high school at the time, on a debate team arguing the merits of "free trade" - and I was puzzled by my analysis of the unsupported arguments used to attack Stevenson.

At the same time I noticed that classical music was much less popular than "rock music." One form spoke to the intellect of smart people and the other spoke to the heart of simple folk. Movies also celebrated the simple-minded "rebel" instead of the conscientious citizen. What happened, I wondered, to the patriot who saved civilization from tyrannical Nazi fascism just a couple decades earlier.

The cause for conscientiousness and civility wasn't helped by the growth of a war in Vietnam and mandatory military service if called upon to serve by a draft board. A generation of older men who could benefit financially by war was pitted against a less powerful younger generation who would have to fight it. The inevitable protests that erupted brought the concept of civility into question. Folk music became defiant, and it questioned the legitimacy of those who ruled. Hippies rejected their parent's culture, their materialism, and experimented with simpler lifestyles. It is ironic that the Hippy Generation was looking inward for a path away from materialism, while their parents continued to embrace a materialism that was created by inward-looking Roobs.

Appendix B: Roobification of America

Civility

Good manners is a simple concept. "How do you do, Mr. Smith; I'm glad to meet you." And saying "thank you" or "excuse me." Personal cleanliness, and dressing well reveal civility. When entering a building a man removes his hat, and holds the door open for his woman companion. In public people aren't loud (except at sporting events). Also in public there's no burping, or farting, or picking one's nose. In polite conversation there is no swearing, no vulgarity, and no surrender to emotional outbursts. The English have mastered the art of civil conversation. If in doubt, imagine how an English movie would portray a social interaction. If someone wants to put down another, it's not done with overt "name calling" and with a loud voice, but is handled with such subtlety that only a careful notice will register the insult.

Civility must be an important requirement for holding a society together, for it is found in every society. Primitive societies have rules governing social interactions. This would probably surprise most New Yorkers, for example.

Civil is the root word for "civilization." The implication is that a civilization requires civility!

The Loss of American Civility

In retrospect, I now see why the Roobification phenomenon was more advanced in America than anywhere else in the world. It's because America led the world in the growth of wealth for the individual citizen. Because "no good deed goes unpunished" America is the first society that has to face the political victory of the Roobification phenomenon.

The first televised presidential debate was in 1960, when Jack Kennedy and Richard Nixon faced off. When snippets of that debate are shown on television today, it is jarring! Kennedy and Nixon were civil with each other in a way that would not be expected in a debate that included Donald Trump. What has happened during the intervening 56 years?

The transition was well underway when Price wrote his book *The Great Roob Revolution* in 1969 (published in 1970). There's something about "the 1960's" that defy complete understanding. It was a tumultuous time, or, to quote the opening of *A Tale of Two Cities* (Dickens, 1859): "It was the best of times, it was

144

the worst of times, ..." I recall telling a friend at the time that the 1960's would be remembered for being the peak of Western Civilization. It was an awakening of many things: civil rights for blacks, women's rights, the folly of war, the corruptness of the military-industrial-congressional complex (Eisenhower's phrasing in an early draft of his presidential departing speech), the dangers of over-population, the dangers of global thermonuclear war, the opportunities for space travel - but most important, it was the awakening to the idea that humans were enslaved to the genes that assembled us for engaging in tribal gene pool competition. This last awakening was occurring within a small academic discipline that would be known a few years later as "sociobiology." I won't claim that sociobiological thoughts were motivating the common man in any way, because they weren't. But the same audaciousness of thought that influenced those in academia was also influencing the common man, so there is a common-cause connection.

The 1960's was a time for unleashing high expectations for the future! This was a result of the fastest growth of personal wealth for Americans in living memory (starting after World War II). But in an open society, a democracy where public protest was possible, competing factions clashed and sparks sure did fly. Assassinations of public heroes, race riots, Vietnam war protests, student speeches and protests on college campuses - these social disruptions and threats to civility led eventually to a vote for "law and order" presidential candidate Nixon (in 1968). War protests continued in front of the White House, and Nixon's hatred for everyone unlike him, everyone from hippies to reporters, became obvious. This was the social climate when Price wrote his Roob book.

The Rise of Sociopathic Megalomaniacs

As I wrote in my book *Genetic Enslavement* (2014) "A wealthy Roob is less of a threat to social stability than a recently impoverished Roob" (pg. 264). This observation was inspired by a reading of early 20th Century history. After The World War, as it was called at the time (since no one believed humans would be stupid enough to repeat such a calamity), the victorious Allies punished Germany with the Treaty of Versailles, which imposed harsh reparation costs on the German economy (mostly in response to the French, who wanted to dismember Germany so that it could never start another war). The Germans, who were the best-educated population in the world, and who enjoyed a relatively high standard of living before the war, became paupers in less than a decade. This sudden poverty created a situation ripe for revenge by those with a Roob mentality. Hitler was mocked as a clown during the 1920's, when he was an amateur activist trying to rouse the discontented rabble. But his psychopathic, conniving talents eventually prevailed in 1934, when he became Fuhrer. It has been said that Hitler was kind to his mother, and liked dogs (although his German Shepherd dogs acted wary of Hitler, as revealed in home movies). A more accurate description of Hitler is that he was a psychopath.

Benito Mussolini was more successful, for he became Italy's prime minister in 1922, which he maneuvered into a dictatorship in 1925. His goal was to re-create the Roman Empire through fascist rule. However, he suffered from "megalomania" and lacked an understanding of the use of power. Still, he hung onto his dictatorship rule until 1945, when he was hung to death. Mussolini's trademark posture and expression is irresistible for psychological analysis.

These postures and expressions prompt many words: arrogance, contempt for others - but mostly (for me) psychopathy.

Approximately 4% of Americans meet the diagnostic requirements of "psychopathy" (also commonly referred to as "sociopathy"). Another several percent have "borderline personality disorder" (BPD); these people share many of the personality traits of psychopaths. Serial killers are psychopaths; sociopaths don't kill as often. Most successful businessmen (e.g., CEOs) are psychopaths, some are sociopaths and few are normal (Dutton, 2012 and Murphy, 2018).

Appendix B: Roobification of America

Leadership qualities overlap amazingly well with psychopathology. Hitler, Mussolini and Stalin come to mind as the most infamous psychopathic leaders of the 20th Century. Attila the Hun and Genghis Khan would be earlier examples.

I do very much want to talk about 21st Century psychopathic leadership, but before that I think it's important to provide some insight into why some people are attracted to psychopaths to be their leaders.

Feudalism and Psychopaths

When the Earth's climate warmed 11,700 years ago, ushering in our present Holocene Epoch, the Middle East and Southern Europe turned into great places to live. Melting glaciers fed rushing rivers, and great green forests increased the population of animals for hunting. By 8000 BC herding sheep in green fields became feasible and farming was discovered. Irrigation followed, and settled lifestyles became common. Because an acre of land could support more people than before, a combination of tribal territory shrinkage and tribal size increase occurred. As tribes were forced together, and became larger, coalescence became an imperative because larger tribes were usually victorious over smaller ones. By the mid-Holocene large settlements that were sustained by farming and herding were common. Their need for storing and transporting food became a magnet for marauding nomadic tribes. The settlements responded by increasing the power of their rudimentary governments. Whereas the original form of protection from marauders was a banding together of neighboring farmers to defend themselves, it became clear that a more formal form of defense was needed. Feudalism was the answer: a wealthy landlord would allow a vassal to farm a portion of his land in exchange for defense from marauders by a "standing army."

Before the Holocene people lived as "hunter/gatherers" with an egalitarian social structure. During the Holocene the HG structure was transformed into a hierarchical social structure with a strong man in a leadership role at the top and levels of designated powerful people loyal to the top man who administered the leader's commands. Of course, the "man with the hoe" resented this, but he had no choice!

The new structure for governance created opportunities for people with a genetic disposition for leadership. It doesn't take many generations for evolution to reward a coveted niche, especially considering that the leader will have many more offspring than the farmer. Any young man who is inclined to achieve the

Appendix B: Roobification of America

rewards of status, acclaim, and an informal "harem," who is also willing to accept responsibility for giving commands that appear to make sense, will be favored when he is successful. Climbing to the top of such a social pyramid is, however, no easy task. It requires a willingness to "use" people, to manipulate them, to create an illusion that the used person will share in the winnings, and then to trample them when they are no longer useful. This, I claim, is a ready-made role for the psychopath!

During the past 8000 years there have been ~ 270 generations. Surely, during that time, the first few men who were both charismatic and lacked empathy, would have prospered.

21st Century Psychopathic Leadership

The most commonly used test for identifying psychopaths is the Hare Psychopathy Checklist. The checklist consists of 20 items, that can be scored as either 0, 1 or 2. The range of scores for any person is therefore from zero to 40. A score of 30 or more is accepted as "psychopathic."

Keith Olbermann has subjected presidential candidate for the Republican Party, Donald Trump, to the Hare Psychopathy Checklist. His results are available in an article for *Vanity Fair*, and also at a web site:

http://www.vanityfair.com/news/2016/07/donald-trump-keith-olberman-sanity-test.

Here's how the scoring went, with score preceding the trait (details of the reasons for the scores is given in the article and web page).

2 = glibness and superficial charm
2 = grandiose sense of self-worth
2 = need for stimulation/proneness to boredom (e.g., short attention span)
2 = pathological lying
2 = cunning/manipulative
2 = lack of remorse or guilt
2 = shallow affect (not understanding of human relationships)
2 = callous lack of empathy
2 = parasitic lifestyle (e.g., taking credit for work done by others)
2 = poor behavioral control (as in tweeting before thinking)
2 = promiscuous sexual behavior (e.g., boasting about it)

2 = early behavioral problems ("I punched my music teacher because I didn't think he knew anything about music...")
1 = lack of realistic long-term goals
2 = impulsivity
1 = irresponsibility
2 = failure to accept responsibility for one's own actions
0 = many short-term marital relationships (3 marriages lasting 14, 6 & 11 years doesn't qualify)
2 = juvenile delinquency (father says "He was a pretty rough fellow when he was small." and more)
0 = revocation of "conditional release" (by a parole officer)
0 = criminal versatility

Total points = 32. Donald Trump, by this scoring, is a candidate for being considered a psychopath.

An even scarier article was recently published in the *New Yorker*, 2016 Jul 25 issue, by Jane Mayer, based mostly on an interview with the person who wrote *The Art of the Deal*, Tony Schwartz (hereafter, TS). For the record, in spite of repeated claims by Donald Trump (hereafter, DT) that he wrote the book, TS insists that DT didn't write any of the book, but merely made a few red marks for changes, to make him look better, and TS made the changes. TS thinks that DT may not have read the entire book, since there's no evidence that DT has ever read any book. The article can be viewed here:

http://www.newyorker.com/magazine/2016/07/25/donald-trumps-ghostwriter-tells-all.

Some highlights from the article are that TS spent 18 months trying to get DT to provide interviews, but DT had such a short attention span that all interviews were cut short with almost nothing to show for them. After deciding to give up on getting enough material for the book, and on a flight home, he had the idea of listening in on DT's phone conversations. DT loved that idea, and so the book project resumed. Unbeknownst to the callers DT was talking with, TS finally was able to obtain enough information to write the book. The TS interview for the *New Yorker* includes the following.

DT is pathologically impulsive and self-centered. If TS were to write the book today he would title it "The Sociopath." "I genuinely believe that if DT wins and gets the nuclear codes there is an excellent possibility it will lead to the end of

Appendix B: Roobification of America

civilization." "Trump's first wife, Ivana, famously claimed that DT kept a copy of Adolf Hitler's collected speeches, *My New Order*, in a cabinet beside his bed." "Lying is second nature to him." "He lied strategically. He had a complete lack of conscience about it. DT's indifference to it gave him a strange advantage." "Trump stands for many of the things I abhor: his willingness to run over people, the gaudy, tacky, gigantic obsessions, the absolute lack of interest in anything beyond power and money." DT has an insatiable hunger for "money, praise and celebrity." "He's a transactional man - it was all about what you could do for him." In a TV interview (Lawrence O'Donnel's "The Last Word," TS said that that DT has a black hole at his center, that needs to be filled with attention from others ("all publicity is good publicity"), and that he has no capacity for empathy. This was brave because TS was inviting a lawsuit by Trump for violating a non-disclosure agreement, but TS said he has kept quiet until now because DT's mischief until now was mostly limited to failed building ventures, but now TS felt a moral obligation to warn the nation about someone with a serious possibility of winning an election for president of America.

I'm not trying to pick on Trump. He's just the easiest "leader" to study because so much is known about him. Other 21st Century leaders that appear to be psychopaths include Dick Cheney (Bush's VP), Vladimir Putin (Russia), Tayyip Erdogan (Turkey) and many in Africa. The 20th Century has many dozens of examples.

The question that interests me more is "Why are so many people attracted to psychopathic leaders?"

Appendix B: Roobification of America

What's Wrong with Voters?

Anybody can blame the victim of a crime on the criminal, but when victims are so willing and clueless, then another question has to be asked: Why do so many people fall victim to psychopaths?

The Donald Trump type was just waiting for America to evolve a readiness for his pitch! Recall what I wrote in my 2014 *Genetic Enslavement* book, in the chapter about Roobs: "A wealthy Roob is less of a threat to social stability than a recently impoverished Roob" (pg. 264). Before the 2008 global financial collapse (that started in America because of greedy and illegal behavior by unregulated investment bankers) America wasn't quite "ready" for a full-blown psychopath leader. The prerequisites for that readiness had been building slowly for 30 years, ever since the Ronald Reagan presidency. During that time wages had stagnated and large corporations had become international, and had begun to move manufacturing jobs overseas. Workers without a college education couldn't adapt to such a change; they couldn't learn MS Word or Excel, for example, and their options were thus limited. With an oversupply of less educated workers they couldn't demand raises if they had a job, and if they didn't have a job they had to accept a lower-paying job to remain employed. Household income had been increasing during most of the second half of the 20th Century due to women entering the labor force. But by century's end most households had already made that transition. Early in the 21st Century household income for the Middle Class began to shrink. But how many of these financially desperate people in America are Roobs?

Recall the definition of a Roob. He's someone who doesn't trust what educated people have learned through centuries of inquiry, by observing the way the world is and using disciplined thinking to figure things out. The Roob prefers to search inside himself for an inner truth. And if he has achieved wealth sometime during his life, his inner truth will have been vindicated, and no other person, regardless of his learnedness, and <u>in spite</u> of his learnedness, can change his mind. How many Americans are Roobs? Our best guide on that comes from polls on what people believe, or know. Here are some data on that: 1) 60% of Americans know that Superman comes from Krypton, but only 37% know that Mercury is the planet closest to the sun (Zogby poll). 2) 74% know the names of The Three Stooges (Larry, Curly and Moe) while only 42% can identify the three branches of government (Zogby poll). 3) 41% of Americans believe that Saddam Hussein

Appendix B: Roobification of America

had strong links to Al Queda, and 22% believe he helped plan the 9/11 attacks (Harris poll). 4) 20% of Americans think the sun revolves around the Earth. 7) 29% of Americans can't name the vice-president (Newsweek, 2011 Mar 28). Considering these statistics, it is fair to imagine that something short of half of Americans are uneducated, uninformed and unconcerned about the matter - in other words, a self-satisfied Roob!

Trump does a masterful job of mimicking the uninformed voter who he hopes to win over. A little-known discipline, called Neuro Linguistic Programming (NLP), urges salesmen, or anyone trying to influence a target person, to observe closely the target's mannerisms, such as their speech patterns, and to then mimic them. The NLP user will note which of three word categories is most used by the target (seeing, hearing and feeling - corresponding to the three posterior lobes of the brain), and to intentionally engage that person with an emphasis on the same word categories. In a similar manner the target's posture is to be observed, and mimicked (arm folding, etc.). I doubt that Trump has studied NLP, but he seems to practice it well. When the voter sees Trump, he sees himself. For example, Trump proudly proclaims that he gets his information from TV, not books or newspapers (and certainly not from experts). Trump's language and demeanor is unsophisticated, low-brow. His words are simple, and often vulgar, like the voter he's trying to mimic. He makes fun of people who are threatening to the uninformed voter, such as intellectuals. Trump's disdain for intellectuals, and those people in government who are blocking the average man from succeeding, is reassuring to the low-information voter. The regular guy believes that Trump is like him, but just brave enough, due to his business success, to speak the truth without regard to "political correctness." When interviewed, Trump supporters often say that "he's like me; just more successful." It's a clever trick, persuading the average guy who's temporarily down on his luck that he could someday become successful, like Trump, if only those educated people would stop blocking the little guy's path to success.

Once a Roob is created, he cannot be uncreated. The Roob who saw his prospects for prosperity fade after the 2008 recession didn't question his ideas and beliefs; by then he was confirmed in his rightness on all fundamental matters. He knew at some unconscious level that people in government couldn't be trusted. Of course there was some truth to this, because humans in general can't be trusted; but there's a nuance to this problem, and Roobs don't understand nuance. There was a growing segment of the American population who didn't know who specifically to blame, but they knew it couldn't be themselves.

I experienced this first-hand when I was credited with making the first recovery image of Comet ISON ("Comet of the Century"), ahead of NASA, and this notoriety produced a "fan club" who celebrated my revelation that NASA was hyping the comet to get more money; and NASA knew things about the comet's danger to humanity but wasn't telling the public, because the public couldn't handle the truth. I tried to explain to my cynical fans that NASA was a reputable organization, in spite of being part of the government, and they were only guilty of hyping the comet to get publicity. I also saw how news organizations exploited opportunities for improving their ratings by reporting my updates on comet activity with completely fabricated stories that they bought from unscrupulous freelance "journalists." Everyone behaved badly: the news media, bloggers trying to get attention, the readers who were clueless about comets, and to some extent NASA for hyping the comet more than was warranted. My "takeaway message" from that experience was that very few humans are capable of good judgement and good behavior.

The point I'm driving at is that today, in 2016, most Americans are incapable of understanding why the economy is unfair to them, because they're incapable of questioning their beliefs and seeing the connections between their past voting behavior and the forces that shape our evolving economy to their disadvantage. The Republican Party has snookered them into voting against their best interests. Most voters are unaware of the gerrymandering of district lines by Republican state governments in a way that promotes conservative extremism and a disregard for the middle class worker.

Most American voters remind me of the early Holocene farmers who feared the next wave of marauders, and who are therefore looking for that "strong leader" who would protect them. Trump is merely an opportunist, seizing the moment by inflaming fear about those marauders, who come from Mexico and the Middle East. The Roob voter hates intellectuals, so Trump mocks educated people, the government, newspaper and TV reporters and everyone else in the media who asks difficult questions of him. The Roob is tribal, and is ready to wage war upon that neighbor tribe, whoever they are.

Appendix B: Roobification of America

Summary

I have described Jose Ortega y Gasset's puzzlement over people's preference for ideas that come from within themselves than those presented to them by others with academic expertise on the matter in question. In his book on this, *Revolt of the Masses* (1930), Gasset asserts that this preference was a new and troubling trend. Four decades later Roger Price published *The Great Roob Revolution* (1970), which updated the trend with an extra dimension of explanation: people who have achieved some measure of wealth place greater reliance upon their beliefs than the beliefs of others. He coined the term Roob for referring to an unsophisticated rube who has undergone this change. Price also expressed concern that because of the Roob's buying power he was having too much influence over culture. Another four decades later I published *Genetic Enslavement* (2014) with a chapter updating the Roob's influence on American culture. I suggested that the downside to America's success was a triumph of Roob culture in so many aspects that the foundations of America's greatness was being undermined. Vulgarity of taste in every aspect of culture, and a disdain for objective information, threatened to unravel the fabric that kept America alive.

In this essay I have described psychopaths as opportunists who will seize upon weakness in others in order to feed their own growth. The leadership of a society is the grandest example of a psychopath's pernicious destructive power. But a psychopath's success requires certain conditions, namely, that his victims become ready for unthinking surrender. The rise to leadership by psychopaths had its origins during the mid-Holocene Epoch, when the hunter/gatherer lifestyle was replaced by a settled farming lifestyle, because these settlements were besieged by nomadic marauding invaders that required strong leadership for protection.

Now, late in the Holocene, conditions are again becoming especially favorable for psychopathic exploitation. The rise of wealth, combined with democracy, gives undue influence to Roobs over a society's culture. The Roob has disdain for enlightened governance, for he trusts only those things that seem true to him that come from within himself (the reason for this is another story, related to millions of years of tribal gene pool competition, which hasn't been addressed here). The Roob now dominates not only American culture, but also American politics; he is a willing victim of the opportunistic psychopath who comes seeking leadership of America. My fear is that the Roob will deliver America to psychopathic rule, called fascism - a 20th Century form of dictatorship. If this happens, America will slide into irrelevance, and could take down the rest of Western Civilization with it.

We live in interesting times!

Closing Thought

I've had a lifelong fascination with the matter of how societies unravel, and how civilizations collapse. During the Holocene Epoch hundreds of civilizations have arisen and fallen; their median lifetime seems to be about 5 centuries. Following the Dark Ages was the birth of our present civilization, defined by the beginning of the Renaissance in 1453. We're approaching the 6 century mark, and I feel like the unraveling is underway. I have a ring-side seat for observing and studying the process. What a sad time to be alive, if aware.

Appendix C: The Fragility of Democracy

Bruce L. Gary, 2016.12.20; 2017.06.27

Our prehistoric inheritance can't be ignored for any accounting of contemporary dysfunction. Some genes that evolved for living in small hunter-gatherer tribes are unsuited for life in an industrial society with a large population. Democracy is an attempt to recover the "equal voice" of the hunter-gatherer setting. There may not be any form of governance of the modern society that is stable, and capable of enduring for more than the typical 3 to 5 centuries of most past civilizations. Most humans are simply unsuited to the requirements of civilization.

Introduction

Just because humans are capable of creating a democratic form of governance, occasionally, we should not assume that a democracy can be sustained any longer than for other forms of governance. I approach this subject mindful that humans are assembled by genes that have survived within the human gene pool for the last ½ million years of the Pleistocene epoch. As such, human behavior is adapted to a setting that disappeared 12,700 years ago. We are now like "fish out of water," and just because human tribes survived millions of years is no guarantee that we will be able to manage human affairs during the present Holocene epoch. Democracy was supposed to be our winning ticket, the way to survive the rest of the Holocene, but the American version may crumble as quickly as it was created 240 years ago.

Anthropologists tell us that hunter-gatherer (HG) tribes are egalitarian. When a tribal decision needs to be made, such as whether to relocate, each male tribesman is allowed to speak. There will always be someone with a more insightful perspective and persuasive argument than any of the others. The group benefits from any decision arrived at in this manner. To me, this process seems like a good evolutionary adaptation. Since humans have probably lived in small HG tribes for millions of years, the concept of "equal voice" for group decisions must be genetically inscribed in our thinking.

Tribal Mentality

For millions of years our ancestors lived in small tribes. Everyone in the tribe knew everyone else, and the strength of the tribe required that inter-personal relationships were well-established and stable. Tribes competed, or as I prefer to say, tribal gene pools competed. Of course there was some intra-tribal competition, but the greater the threat from a neighboring tribe the greater reward there was for intra-tribal cooperation. Therefore, each tribe became a competing force on the stage of evolution, and members of each tribe had to be loyal to the imperative of tribal survival.

Because of the need for tribal members to quickly identify same-tribe versus other-tribe affiliation, tribal cultures diverged in ways that were otherwise unnecessary. Differences evolved in dress, language, beliefs, rituals, religion – in every aspect that could distinguish members of one tribe from another. For the most part, relationships between members of the same tribe were supportive, whereas encounters with members of a neighboring tribe were unpredictable and often confrontational. The outcome of other tribe encounters would depend on which group outnumbered the other. If a single individual from the neighboring tribe was encountered by a group of home tribesmen, murder was a possibility. Mob murder is instinctive, and it is triggered by the encounter of someone who shows all the signs of belonging to another tribe.

The term "tribal mentality" has been recognized for more than a century as a hallmark of our heritage (Spencer, 1892). It was described as "intra-tribal amity and extra-tribal enmity." It is so prevalent among known primitive tribes, as well as cultures throughout the world, that it should be on the list of "human universals" (Brown, 1991).

Tribes that failed to evolve a strong tribal mentality would have been at a disadvantage when they encountered another tribe, and competed with them for territory. Since this evolutionary dynamic has been at work for at least hundreds of thousands of years, we should view tribal mentality as an instinct that cannot be extinguished in as short a time as the Holocene epoch's 12,700 years.

Super-Tribes Replace Small HG Tribes

The Holocene epoch is just the latest global warming event that has occurred every 120,000 years during the past ½ million years. Each warming lasts for about 10,000 years, typically. (These warmings are not to be confused with the current man-made global warming, which is a much faster and greater warming than has ever occurred.) When a climate warms, large areas of land become habitable. Grass and trees grow where glaciers once existed. The limit to human population density rises with each warming epoch. Small tribes can grow in population, and they can exist closer together.

The Holocene warming was good for everyone, except when the proximity of tribes aroused ancient enmities. The Holocene differed from previous warming epochs because herding and agriculture was discovered by at least one tribe, and this new lifestyle permitted an even greater population density than hunting and gathering. Perhaps tribal coalescence had occurred before, but with the advent of herding, and especially agriculture, the rewards for coalescence were greater than ever. As in the past, during the Holocene a larger tribe was usually more successful in warfare with a smaller tribe. In addition, during the Holocene, an agricultural tribe had to protect itself from marauding tribes desperate for agricultural food stores.

But if members of another tribe must be absorbed into a home tribe, imagine the mental stress produced by tribal mentality instincts! Picture a home tribesman faced with a new neighbor who looks different, dresses differently, speaks differently and worships differently. The new person could easily be hated before any meeting, and because the home tribe has agreed to welcome the small tribesmen there must be a feeling of resentment toward him. Some home tribesmen were better able to "bite their tongue" and not outwardly complain, and thus preserve harmony within the larger tribe. At least the appearance of harmony within a tribe would be helpful in repelling marauding tribesmen.

Origin of Political Correctness

The home tribe chief, and his buddies, had an interest in enforcing acceptance of the new tribal members. Their edicts are the beginnings of "political correctness." A tension within the home tribe had to be kept below the surface in order for the imperative of tribal coalescence to render the larger tribe successful in subsequent inter-tribal conflicts. Tribal harmony was a somewhat superficial state. Resentments festered below a calm surface.

As more tribes saw the wisdom of becoming larger by coalescing with their neighbors, an arms race of sorts led to super-tribes. Super-tribes controlled larger land areas, and economy of scale favored those who could manage the larger numbers of people and larger land area. These changes enhanced security from external threats, but they created new internal threats.

Appendix C: Fragility of Democracy

Origin of Governance - A Theoretical Treatment

In this section I want to illustrate some of the challenges posed by the creation of super-tribes by imagining that our ancestors followed a rational approach to finding solutions. This is not the way it happened, but this idealistic approach will be helpful in identifying some of the challenges that had to be solved if the super-tribe was to be successful in fending off attacks by small tribes.

In a super-tribe, where the population exceeds about 150 individuals, it is impossible for everyone to know everyone. The "Dunbar Number" of about 150 is the maximum number of people in a group that permits personal relationships between all members (that matter). Tribes this large place an uncomfortable demand upon its membership when it demands trust with strangers. For the first time in human history, people were expected to trust strangers as if they belonged to the same tribe – because the super-tribe was acting as if everyone was a fellow tribesman. The requirement to trust strangers created resentment of the super-tribe imperatives, and was an additional threat to internal security.

Misbehavior by an individual super-tribesman could not be punished in the small tribe manner. The tribal chief had to assume additional duties, and enlarge his staff to handle disputes and enforce punishment. The agricultural lifestyle placed new demands on the tribe. Storage of grain and other food was needed, and record keeping for rewarding the most productive farmers was required. Farmer's markets were organized, and exchange methods had to be invented. Defense against marauders had to be organized. Farmers had to be taxed to pay for their protection. All of these new needs required the creation of governance.

Governance involves making rules that everyone agrees to abide by, identifying cheaters, and administering punishment of the guilty. These are the three branches of government. The larger the super-tribe, the larger are the number of governing issues that have to be dealt with, and the larger government has to be.

Creating rules, the legislative duty of governance, can't be done in the old-fashioned, small tribe way. It's simply not practical because there are too many people who would want to speak about each law under consideration. I can imagine how this was first discovered: a large meeting was called and only a few were allowed to speak. The shy tribesman, who in the small tribe setting would nevertheless have spoken, would in effect be silenced in the super-tribe. If he had something important to say it was overshadowed by the less shy blowhard. It is reasonable to assume that the quality of group consensus suffered.

Representative government would be a natural response to this shortcoming. Small groups, possibly resembling the long forgotten small tribe in size, would represent the opinions arrived at in a setting where everyone had a voice. The representative would meet with other representatives to formulate super-tribe laws. The same process could be used to arrive at all manner of decisions affecting the super-tribe.

Origin of Governance - The Way it Really Happened (Feudalism)

When farmers first noticed that they were a target for marauding tribes they probably at first agreed among themselves to protect each other. But a few farmers would be no match for a warrior-based marauding tribe. That's when a "strong man" who lived among the farmers, and wanted them to succeed, presented himself as a "king" with his warrior buddies serving as his standing army to protect the farmers, provided the farmers agreed to a tax that was sufficient to maintain the king and his army. This "protection racket" made sense to everyone involved. Consider the analogy: the farmer is to the king, as the farmer's cow is to the farmer. Each is useful to the other. This is called "feudalism."

The only problem with feudalism is that the arrangement can be abused. The king can raise taxes to an unreasonable rate, and what then can the farmer do? Human history is a repeating story of clever people taking advantage of "the man with a hoe." And don't believe that the farmer doesn't know this!

The first king may have been fair-minded, but his arrangement with the farmers created an opportunity for the unscrupulous opportunist who envied the king's position. We now refer to these people as psychopaths if they lack concern for group welfare, while succeeding in conveying an opposite impression to a population of individuals who have no personal experience with him. The psychopath was a constant threat to HG tribal stability, but they had a way of dealing with the psychopath who was too destabilizing: they killed him! Within the new super-tribes this cleansing of parasitic individuals did not occur.

The psychopath may in fact have been a more effective king than the kindly type of person. After all, a king with a fierce reputation will give pause to a marauding tribe that knows of the king's reputation. I wonder if the farmer ever came to a realization that he needed a psychopathic leader.

Feudalism has its vulnerabilities to stability. Psychopathic leaders are common, for the non-psychopaths are out-maneuvered or killed if they get in the way of the psychopath's rise. The genes yield up a wide range of psychopathic phenotypes every generation, and each has a slightly different appeal to the farmer. One sub-type of psychopath is good at appealing to the commoner's resentment of civilization. The little man who works hard and suspects that he's being cheated by those in power is looking for someone, or something, to blame. This psychopathic leader who accuses the "governing elite" of abuse may create a following. But inevitably, each of these clever psychopaths change when they become king.

The thoughtful leader who urges reform of governance so that it's more responsive to the little man's needs has a smaller audience. Unlike the psychopath, who shouts his message to rouse the rabble, the thoughtful leader can only reason with the little man. Since the little man has little reasoning ability, the first leader is more persuasive, and always wins.

Origin of Democracy

Democracy is an attempt to recover the "equal voice" aspect of the HG setting. It's a rejection of the abuses of feudalism, and its tyrannical outgrowths, such as fascism.

The democracy experiment has made at least two appearances in history. The first democratic society might have been the Minoan, but we know so little about that 2nd Millennium BC civilization that we can't learn from their experience. The first one we know about is ancient Greece, which had cultural similarities to the Minoan and may in fact have been inspired by their memory (the Minoans were decimated by the volcanic eruption on Thera, in 1646 BC).

The Greek city states may have been a reaction to millennia of frustration with tyrannical oppression during the early Holocene. As always happens when humans are in charge of human affairs, the Greek democracy became flawed by

Appendix C: Fragility of Democracy

the corrupting influence of the wrong people. Socrates was found "guilty of impiety, and for corrupting the youth." His questioning of everything was a threat to "group think" conformance, a leftover requirement for small tribes. Plato may have been motivated to question the underlying theory for democracy as a fair and stable governing principle due to its role in the death of his mentor, Socrates. This is described in the brilliant essay by Andrew Sullivan (2016). Plato foresaw that democracy undermines the notion that some people have better ideas than others. It's obvious to anyone who thinks that all men are <u>not</u> created equal, yet in a democracy everyone's vote is equal. The greatest apparent beneficiary of this fiction is the person who votes with the least thought behind it and is made to feel equal to those who are smarter, or more educated, or who have more wealth and influence in the affairs of society. The "equality fiction" is a trick to keep the great numbers of *hoi poloi* content with the status quo.

The Commoner's Rise to Power

Perhaps we can gain some insight into what happens to any experiment with democracy by inspecting our own experience, so far.

In 1930 Jose Ortega y Gasset published his book *Revolt of the Masses*. He argued that people were losing respect for academics, or anyone with intellectual expertise. He suspected that the readiness to discount a person with more knowledge had its origin in the growing wealth of the common man. If a person equates wealth or power to individual merit, then the newfound economic success of the common man must attest to the validity of his opinions. The common man was emboldened, and went further by suggesting that knowledge corrupts, and only the uneducated can be trusted for knowing Truth and being in charge of governance.

Roger Price wrote *The Great Roob Revolution* (1970) 40 years later. This book was an update on the growing boldness of ignorant people. He strengthened the case for explaining the certitude of the uneducated person by his observation that the marketplace was catering to him. Not only the marketplace of movies, music and TV, but the marketplace of ideas. New insults to the academic included terms like "egghead."

My book *Genetic Enslavement* (2014) includes a couple chapters updating this phenomenon. My interest in the subject was inspired by the possible role the new

Roob class might have in pushing Western Civilization over the edge to inevitable collapse. I speculated that the Roob's belief in the worth of his ideas is added to by living in a democracy; the reason is subtle: since society gives him a vote, with equal value to all others, then this must mean that his opinions have equal value.

A Roob differs somewhat from a rube. Whereas a rube behaves badly in public for lack of knowing better, a Roob delights in throwing his weight around as he intentionally flaunts his coarseness. The Roob knows that he can't be put back in his place because there are so many of him, and he has re-fashioned all aspects of culture to his unsophisticated taste. He feels comfortable in his dominance of American culture, and has no intention of feeling shame or apologizing to anyone. Anti-intellectualism is the subject of many books, most notably *Anti-Intellectualism in American Life*, by Hofstadter (1969). Robert Sheaffer, in *Resentment Against Achievement: Understanding the Assault Upon Ability* (1988), wrote *"Throughout recorded human history the ebb and flow of the love of achievement and the resentment against its successes have been major forces behind the rise and fall of civilizations and empires. Achievement-oriented values like tolerance, liberty, and the freedom of the individual to work hard and enjoy the fruits of his labor provide the motivation necessary for a civilization to grow and flourish."*

The Roob votes, and this is why I've devoted a few paragraphs to describe him. His vote, as can be imagined, is not nuanced or influenced by erudite policy philosophies. His vote is emotion-based, and it reflects whatever makes him feel good. This means that the Roob's vote is rooted in instincts that evolved during thousands of generations of life in small HG tribes, and his resentment for being dis-respected by a ruling elite during a few generations of super-tribe governance. Any politician who wants his vote will have to pander to the Roob's feeling of inferiority and resentments. Probably no one seeking votes shares the Roob's feelings on this matter, so the politician who can fake it better will win their vote.

Trump

Donald Trump is a "city slicker" who claims to be wealthy, and has a demonstrated history of disdain for the little man. How ironic that he became the little man's hero during the 2016 presidential campaign. Trump is a salesman with experience manipulating others. A good salesman is able to read his mark, and adjust his persona to maximize his persuasive influence on the hapless victim. Some people are "born salesmen" and Trump must be one of them.

Neuro Linguistic Programming (NLP) is one of the tools used by persuasive salesmen. Although NLP practitioners claim to be unaware of the neuropsychology underlying their techniques, it should be obvious to any neuropsychologist. For example, NLP asks the salesman to give careful attention to his mark's word usage. There are three categories, as illustrated by the following: "That sounds right to me." "I see what you mean." "I feel that you're right." Sound, sight and feeling are the three sensory modalities, and they are processed by the three posterior lobes of the brain (temporal, parietal and occipital). People tend to rely more heavily on one of those modalities for perceiving the world, and the modality they favor is revealed by their choice of adjectives. So when a salesman notices that his mark is a "feeling" sort of man, he will shift his speech by invoking more feeling adjectives. For the mark, this increases his comfort level with the salesman.

The salesman has a larger arsenal of tricks besides NLP. If the mark gestures a lot, the salesman will ramp up his gesturing. If the mark has a simple vocabulary, the salesman will limit his vocabulary. If the mark swears a lot, the salesman will use vulgar profanity. But more important than this superficial mimicking is the salesman's need to understand his mark's underlying frustrations.

Everyone is familiar with the shrinkage of the American middle class during the past several decades. Large corporations took advantage of weakening unions, and suppressed worker wage growth while raising salaries and benefits for company executives. International corporations moved manufacturing overseas, to countries with low-wages and fewer regulations (safety, environmental, hours, etc.). Factory workers didn't have the high technology skills that emerging jobs required, so they couldn't maintain the same income level. The government made things worse by entering into treaties that overlooked the American worker (NAFTA is the standard example). Affirmative Action laws favored minorities, which angered some white workers. It became apparent that the federal government was playing a role in worsening the plight of the American white worker. The recession of 2008 worsened things for nearly everyone, but especially those whose jobs that were already precarious. The Tea Party may have been partly in response to a black man becoming president. Visions of more affirmative action preferences for black people and other minorities provided a basis for mistrusting the federal government. If taxation shrank, so would federal benefits to minorities, and maybe the forgotten worker would have more income left over to live on. The Tea Party was comprised of a "forgotten white majority" who viewed the government as run by elites who were more interested in helping others (immigrants, homosexuals, Muslims, disabled) than the workers who made America great during past decades.

Either Trump understood this, or during his campaigning he figured out what to say, and how to talk, for producing the greatest applause. No one disputes that he's a narcissist, and applause is perhaps the most powerful reward for such a person. The Trump following had origins so misunderstood by elites, people with education and influence over the American society, that the elites discounted Trump as a buffoon – somewhat resembling the way Hitler was discounted as a buffoon prior to his rise to power in 1933. The elites would say, in various ways, how could anyone take Trump's run for the presidency seriously when he did things that in past campaigns had immediately disqualified candidates? But Trump's message resonated with the Roob who resented being ignored and made fun of by elites. The Roob is sensitive about his status in society; he knows that others, with more education, or better jobs, look down on him. That's why the Roob is quick to proclaim that "I'm as good as you!" and by voting for Trump the Roob finally had a way to make himself heard.

Other Factors Undermining Democracy

I hate to bring this up, but since no one else does, and since it's relevant to any consideration of how enduring a democracy can be, here goes: Half of Americans have below average IQ!

For anyone who spends their entire work life among highly educated work associates, as I have done (employed by Caltech for 34 years), it is easy to believe that everyone brings a high level of intelligence and critical thinking skills to their assessment of important matters: "On the one hand this, on the other hand that." All of my colleagues were able to suspend judgement as alternative ideas competed with each other in our deliberations. Even when we came to a position, we viewed it as provisionally correct. In other words, nuance and a minimal amount of bias was just an automatic way of thinking for us. Even after I published a paper on a scientific subject I was open to an alternative conclusion. Everything, including my own findings, deserved skeptical reconsideration. This

Appendix C: Fragility of Democracy

extended to newspaper articles, TV, news, and most certainly other people's statements of fact and opinions. I would sometimes be puzzled by a less informed person expressing himself with an excess of certitude, but that was a reminder that other people approached important questions differently.

When the internet came into existence I brought the same habit of skepticism to everything that was presented as true on web pages. The new internet age puts too much "information" into the public domain. People who browse the internet without a habit of skepticism can "fall into the rabbit hole." These people risk entering a realm of intellectual chaos and confusion. At worst, they may be sucked into cults that normal people have never heard of.

Half a century ago the TV Evening News was viewed by ABC, NBC and CBS as a business "loss leader." The FCC also viewed the major networks as having a social responsibility to present national and international news without political bias. Major city newspapers were similar in keeping opinions in their editorial section. Editors for both TV news and newspapers were conscientious in judging the factual basis for truth, as well as newsworthiness. By the end of the 20th Century this cultural tradition was changing. Corporations that owned TV networks shifted emphasis from public service to shareholder profit. At the same time, the internet was beginning to compete with TV news and newspapers. The end result is the gradual disappearance of information-based and editorially-crafted evening news programs, and in their stead Fox News. A younger generation is getting much of their news from Facebook, or Yahoo. People live in different "bubbles," with different facts, yet they are asked to vote for the same set of candidates. Can a democracy survive under these conditions?

The present environment with an ocean of mis-information places a greater burden than ever upon everyone to be cautious, and deliberate, in forming an opinion. The person with an IQ of 85 is less likely than the person with an IQ of 115 to bring the same amount of judgement to assessments of what's on the internet or TV news. There are the same number of people with IQ less than 85 as there are above 115, and the disparity of thinking skill is even greater for these two populations. Yet, they both have the same voting power. This doesn't make sense! Democracy's equal voting voice is different from the HG tribe spending an hour in a big tent taking turns giving opinions and later arriving at a consensus. Those in the tent who didn't understand what was said were too ashamed to object, and look foolish; in a democracy the voting booth invites making that mark regardless of how much is understood, because nobody knows how you voted and you don't have to defend your vote in front of more knowledgeable people.

If voters were vetted with simple questions, such as "How many branches of government are there?", and if their vote was assigned a value based on their answers, the prospects for democracy's survival might be improved. But such a change would never be voted for where half of everyone has a below average intelligence. Besides, such a proposal sounds "elitist" - which it is; and the Roobs of America are already wary of elitist tricks.

Has Hitler Returned?

Sometimes while waiting in a grocery checkout line I wonder if the person next to me is basically the same person who cheered Hitler in 1933. Could just anyone in America today behave as the Germans did some 80 years ago? After all, at that time the Germans were the most educated country in the world, and they had a long history of cultural contributions in such fields as music, philosophy, literature and science.

The German people felt humiliated by their loss of The World War, as it was called then. The Treaty of Versailles was designed to prevent the Germans from rising from the ashes to threaten Europe again. Inflation, joblessness and an economy that could not reconstruct itself added to humiliation. Hitler claimed that Germany still could have won the war when the German government surrendered. By this means he endeavored to discredit the ruling German elites. It was also obvious that those elites didn't endure the same insufferable standard of living as the average German. It's understandable that following the war's end resentments and discontent grew during the following decade and longer.

My father led a bicycling trip of American high schoolers through Germany in 1937. He wrote back to a local newspaper how stoic the Germans were in their hardship. A German family was welcoming when a bicycle breakdown stranded the group far from their intended Youth Hostel. People can be simultaneously kind, and clueless. My father wrote that "Herr Hitler is a smiling individual, contrary to American press reports. This I know to be true because yesterday I was in his presence for 30 minutes while he was reviewing 10,000 of his fervent, exultant German admirers at his residence at, or near, Berchtesdaden. ... Also, he

Appendix C: Fragility of Democracy

is shorter than we popularly suppose." The "fervent exultant" admirers were clueless about what would happen to them a few years later.

Many Germans of the Nazi era saw Hitler making Germany great again. The businessman saw improvement, because factories were being constructed, government contracts were creating new work, and workers were being hired (for making tanks, bombers and innovative new weapons). It was tempting for the businessman, and worker alike, to overlook Hitler's hate-filled speeches, his Brown shirt storm troopers trashing of Jewish businesses, and the Kristallnacht (that occurred one year after my father's visit). Hitler's party went by the name National Socialist German Workers Party, so its appeal was aimed at discontented workers with hope for "socialist" help.

Historians of the Nazi era cite a phenomenon called "alignment." After Hitler consolidated power with the 1933 Enabling Act, giving him power to enact legislation that had formerly resided with the Reichstag, critics gradually accepted him. They would explain his excesses as just theatrics. Even some Jews would discount his rants about Jews. "Give him a chance" to improve our lot. There are two reasons leaders can get away with such abuse of their followers. 1) Tribes thrive and survive inter-tribal warfare when their internal workings are harmonious, 2) Strong leaders won't tolerate critics who might undermine their rule. Compare the likely fates of tribes consisting of individuals who accepted the inevitable, regardless of how unfair that inevitable condition is, and who got on with life and contributed to the tribe's welfare, with tribes consisting of individuals who remained divided after takeover by a strong leader. Tribes of the former type will be victorious over the latter type, assuming other conditions of tribal strength were similar. We are descendants of the first type of tribe. We therefore "conform" to whatever has become inevitable for our tribe. "Conformance" is a technical term used by sociobiologists to describe this trait.

I view Trump as playing a similar role in America today. Probably the business community views Trump in the same way the Nazi era business community viewed Hitler. If Trump can implement the policies he campaigned on then probably the economy would be stimulated in the short term, without regard for the inevitable longer-term indebtedness and corporate over-reach that would result. Trump's outrageous behavior, which no person would accept among their friends, is excused as just attention-getting theatrics. Trump voters said he would never do some of the things he threatened to do. "Now that he's elected" they would say, "just give him a chance." Indeed, some liberals are saying the same thing: "Just give him a chance" - as if he will become a normal human, and abandon his psychopathic ways. Some liberals are going further, and crediting Trump with drawing attention to issues that liberals had neglected (too much PC, trade agreements that hurt workers, etc), and blaming themselves for Trump's rise. This is the same "conformance" that occurred after Hitler secured power. An article by Shawn Hamilton (2016) describes this, using the current terminology for conformance: "alignment." Even liberal TV commentators are "aligning." As both conservatives and some spineless liberals "align," American culture will coarsen, intolerance for others will grow ugly, neighbor will hate neighbor, snitching to authorities could become common - as happened in Nazi Germany. Trump's criticisms of intellectuals, and especially journalists, is designed to inoculate him from thoughtful criticism. Free thinkers should be on notice: book burning could once again become common, and my books will belong to the category that's thrown on the bonfire.

In spite of these comparisons of Trump with Hitler, it's my sense that these two psychopaths are fundamentally different. Hitler was an ideologue, and remained true to long-held beliefs. Trump is not an ideologue; he is mostly a narcissist who seeks applause. In theory, therefore, if Trump pursues strategies that maximize applause, he may actually do some good in the short-term. He might actually persuade Congress to invest in infrastructure spending, and this job stimulus might have other beneficial effects. He may actually preserve some health care provisions in Obama's Affordable Care Act, because the masses will applaud him for that.

However, Trump seems oblivious to long-term consequences, especially if they don't affect him. So he may allow himself to ally with Republicans who want to "modernize" Medicare (privatize it with vouchers), de-regulate the banking system (repeal Dodd-Frank), eviscerate the EPA, withdraw from climate change agreements, appoint Supreme Court justices who think outlawing abortion is legal, and generally take America backwards for a couple generations.

A Disintegration Scenario

America is like a cookie poised to crumble. How might this happen?

Appendix C: Fragility of Democracy

Recall the oft-cited description of America being a bi-coastal country: The New York/Washington DC region and the West Coast have a vibrant business relationship, dominated by liberal politics. Businessmen who fly back-and-forth derisively refer to the vast land in-between as "fly-over" country. People living in the fly-over region have heard the terminology, and some have described their vote for Trump as a fly-over revolt. This illustrates the growing divide between the Two Americas.

People in the West Coast states of California, Oregon and Washington are beginning to talk about secession. For decades there has been discussion of a more limited secession of Northern California, Oregon and Washington to form a new country called "Cascadia." Southern California has recovered from the Birch Society movement that painted the political map conservative for a while, so now essentially all of California is liberal, and the new Cascadia would include Southern California. Even Hawaii might be included in a secession, because that state is possibly the most liberal in the nation. Conservatives have always championed local determination, so secession is an ultimate expression of this sentiment. Conservatives would probably welcome the Cascadian breakaway. Having lived in California for most of my life, and in spite of having grown up as a farm boy in Michigan, I would favor the proposed secession.

If a major secession like Cascadia did occur, there would be pressure for the East Coast to do the same. However, the political establishment in Washington, D.C. would object because they wouldn't want to lose the power they now enjoy by presiding over almost an entire continent. New York City might consider a new form of secession, that of a city becoming a country – somewhat resembling Singapore in its relationship to their region.

The entire secession process would be driven by the mutual resentment of people who embrace diversity and those who abhor it. One faction wants to march forward, and the other wants to march backward. One is open-minded, and the other is closed-minded. Each faction has ancestors who had different reactions to the past 12,700 years of tribal coalescence leading to super-tribes, and eventually civilizations.

While Cascadia pursues a space program for colonizing Mars, the redneck southeastern states will celebrate NASCAR racing, cotton plantations, and they will embrace the Confederate Flag as they attempt to re-institute slavery. The

Appendix C: Fragility of Democracy

Two Americas will become two countries, with trade agreements and border check-points.

Summary and Conclusion

Humans may not be capable of any form of governance. This is due to their Pleistocene inheritance, instincts that were adapted to small HG tribal life for at least a half million years. The last 12,700 years of Holocene warming allowed invention of farming and other new lifestyles, and this is too short a time for our primitive instincts to have been replaced with newer ones that are better adapted to a civilized way of life. A minority of humans feel comfortable being civilized, but a majority is best described by Freud's famous terminology: "discontent with civilization."

Given that most people have a subconscious longing for "going back" to their primitive origins, to life in a small HG tribe, the prospects are dim that a winning place can be found for those of us who prefer to "move forward" to an evermore civilized society.

The *hoi poloi's* simple-minded appeal to unsophisticated things, and their re-moulding of our culture to their unsophisticated and vulgar taste, means that they cannot be persuaded to move forward. For them, democracy was a disappointment, because those in charge of governance ignored them. They are gullible, and a sophisticated psychopathic salesmen, like Trump, can arouse their hopes for something resembling a backwards move, a retreat from civilization, while calling it "Making America Great Again."

America is now on a course of retreat. Our dis-assembling will begin in earnest in 2017. After World War II America helped preserve global peace by restraining dictators. This era will start to fade in 2017, as the world begins a return to the 19th Century, and earlier ones, with incessant wars waged by dictators whose only interest in peace is unchallenged rule.

Those of us alive now, adults who experienced the second half of the 20th Century, are the lucky ones. Conditions may never improve, and even though our standard of living may remain high for a few more decades, being on the rise, with hope for the future, is always better than being on the decline with futures foreclosed.

Appendix C: Fragility of Democracy

Time will tell. At my age of 77 I won't know what time will tell. But it still concerns me, and I'm upset.

Appendix D: Confessions of a Misanthrope

Psychopaths aren't responsible for the entirety of human horribleness. Most Normaloids are capable of despicable behavior under certain conditions. This is most dramatically illustrated by Nazi Germany.

World War II began when I was 3 months old. Throughout childhood I browsed picture books documenting the horrors of war. Before I started grade-school there were pictures of Nazi concentration camps where Christian Germany was exterminating Jews. This is how I came to the realization, by the age of six, that humans could be evil.

In high school I learned about my ancestors invading America, and massacring people who had lived here for thousands of generations. We also learned about plantation owners abducting Africans to work as slaves on plantations. History class also gave passing notice about the Crusades, and the Inquisition. These revelations further confirmed by disappointment in human nature.

I sensed that everyone believed in religious stories about how God created everything: the Earth and all the stars in the heavens, all the animals, and especially humans. He was watching people to see who was naughty or nice, and like Santa Clause he would pass judgement for future punishment or reward. This "fairy tale" involved the magic of prayer, angels, the Devil (Satan) and mythical places like Heaven and Hell. Explanations from science, such as astronomy or evolution, were forbidden. I learned that it was essential for me to hide my wariness of humans for their stupid beliefs because they were intolerant, and capable of nastiness in the way they punished people with ideas that deviated from their stupid beliefs.

My childhood disappointments with humanity placed me on a path to misanthropy. I nurtured the default assumption that everyone I didn't know well was secretly evil, regardless of their superficial niceness, and that they were also stupid, regardless of their appearance of having normal intelligence. I wondered if these assessments were correct 90 % of the time, or 99 % of the time. In other words, I was considering that only 1 to 10 % of people were both nice and smart. As I grew older I favored values even lower than 1 %. This meant that at least 99 % of people were in the bad or dumb categories.

Today it amuses me to read that only 1 to 4 % of people are bad, using the definitions for sociopathy and psychopathy. The discrepancy between my assessment and the generally accepted one must be related to differences in defining bad. My definition is that 99 % of people will behave well under everyday circumstances but can behave badly under certain other circumstances. Nazi Germany comes to mind for the latter. Whereas the more generally-accepted definition is that 1 or 2 % of people lack a conscience and will manipulate people without mercy, as psychopaths do, those so-called Normaloids who have a conscience are able to overrule it under certain circumstances.

Appendix D: Confessions of a Misanthrope

In this appendix I want to present a better "balance" in characterizing human nature.

Human nature evolved to serve the survival of small tribe gene pools. Conformance with tribal customs helped secure patriotic behaviors, such as joining a war party to attack a neighbor tribe that was vulnerable. Anyone who questioned tribal mythologies, for example, would be subjected to extra scrutiny. "Individualism" must have been somewhere between rare and non-existent during the AE.

The men of a tribe were "tribe's men" – i.e., owned by the tribe. They were enslaved to the tribe, and when the tribe called on them, they heeded the call unthinkingly. Such tribes must have been victorious more often than any tribe that valued the critical thinking skills of individualism. An individual will hesitate when the "call to action" is issued; he will consider the pros and cons of action, and he might consider whether he, as an individual, has more to gain or lose by heeding the call.

The unthinking individual is prone to reacting to situations in accord with instincts. It is instinctive to wish for the death of *other* tribesmen. It must have been easy for the Roman Empire citizen to attend the coliseum and cheer gladiators who fought for their lives, who appealed to the emperor for permission to kill the vanquished gladiator. The cheering crowds may have included a few psychopaths, but for all practical purposes they were Normaloids, acting as Normaloids will under certain conditions.

The witch hunts by Eighteenth Century New Englanders could not have been exclusively by psychopaths. They had to be an expression of Normaloid idiots motivated by an inner nastiness found in most people.

The human appetite for oppressing others can be abused by unscrupulous leaders. The Inquisition was started in 12th Century France by the Catholic Church. It was initially a way to punish heresy among Catholics, sometimes including the death to heretics by being burned at a stake. It occasionally took the form of religious wars, culminating in Crusades of armed marches into areas with different religious beliefs. The Catholics weren't psychopaths, they were Normaloids with the same idiocy and nastiness of most humans.

The 1971 "Stanford prison experiment," conducted by Philip Zimbardo, showed that ~ 1/3 of randomly chosen student volunteers could behave with sadistic abuse toward "prisoners" who had also been randomly chosen from volunteers. The "Milgram experiment" on obedience to authority, conducted by Stanley Milgram at Yale University in 1961, illustrated that most volunteers would administer painful electric shocks to subjects (actors, pretending to show pain) who didn't perform well on tasks.

Examples of Normaloids being led by psychopaths can be found throughout history. The genocide in Rwanda by Hutus against Tutsis, between 1990 and 1994, may have been instigated by psychopaths, but the bulk of it must have been carried out by Normaloids. The 1968 My Lai massacre in Vietnam was carried out by presumably Normaloid American soldiers, led by a possibly psychopathic platoon leader William Calley Jr. American soldiers in Iraq committed degrading acts of abuse at a military prison at Abu Ghraib in 2003. Catholic priests have been sexually abusing young boys for decades, and presumably most priests are not psychopaths. For more than a century in "the south" negros were lynched while large crowds of Normaloid "whites" watched.

The most famous 20th Century example of Normaloid atrocious behavior was led by psychopath Hitler with his appeal to Nazi fascism. The unthinking German Normaloids responded to Hitler's "call to arms." The Nazi message was that everyone else, those others, the Jews, were taking advantage of loyal countrymen, the true Germans. The others, the social parasite intruders, deserve to be expelled; the homeland must be cleansed. In this way Hitler promised to make Germany great again!

During the years that Hitler controlled most of Europe Nazi were assigned to going from village to village and hiring pit diggers from the local population. When the pit was ready the townspeople would gather to watch as Jews were escorted to the edge of the pit and shot. Most who fell into the pit were still alive, but the Nazi's orders followed to shovel dirt back into the pit to cover it up. One wonders why the local population didn't defend their neighbors, the Jews, by driving the Nazi away from their village. Could the locals have been looking forward to rewards of the spoils left behind by wealthy Jews? In any case, we must assume that most of the local onlookers and pit diggers were normaloids.

Germany was a democracy when Hitler gained a foothold in Germany's power structure. His 33% of the 1933 vote was more than the other five candidates, so he won that election. Germany made the transition from a democracy to a fascist tyranny within a year. Hannah Arendt wrote about the "banality of evil" (1963), describing the "chilling ease with which seemingly normal people (in Germany) did atrocious things" (Kelly, 2018). The German people got the government they deserved, and the millions who died in the war that they started paid the price for being who they were.

America, the USA, is poised to cross the same threshold. Americans come from the same "stock" as the Germans, and we are also capable of answering the same "call of the wild." Trump's loyal support is currently the same as Hitler's original 33 %. When half of voting age people don't vote, and the other half are clueless, significant change to a democracy is possible.

If Trump can accomplish a fascist take-over he can be expected to foment racial and class discontent similar to what other tyrants have done. The "corrupt elites" will be targeted, along with the Mexicans, Muslims, African Americans, intellectuals, or any other group that doesn't resemble the poor and struggling rural Caucasian who remembers how great America was in 1950.

I will be targeted because I'm an intellectual, and because I'm a misanthrope, an individual with critical thinking skills who is unafraid to mock the clueless *hoi poloi*. The ugliness of human nature will assert itself, and we will have a repeat of Nazi Germany!

I don't know if this will happen, but it could!

Appendix E: Futility

Bruce L. Gary, 2017.06.26; 2017.07.10

If a society doesn't rid itself of psychopaths they will eventually take-over and destroy the society, for the same reason that a cancer cell, left unchecked, will take-over and destroy an organism. Since a civilization requires a suspension of primitive intolerance, psychopaths will be tolerated instead of shunned, banished or killed, so their numbers will rise and cause an eventual collapse of the very civilization that allowed them to prosper. These Forces of Destiny are more powerful than any well-meaning individual, so the impulse to make things better is futile!

After 78 years the word "futility" is finally entering my vocabulary. I recognize the futility of trying to make things better. Maybe in a small tribe this was feasible, but not in an increasingly-connected world of 7 billion people with fundamentally flawed natures.

I have become inclined to think in terms of a chronic conflict between good and bad. It's tempting to portray the world as favoring "bad" in all manner of things. Although "bad" is always the ultimate winner, good can exist temporarily. Life is good, yet a person's life is brief; civilizations arise, but they always collapse; the Earth is life-bearing, but in a few billion years the oceans will boil away and later the sun will swell to evaporate everything. A "game theorist" might use computer simulations to arrive at the conclusion that for a wide range of settings bad is favored to prevail.

Single Cell to Multi-Cellular Life

Imagine starting with a cell that lives in the ocean, and reproduces by splitting to produce clones of itself. It has genetic immortality for as long as non-living nutrients are plentiful in the ocean water. Then, mutations lead to a type of cell in the ocean that could eat the other cells, which is the first occasion for life consuming life. But then a mutation occurs that leads to cells sticking together to form a more formidable group of cells. It thrives because attacking cells can't destroy the stuck-together group. New mutations cause the cells on the surface of a stuck-together group to become better at defending against attacker cells. This protective "skin" is the beginning of the evolution of a multi-cellular organism.

A multi-cellular organism is "cumbersome." It not only moves slowly, but it takes time to assemble itself from a single cell. The assembly is, of course, under the

Appendix E: Futility

direction of the genes within the cells. Each cell has the same genes, so it is necessary for only a subset of genes to be "active" in each single cell. For a skin cell, only the skin cell genes are active; for a heart cell, only the heart cell genes are active, etc. For present purposes it's not necessary to describe how most genes are kept inactive by being surrounded by a methyl molecule covering. But it is necessary to state, without proof, that one of the organs is devoted to preserving a set of genes for a sexual reproductive process. Sexual refers to the fact that the organism doesn't reproduce by splitting apart, the way a single-cell reproduces. Rather, the multi-cellular organism has to use the special cells reserved for this purpose to combine with analogue cells from another organism to form a complete cell that will duplicate itself, over and over, to form a new multi-cell organism. In theory a single organism could achieve this, and produce an identical offspring organism, but a species that did this could not adapt to changes in the environment as quickly as the sexually reproducing ones. Remember, a multi-cell organism is cumbersome, and its individual lifetime is longer than the ancestral stock of single-cell organisms. Sexual reproduction therefore overcomes the evolutionary disadvantage of long individual lifetimes while preserving the evolutionary advantage of fast-mutation agility.

Individual/Group Conflict

Game theory has revealed some interesting subtleties relating to the coming together of elements to form a group. When the group thrives or dies as a group, it is found that certain traits for the individuals are favored. Individuals that serve the group when it competes with other groups are more successful, and the individuals constituting these groups remain in existence after several rounds of gaming. An individual that disrupts the group's performance threatens not only the group, but all the individuals that came together to form the group. Therefore, a new dynamic of "group conformance" is required, and those groups that come together from individuals who are vigilant in identifying and destroying "cheaters" will prevail during inter-group competition.

Let's apply this to a multi-cell organism. It is theoretically possible for a cell to exist within an organism even when it doesn't cooperate and with the function of the organ in which it is found, and instead use resources to reproduce itself, and in effect form its own group within the organism. We refer to such a cell as cancerous!

A cancer cell, left unchecked, will destroy the organism that gave the cell its opportunity to exist. Organisms have evolved strategies to identify and destroy cancer cells. The immune system includes "killer T cells," and it's their job to identify cancer cells, and initiate their destruction. The process used for cell destruction is interesting: it's called apoptosis. The killer T cell marks the cell to be destroyed with a chemical signal, and the internal response is self-supervised cell death. The marked cell commences to chop-up its DNA, rendering it functionally useless, and the cell quickly dies for lack of instruction for doing anything. Killer T cells also identify cells that are too old to function efficiently, senescent cells, and they also self-destruct when marked.

Tribes and Organisms

A tribe is a group of genetically similar individuals, analogous to an organism being a group of identically genetic cells. Individuals in a tribe have a "shared fate" in the sense that when a tribe is vanquished its individual membership is killed, or enslaved, rendering the vanquished individuals evolutionary dead-ends. The demise of a tribe is analogous to the death of an organism. Game theory predicts that the interaction of individuals in relation to a tribe should resemble the interaction of cells within an organism.

Indeed, what we find in an organism is also found within a tribe. The cancer cell's analogue is a cheater person, or psychopath. The psychopath is a master manipulator. He steals resources from others, and thus grows in strength at the expense of the group. The psychopath will pretend to be patriotic, but when talk is supposed to translate to action, the psychopath disappears. The group, in response, has the analogue of killer T cells. These are individuals who are vigilant in identifying cheaters, or imposters, and marking them for a targeted harassment and ultimate banishment from the group. In the ancestral environment the small tribe had ways of dealing with the man who was "too big for his britches" (the blowhard bully): ambush murder.

Any group that provides respite for the injured is potentially vulnerable to freeloading by psychopaths, so vigilantes are also quick to identify freeloaders. Calling an individual a freeloader is analogous to the killer T cell marking a non-functioning cell, or senescent cell, for apoptosis.

Appendix E: Futility

Since neighboring tribes are in almost chronic conflict, it occasionally happens that an individual from a rival tribe will seek membership in another tribe for the purpose of doing damage; vigilantes are quick to identify spies, or treasonous enemies, and kill them. This is analogous to the response of killer T cells in identifying a virus that has invaded the organism.

I hesitate to call attention to two sad analogies. School yard bullies identify weaklings and humiliate them in an effort to cause the weakling to commit suicide. This is analogous to the killer T cell identifying cells that are low-functioning because they underwent a deleterious mutation when they formed. It is well known that under-performing cells sometimes identify themselves as defective, and by themselves initiate apoptosis. The analogy for people is depression, a form of self-identification of low-functioning; depression puts a person at heightened risk of suicide.

Super-Tribes

Super-tribes began to form for the first time ~ 12,700 years ago, when Earth's climate warmed and the glaciers receded, resulting in an acre of land at mid-latitudes being able to support more people. With an increased "carrying capacity" tribal size could increase, even while shrinking its territory. This brought neighboring tribes closer together, and this triggered inter-tribal warfare due to old instincts. The coalescence of two tribes, if it could be successful, led to the reward of assured victory over any challenging tribe. It also meant that the new super-tribe could attack the old-fashioned smaller tribe with impunity.

The trick for super-tribe formation was finding a way to overcome the instinctive distrust of strangers. A traditional tribe was never larger than the Dunbar Number, about 150 adult individuals. Anyone in this small a tribe would have had sufficient interpersonal relationships with all fellow tribesmen to accurately judge their trustworthiness. No one in such a tribe is a stranger, and presumably all the sociopathic cheaters would have been identified and either shunned, banished or killed; this permitted an almost automatic mutual trust of any adult who remained in the tribe. When two tribes join, however, all new tribesmen will be strangers, and most will remain so. They will be easily identified because they will dress differently, talk differently, and have different customs and beliefs. When a super-tribe enters into battle with another tribe, even if that other tribe is smaller, there will be a hesitance by the super-tribe warriors to totally trust each other, or even to identify each other since some fellow tribesmen will be strangers.

Since super-tribes did in fact form, and prevail, we must assume that these difficulties of coalescence and assimilation were sometimes achieved. For a successful coalescence of tribes to occur, the individuals must suspend their primitive distrust of strangers, driven by an instinctive intolerance, and nurture the notion that tolerance is good.

Discontents with Civilization

The super-tribe allowed some individuals to specialize. For example, whereas in the small tribe every warrior made his own weapons, in a super-tribe a master weapon-maker would provide warriors with superior weapons: spears, bows and arrows, chariots, guns and eventually atomic bombs. Completely new occupations were feasible within the super-tribe setting: farming, warriors to defend the farmers from marauders, markets, factories and bankers.

But the people born into a super-tribe had brains that were adapted to the small-tribe, hunter-gatherer lifestyle. It didn't come naturally for these people to be comfortable encountering strangers every day. Learning the newest trade, such as a flour grinding mill, or computer programming, is unsettling for the small-tribe brain. People differ in their ability to adapt, or feel comfortable with "modernity." Just as a dog may hear a "call of the wild" when hearing a distant wolf calling, the person with a primitive brain will feel discontent with this thing he's supposed to embrace, called civilization.

Hyper Liberalism

The most successful super-tribes must have been the ones that were able to restrain the "tribal mentality" instinct. This is the instinct that promotes amity for interactions within the tribe, and enmity for extra-tribal interactions. It's an extreme form of "intolerance" because other tribesmen are slightly different in dress, behavior, beliefs, etc., so it's these differences that trigger an intolerant reaction. Everyone's brain has a tribal mentality module, hard-wired via neuronal connections and synapse sizes set at birth. But some people have a weaker tribal mentality module, and a super-tribe dominated by those people will stay together better, and prevail upon their neighbor tribes.

Appendix E: Futility

Super-tribes must have appeared first where the climate change was most dramatic. That would be Europe. The greatest rewards for super-tribes with tolerant individuals would have been in Europe, and especially Scandinavia. Guess where the most liberal societies are? Scandinavia and Europe.

But there can be too much of a good things. A liberal is prone to demand tolerance of things that shouldn't be tolerated. For example, an extreme liberal will object to someone criticizing "honor killings" because that's part of someone's religion, and religions are to be tolerated. Ultra-liberals may demand "safe zones" on college campuses, where their sensitivities to shocking ideas won't be offended. They have made a bad name for themselves by curtailing the "free speech" of speakers with ideas that I think merit consideration (e.g., Charles Murray, who co-authored *The Bell Curve*.)

Extreme positions in any direction, with a visceral hatred for the "other," are not good for maintaining societal stability. Anything that promotes the growth of differences within society is de-stabilizing. The replacement of newspapers by the internet is destabilizing. The growth of wealth inequality is destabilizing. But the most destabilizing force in contemporary society is from something nobody dares talk about: the rise of psychopathy.

The Rise of Psychopathy

In small tribes people know each other, and a cheater is identified and gossiped about. Cheaters in small tribes were rendered less harmful because everyone else knew who they were, and social pressure constrained how much cheating they could get away with. Cheaters are thus handicapped in a small-tribe. But in the super-tribe a sociopath can cheat in one region until he is discovered, then move to another region where the gossip hasn't spread, allowing him to repeat his cheating trick. Thus, on theoretical grounds, or as game theorists would say, civilization invites sociopathology.

I have no information about the incidence of psychopaths in small-tribes, or even the early super-tribes. Today, however, we have an accurate measure. Psychopaths, and their less extreme cousin, sociopaths, constitute 6 to 10% of Americans. There are ~ 2% of the hard-core type, the psychopaths. Sociopaths are technically referred to as "borderline personality disorder." On the 40-question "Hare Psychopathology Checklist" (see Fig. 1, next page) a psychopath is anyone who scores at 30 or above, and a sociopath is someone who scores between 7 and 29 (this last is my suggestion). Together, the sociopaths and psychopaths are often referred to by the term "sociopathy."

There's apparently no correlation of sociopathy/psychopathy and IQ. This makes sense, because IQ is determined entirely by the capability of the three posterior lobes (parietal, temporal and occipital), whereas "executive function" is controlled exclusively by the frontal lobe. I like to say that dumb psychopaths end up in jail while smart ones become CEOs of big companies. There are plenty of opportunities for sociopaths and psychopaths today. The incompetent female ones manipulate husbands to buy them things, or they shop lift, while the more innovative ones become TV evangelists or cult leaders; with even greater luck a psychopath can become president.

```
2 = glibness and superficial charm
2 = grandiose sense of self-worth
2 = need for stimulation/proneness to boredom (e.g., short attention span)
2 = pathological lying
2 = cunning/manipulative
2 = lack of remorse or guilt
2 = shallow affect (not understanding of human relationships)
2 = callous lack of empathy
2 = parasitic lifestyle (e.g., taking credit for work done by others)
2 = poor behavioral control (as in tweeting before thinking)
2 = promiscuous sexual behavior (e.g., boasting about it)
2 = early behavioral problems ("I punched my music teacher because I didn't think he knew anthing about music...")
1 = lack of realistic long-term goals
2 = impulsivity
1 = irresponsibility
2 = failure to accept responsibility for one's own actions
0 = many short-term marital relationships (3 marriages lasting 14, 6 & 11 years doesn't qualify)
2 = juvenile delinquency (father says "He was a pretty rough fellow when he was small." and more)
0 = revocation of "conditional release" (by a parole officer)
0 = criminal versatility
```

Figure E1. *Hare Psychopathology Checklist, scored for Donald Trump by Keith Olbermann.*

Cancer on Civilization

Pschopaths are analogous to a cancer cell that threatens to grow, multiply, and kill the organism that gave it life. Where are the "ambush killers" when we need them?

Appendix E: Futility

Essentially every news story that makes me "shake my head" has a psychopath or sociopath in it. From local news stories, like the robber who shoots a clerk, to major ones, like congressmen dismantling an environmental program, the underlying problem is someone with power who doesn't have empathy for others, because they just don't care. They can't care, because they're missing the gene, or genes, that create a moral sense, an intuitive understanding of right and wrong, the attitudes that hold a group together.

The old-fashioned sense of responsibility cited by nobility, called "noblesse oblige," held that the strong had a responsibility to help the weak within their society. The reverse of that sentiment drives the sociopath, and especially psychopath: The strong are entitled to victimize the weak. When pressed for an explanation of some egregious act of victimizing someone, a sociopath or psychopath might say "It's their own fault for being clueless."

Consider the opposite sentiment, expressed in following passage, written by Bertrand Russell in 1903 ("A Free Man's Worship"):

The life of Man is a long march through the night, surrounded by invisible foes, tortured by weariness and pain, towards a goal that few can hope to reach, and where none may tarry long. One by one, as they march, our comrades vanish from our sight, seized by the silent orders of omnipotent Death. Very brief is the time in which we can help them, in which their happiness or misery is decided. Be it ours to shed sunshine on their path, to lighten their sorrows by the balm of sympathy, to give them the pure joy of a never tiring affection, to strengthen failing courage, to instill faith in hours of despair. Let us not weigh in grudging scales their merits and demerits, but let us think only of their need - of the sorrows, the difficulties, perhaps the blindnesses, that make the misery of their lives; let us remember that they are fellow-sufferers in the same darkness, actors in the same tragedy with ourselves. And so, when their day is over, when their good and their evil have become eternal by the immortality of the past, be it ours to feel that, where they suffered, where they failed, no deed of ours was the cause; but wherever a spark of the divine fire kindled in their hearts, we were ready with encouragement, with sympathy, with brave words in which high courage glowed."

Both sociopaths and psychopaths would be puzzled by these sentiments. He would of course pretend to understand, and say some robotic thing of praise. But by his actions we would know that he is deeply imbued with the cancerous attitude, willing to cleverly destroy anyone, or anything, that gets in his way. The sociopaths and psychopaths rob society of the glue that holds it together. Without the caring glue, a society, or a civilization, will come undone.

Have good people become intimidated by the psychopathic bullies who control much of contemporary society, to an extent that these good people are afraid to call the bullies out, and use the name <u>sociopath</u> or <u>psychopath?</u> Have the ultra-liberals created such a strong force of "political correctness" that a politician who cares about people's welfare, and society's, cannot call his opponent a sociopath or psychopath when it is appropriate?

Roobs are Enablers

In 1930 the Spanish philosopher, Jose Ortega y Gassett, published a book *Revolt of the Masses*. His main message, or warning, was that people without education, but rising wealth, were voicing their <u>opinions</u> as if they deserved as much consideration as carefully arrived at positions by academics. If the layperson's opinion was discounted, they would speak it louder. It's as if the truth was to be found by looking inward instead of by an outward search for evidence which would then be judged by a disciplined academic process. This new form of anti-intellectualism was on the rise according to Ortega y Gassett.

In 1970 the TV comedian and commentator Roger Price published the book *The Great Roob Revolution*, which in essence was an update of *Revolt of the Masses*. He wanted to change from use of "rube" to "Roob" to distinguish between the innocently clueless from the intentionally boorish. The Roob sensed his buying power, and the reticence of the marketplace to insult him, and instead cater to his uneducated taste. This caused a coarsening of not only music, movies and entertainment, but the realm of ideas, and – most dangerously, politics. The Roob voted, and politicians dumbed-down their rhetoric; they embraced false notions of how the "eggheads" were secretly mocking the earnest and hard-working man without education. A feedback of ignorance was displacing academic discourse.

Sociopaths and psychopaths are master manipulators. They resemble the much maligned car salesman, who reads his mark, imitates his gestures and speech, in order to nurture a comfort level that feeds trust. Whether politicians figured out that this is the best way to play the game, or the politicians who were just naturally slick salesmen were more successful, the end result is the same: a growing dominance of politics by sociopaths and psychopaths. This success owes itself to the Roob, who lacks critical thinking skill and is sold on the most convincing imposter.

Figure E2. *Cover of 1970 book introducing the term "Roob."*

 "God must have an inordinate fondness for Roobs, for why else would he have made so many?" I don't know who said that (JBSH, of course, referring to beetles), but there's truth in the refrain. Sociobiologists have the answer: most men are meant to be warrior fodder. A good warrior doesn't think, he just says to himself "My country, right or wrong." Also, most women are meant to be baby makers, and again, thinking isn't an asset for that task. That's why so many of today's voters are clueless Roobs, who become enablers of sociopaths and psychopaths aspiring to leadership.

Can Democracy Survive?

Consider the make-up of American voters: 1) Half have below average intelligence, 2) at least 10 % are either sociopaths or psychopaths, 3) about 40 %

are Roobs, 4) 74 % know the names of The Three Stooges (Larry, Curly and Moe) while only 42 % can identify the three branches of government, 5) about 20 % of Americans can't find the U.S. on a world map – and the list of American ignorance goes on! Maybe it's good that half of all qualified voters don't vote. But which half is voting?

When Germans voted for Hitler in 1933 their society was considered the best educated in the world, with a long history of cultural contributions. What were they thinking? Couldn't they see that Hitler was a mentally-disturbed buffoon (a term sometimes appearing in newspapers), a hate-filled bigot, and an aspiring dictator? Those who criticized Hitler were treated like unpatriotic infiltrators from a neighboring tribe. An amazing array of intelligent people supported Hitler, not only in Germany, but in England, America and other countries.

In hindsight we know that Hitler had a "schizotypal" personality; he was a rabble-rousing psychopath which sociobiologists would describe as having a purpose when a tribe in the ancestral environment became too large and needed to fission with the help of a charismatic leader making up stories about a "promised land." Hitler had a ready audience because most contemporary humans have brains no different from their prehistoric ancestors, the ones who lived in small hunter-gatherer tribes, that were in chronic conflict with neighboring tribes over territory and existence. Hitler's "brown shirt" Stormtroopers were thugs given a purpose. Those "marching morons" picked on anyone who frowned. It's braver to speak truth to power than to join the patriots in attacking the lone truth teller. Hence the saying: "Patriotism is the last refuge of a scoundrel" (1775, Samuel Johnson). In retrospect, we can view Hitler as resembling the single cancer cell that metastasized and killed the organism from which it arose; at the end of World War II Germany was a wasteland!

Thankfully, our President Trump is less disciplined than Hitler. He may self-destruct soon, but when that happens the mess he created may not be salvageable. Our congress is dominated by sociopaths, so they will do whatever is in their personal interest, not the national. It's a fair question: will American democracy survive?

Can Civilization Survive?

If democracies can't survive, can a civilization survive?

Appendix E: Futility

The first civilization, however the term is defined, was by definition "not adapted" for survival. It was a fluke, with an uncertain future. It might have occurred 5,000 years ago, or 15,000 years ago; whenever it was, those who brought it into being must have wondered what would happen to it, for they had no history from which to learn or judge. Today we know about hundreds of civilizations, and they all failed to endure. Their median lifetime is approximately 5 centuries. Things happen faster today, thanks to enhanced travel and the internet, so America's 241 years might be close to the new limit.

Sigmund Freud had a good intuitive sense for what ailed modernity. He discerned the important role for subconscious thought, the greater than acknowledged importance of sex, and most importantly, he realized that at a subconscious level people resented civilization. In his book *Civilization and its Discontents* he saw a primitive mentality that was not comfortable with the restrictions imposed on individuals by civilization. If Freud had lived another 30 years I believe that he would have embraced sociobiology, with its theoretical explanations for humans being better adapted to the ancestral small-tribe lifestyle than to a civilized one.

Only the "artisans," who had a small niche in the ancestral environment, feel comfortable with civilized life. The artisan is tolerant, and he played a crucial role in creating civilization, and this happened at the expense of the importance of the non-artisan, who remains intolerant and feels resentment of civilized governance. It's as if the typical man feels betrayed by a promise made millennia ago that civilized life would be an improvement. He rejects the artisan's forward trajectory, and wants to "take us back" on a backward trajectory to those ancient times when life was simple. If they are only half successful they will take us back to another Dark Ages.

World Population Explosion

When I was born, in 1939, the world's population was 2.2 billion. Today it is 7.2 billion! During the 1960's there was public discussion about the negative implications of an explosive rise of world population, about the strain this was having on food supply and environmental degradation. A minor dystopian theme was the fear of future mass migrations from over-exploited land to better-maintained land. A contemporary version of this last concern would be the fear of mass migration from countries with dysfunctional governance to countries with stable governance. In addition, global sea level rise could be 20 feet by the end of the century, and this will produce a migration from coastal cities to interior regions (in countries that border the ocean).

Animals have well-documented strategies for reproduction. At one end of a continuum are the r-strategy reproducers, involving large broods and minimal parental investment - such as fish that lay thousands of eggs and then leave. At the other end are the high parental investment species, referred to as K-strategy, such as elephants and humans. In addition, for some species (e.g., humans), it is useful to consider that the same continuum exists within the species. Some human parents produce lots of babies, with meager investment in each, while others have fewer offspring and invest more in each. There is a strong correlation between family size and parental investment per child, and the correlation is negative. A personal experience illustrates this.

I postponed marriage, and the bringing of children into the world, until my job was secure and I had a savings. This readiness for responsibility began when I was 29 years old. After establishing my family in a rented house, and preparing for the birth of our second child, the next door neighbor was already on the way to having a large family. The patriarch, who worked as a waiter, had at least half a dozen children. A decade later we moved away, and lost track of the next generation of their offspring. When one of my daughters visited them, and spoke with a young woman who used to be a playmate when they were girls, she learned that one of her brothers was in prison, her father, the patriarch, had lost his job, and the total count of children and grandchildren was approximately 30. When I learned this I compared my contributions to society with those of Costello, the patriarch: mine included almost 100 scientific papers, help in understanding the ozone hole, and two daughters who will never have children; the neighbor family's contribution is a population explosion of deadbeats. If the genes could talk they would be happy with Costello and scold me for being their deadbeat.

The Futility of Trying to Make Things Better

Que sera, sera! What will be, will be!

Growing old, as I have done, has taught me humility. It started with a resolve to be a better person. I eventually figured out that all thoughts originate in the subconscious, and the conscious self merely plays the role of giving a green or

Appendix E: Futility

red light on subconsciously-conceived proposed actions. Although this thought isn't "humiliating" it does reinforce my pre-existing feeling of humility.

Humility in youth, futility in old age. Let me count the ways I feel futility, starting with minor ones and ending with the one that upsets me the most.

I sometimes referred to "the starving Africans" to encourage my daughters to finish food on their plate. When they were older, and could reason, I had to admit that the Africans can't be helped, for the poorest people in every country are the ones having the most babies, and saving a starving baby today means adding to starvation in the future. Trying to end starvation in poor societies is futile.

As a parent I learned from my two daughters the limits of parenting. The sage from Lebanon, Kahlil Gibran, wrote in *The Prophet*: "Your *children* are not *your* children; they are the sons and daughters of Life's longing for itself. … You may give them your love, but not your thoughts, for they have their own thoughts." For example, a parent is essentially helpless when an adult child becomes addicted to something that takes the edge off of harsh reality. There are limits to parenting, and trying to exert influence over any adult, including one's own child, is futile.

My cloth shopping bags reduce plastic waste, but the grocery store lobbyists still get their way by obstructing laws that would allow cities to legislate against the use of plastic. By minimizing my "footprint" on Mother Earth I have left room for others who are oblivious to the matter. Being conscientious about reducing one's environmental footprint as a means for helping the Earth is a futile exercise.

I've done my part in combating global warming by publishing an article about it, but some state and federal government agencies have simply forbidden mention of the subject and have recently reduced funding for Earth and environmental science. Lobbyists for the oil and gas industry have more influence than all the world's scientists. Trying to "save the Earth" by publishing environmental science is futile.

My voting in every presidential election since college has provided one increment to the count dominated by millions of others, and none of the elections have been decided by one vote. Conscientious voting is futile.

I have published a half dozen books, and the one of least consequence (*Exoplanet Observing for Amateurs*, 2007, 2014) has sold the most. Promoting important ideas in a noisy "marketplace" is futile.

My daily observations of Comet ISON were meant to provide timely updates on what was happening to the over-hyped "Comet of the Century." My web pages produced a large following, and at first I was pleased by the extent of public interest in an astronomical event. However, as I became familiar with members of my fan club I learned that their principal interest was in my "showing up" the professionals at NASA by telling the truth of the comet's activity level; after all, as my fans would say, "the government couldn't be trusted because they were likely to be covering-up some danger posed by the comet that a public couldn't handle." I tried to "educate" my followers by stating that NASA was one of the most trustworthy of government agencies, and my intent was not to describe things that NASA was covering up. After I assured one caller, he ended the conversation by stating "I'm not crazy, I just want to be prepared for the Second Coming." I might as well have kept my comet updates to myself during that wasted 4-month ordeal because providing innocent updates on an unfolding astronomical event, and as a byproduct reassuring a skeptical public, was futile.

The foregoing are petty complaints. My biggest complaint is that non-sociopaths in a civilization are so tolerant of sociopaths and psychopaths that we are allowing them to take-over the civilization that we have created and that their self-serving greed will eventually destroy! This subject is too impolite to speak about in public, thanks to hyper-tolerant "politically correct" people. I am therefore having a useless conversation with myself when I rant about civilization's fundamental flaw of excessive tolerance for horrible people, the ones who threaten to control and destroy civilization. The suspension of intolerance, something that allowed tribal coalescence and leading to civilization, created a social setting many millennia ago that favored the rise of sociopaths and psychopaths. We, the tolerant champions of civilization, by our very tolerance, are going to blindly watch the sociopaths and psychopaths take-over and destroy civilization. My "call to arms" for banishing or exterminating psychopaths in order to preserve civilization is futile!

I believe that humanity is headed toward tragedy during the next few centuries, and this is happening with an amazing level of minimal concern. The concerns are manifold: it's not just the rise of psychopaths, and their threat to civilization.

Appendix E: Futility

In addition, 1) a global population explosion is underway, leading to a scramble for food, living space and other resources, 2) global warming is on an inexorable march and rising sea level will dislocate people in coastal cities, forcing them to migrate inland, where conflict with people already living inland is inevitable, 3) migration from poorly governed regions (e.g., Africa) to better run countries (e.g., in Europe) is already underway, which is destabilizing the well-governed countries, 4) the "Rise of the Roob" to cultural prominence is already vulgarizing manners, music, movies and politics, 5) the suspension of evolutionary cleansing of the human genome of deleterious mutations, which in the past was achieved by a finite survival rate from birth to adulthood of about 1/3, is leading to a "mutational load" by degraded genetic integrity, and in increase of genetic ailments in each new generation (because "nice" people reject eugenics). All of these threats, plus others, should concern anyone who values the civilized state.

I have argued elsewhere (i.e., in *Genetic Enslavement: A Call to Arms for Individual Liberation*, 2014, Chapter 29) that "Sampling Theory" can be used to argue that there's a 50% probability that humanity will disappear sometime during the interval 2100 to 2600 AD. The most probable year is approximately 2300 AD, when there will have been as many people born between now and then as have ever been born before now. I made that calculation in 1992 using reasonable population projection scenarios, and so far I haven't seen any argument that would invalidate my assumptions or any reason to adjust my calculations. This is illustrated in the next figure.

I am overwhelmed by dismay that humanity may come to a horrible end in a couple centuries! But anything I can imagine doing about it is futile!

Humans have such potential! But as H. G. Welles wrote, when describing the possibility for a good future for mankind *"To me, at least, this is no dream, but a possibility to be lost or won by men, as they may have, or may not have, the greatness of heart to consciously shape their moral conceptions and their lives to such an end."* H. G. Wells, "Human Evolution, An Artificial Process," *Fortnightly Review*, Oct, 1896.

I am a misanthrope, which I define as "Someone profoundly disappointed in human nature, yet still hopeful that a better nature may someday evolve." But, every year that I live, there is diminished evidence that such a future, though theoretically possible, will ever evolve.

Because I believe that titanic forces are at work to extinguish humanity, I feel a futility of trying to make things better. When I place a rant, such as this one, on a web page for possible viewing by internet browsers, my tracker shows that no one is reading it. I wonder if someone was on the bow of the Titanic shouting "Iceberg!" and no one paid attention. It makes more sense to withdraw from such futile rantings and bide whatever time I have left of life by observing peculiar stars and sharing in the publication of results with my colleagues. My contributions to astronomical discoveries and understandings are like Emperor Nero fiddling while Rome burned.

Que sera, sera, and any attempt to make things better would be futile! As Voltaire suggested, it's time to "cultivate my garden."

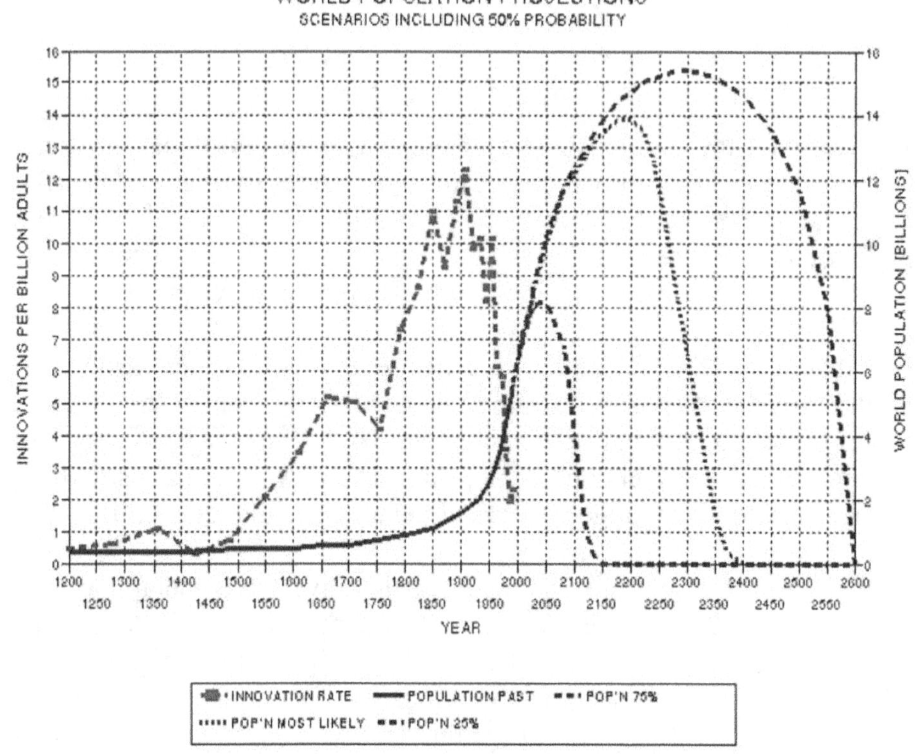

Figure E3. *World population crash scenarios (blue dashed traces), as calculated in 1992. The middle trace divides the 50% probability of prior occurrence from later occurrence, while the earlier and later traces correspond to 25% and 75% occurrences. [from Chapter 29,* Genetic Enslavement, *2014]*

Appendix F: A Free Man's Worship

Bruce L. Gary, 1998.08.27

The following is my "translation" of the greatest essay ever written: Bertrand Russel's *"A Free Man's Worship"* (Russell, 1903). I wrote it when a friend complained that Bertie's version was too difficult to understand. A fuller treatment, with side-by-side passages, can be found in my book Quotes for Misanthropes, Gary (2014). I present it here because it's a classic example of a normaloid's empathic way of viewing the dilemma of human existence. A psychopath would laugh at Bertie's concern for his fellow man; as Bertie wrote: *"One by one, as they march, our comrades vanish from our sight, seized by the silent orders of omnipotent Death. Very brief is the time in which we can help them, in which their happiness or misery is decided."* Only we normaloids have the compassion to care about our fellow man's plight.

Science has removed the veil of mystery from the workings of the universe, forcing Man to accept a view in which all things are the result of cold, uncaring forces. Man must accept that his existence is an unforeseen accident of Nature, and our understanding of the blind workings of these same forces persuades us that Mankind will eventually perish, along with his proud achievements.

How ironic that blind forces created a creature that thinks and aspires to understand the forces that created it, with an understanding denied the creating forces – which are blind. And more, this creature has feelings of good and evil, which also are denied the creating forces. And this new creature uses these insights and feelings to make judgments about the universe that created it.

In spite of being powerless within this mechanistic universe, as metaphorically emphasized by the fact that we die after just a few short years of existence, this thinking and feeling creature is nevertheless "free." He is free to ponder, to understand, to pass judgment, and imagine things that theoretically could exist. All these things are denied to the rest of the universe, and to the forces that bind the sentient individual; this makes the sentient "superior" to the creating and still enslaving forces.

Even primitive people understand that they are subject to forces more powerful than themselves. Those of our ancestors who acknowledged the power of stronger men and prostrated themselves in their worship, were more likely to be spared, and therefore tended to survive. The powers of Nature were dealt with similarly, because of the savages imperfect understanding of the differences between Nature and Man; hence, our ancestors prostrated themselves before the imagined Gods who represented Natural forces and offered sacrifices of valued things as if these would evoke compassion.

The savage relates to Nature the way a slave relates to his master. A slave dare not complain to his master about the unfair infliction of pain. Similarly, the savage dare not complain about the unfairness of his Gods.

The thinking person bravely acknowledges the imperfectness of the world. Unlike the savage, for whom survival is paramount and which constrains his thinking, we thinking people refuse to surrender our wish for the world to be better. We boldly worship "truth" and "beauty" and other concepts which are luxuries for the savage. The savage is enslaved by his excessive concern with the Powers of Nature, which for him are too complex to challenge. We have become "free" by refusing to worship fear-driven Power, like a slave worships his master, and to worship instead an imagined world of goodness, fairness and perfection. Even when the world does not bring forth goodness in our lives, we can at least imagine it, and seek solace from the imagined state. Although we know that we are mortal, we can at least imagine immortality, and be comforted by the thought. No matter how buffeted our lives may be by uncaring natural forces, we can still imagine a tranquil state, and use it's vision to survive the real world with equanimity.

Part of growing-up is surrendering the Mother Love that bathed our self-centered baby years. Our wishes cannot always be met by crying, as they once were. The adult must abandon childhood dreams when Fate denies them, and we must emotionally accept that this is normal. The acceptance of limitations is a precondition for further growth.

After learning that the outer world was not created for our benefit, but that we are mere unintended products of its blind forces, it becomes easier to accept the limitations of living within it. We can forgive it for whatever unintended calamities occur, for the Universe does not seek out its victims. It is unconscious, and uncaring, so there is no point in worshiping it for the purpose of avoiding its anger. This frees us to begin to see beauty within it. Because it is powerful it deserves our respect, but because it does not take notice of us we are free to think about it any way that we want. That which once scared us becomes beautiful, and

Appendix F: Free Man's Worship

worthy of our worship. But this is a new worship, for instead of being driven by fear and the need to propitiate, we are driven by the idealization of beauty, by aesthetics. This is a sort of triumph of the human mind over a once intimidating universe.

Death represents another challenge to the person who has shaken off the shackles of savage thinking. There is no denying that it is inevitable and irrevocable. The vastness of the unlived future, matched by the vastness of the unlived past, would seem to diminish the significance of the short span we do live. How ironic that during our brief span there should be so much travail and pain. Seeing that much of this sorrow is produced by petty strivings, we are less eager to pursue the endless and trivial struggles that once constituted our everyday life. Ever more freed from conventional shackles, and more aloof, it is easier to comprehend the poignancy of the human predicament: we are all subject to the same brief existence, surrounded by an immense and uncaring universe, we invent meaning and work together to achieve imagined goals, but most of these goals are transitory and petty, so in effect we squander our short tenure. And finally, we die alone, carrying the burden of knowledge that our struggles were for imagined causes, and that our final defeat is a passage into an uncaring, inanimate oblivion. However, with our contemporaries we share the realization of the aloneness of Death, and this recognition can bond us. Out of this shared dilemma can arise a new empathy for our fellow Man.

Whereas the savage continues to view the inanimate world as animate, and therefore worships false gods (in the manner of a slave), and whereas the savage continues to be driven by petty strivings with transitory rewards of personal happiness, thereby squandering a finite life, and whereas the savage refuses to accept the inevitable victory of an uncaring universe over his petty struggles, and therefore invents pitiful palliative realities promising everlasting heavenly happiness, the thoughtful man is free of all these false worshippings, false strivings, and false hopes. This emancipating perspective opens the way to the free man's worship.

Thoughtful men, who have freed themselves from the savage's slave worship mentality, are bound together by an acknowledgement of their shared fate. Each of us faces the existential dilemma, each confronts an uncaring physical universe and an evil animate one, each of us endures this for a brief time, and each of us will die alone. To the extent that I understand my individual fate, I also understand the fate of my fellow man. Our shared doom creates a feeling of fellowship. Together we march through the treacherous fields of life, and one by one we fall down to die. We are fellow-sufferers, and it feels right to reach out with a helpful hand to those who we shall later become. We may see their shortcomings, and know that we have ours; and remembering their burden of sorrows, we forgive.

Let our little day in the immense scheme of things be free of unnecessary pain, and be filled with gratitude. Let us worship, during our few precious moments, at our self-built shrine dedicated to aesthetic beauty. If we cherish these few good things during our journey, then we will be less buffeted by the uncaring universe that unknowingly created us. This is the only worship worthy of free men.

YOUR ODYSSEY

1992

From dust to stars, and dust again;
once more a star, with earth in orb,
evolving life, on land and sea,
producing Man, and making me.

Ageless atoms, you leave behind
countless stories, now combined.
Configured thus, you now form me,
providing for my odyssey.

From single-cell, to feeling child,
who learned the skills for living life,
my opened eyes viewed worldly scenes,
I filled with hope, and dreamed some dreams.

I worked and toiled, for decades long,
some lucky breaks, and then achieved!
Triumphant pause, a time to see,
the rush of time, the end of me!

My song is brief, it's almost sung,
deserving rest, my war I've won.
But from within, that short-termed we,
you atoms yearn to wrestle free.

Restless atoms, you must resume
uncharted paths, for endless time.
I give you thanks, and set you free,
as you resume YOUR odyssey.

REFERENCES

Arendt, Hannah, 1963, *Eichman in Jerusalem: A Report on the Banality of Evil,* Viking Press: New York

Arendt, Hannah, 1966, *The Origins of Totalitarianism*, Houghton Mifflin Harcourt: New York

Brown, Donald E., 1991, *Human Universals*, New York: McGraw-Hill, Inc.

Brooks, David, 2017, "The Lord of Misrule," *New York Times*, January 17 editorial

Chagnon, N. A., 1983, Yanomamo: The Fierce People, New York: Holt, Rinehart and Winston

Choi, Jung-Kyoo and S. Bowles, "The Coevolution of Parochial Altruism and War," *Science*, **318**, p. 636, October 26, 2007

Coppins, McKay, 2018, *The Atlantic*, November print edition (see also: https://www.theatlantic.com/magazine/archive/2018/11/newt-gingrich-says-youre-welcome/570832/)

Dawkins, Richard, 1976, *The Selfish Gene,* Oxford: Oxford University Press

Draaisma, Douwe, 2018, *Science*, 2018 Aug 09, pg. 166

Dunbar, R. I. M., 1992, "Neocortex Size as a Constraint on Group Size in Primates," *J. Human Evolution,* **22**, 469-493

Dunbar, R. I. M., 1996, "Grooming, Gossip and the Evolution of Language," Cambridge, MA, USA, Harvard University Press

Dunbar, Robin I. M. and Richard Sosis, 2017, "Optimizing Human Community Sizes," *Evolution and Human Behavior,* in press

Dutton, Kevin, 2012, "The Wisdom of Psychopaths: What Saints, Spies and Serial Killers Can Teach Us about Success," New York: *Scientific American*

Edgerton, Robert B., *Sick Societies: Challenging the Myth of Primitive Harmony*, New York: The Free Press.

Figueredo, A. J., G. Vásquez, B. H. Brumbach & S. M. R. Schneider, 2006, "The Heritability of Life History Strategy: The K-Factor, Covitality and Personality," *Social Biology*"

Gary, Bruce L., 1992, *Essays From Another Paradigm*

Gary, Bruce L., 1995, 2014, 2017, *Midnight Thoughts,* Create Space

Gary, Bruce L., 2014, *Genetic Enslavement: A Call to Arms for Individual Liberation*, Reductionist Publications, Create Space

Gary, Bruce L., 2014, *Quotes for Misanthropes*, Reductionist Publications, Create Space

Gasset, Jose Ortega y, 1930, *Revolt of the Masses*, New York: W. W. Norton and Company (translation)

Gazzaniga, Michael S. and Joseph E. LeDoux, 1978, *The Integrated Mind*, New York: Plenum Press

Geher, Glenn, 2018, "The Psychopath Next Door: Modern Societies are Breeding Grounds for Psychopathy," *Psychology Today*, 2018 February 13, https://www.psychologytoday.com/us/blog/darwins-subterranean-world/201802/the-psychopath-next-door

Ghiglieri, Michael P., 2000, *The Dark Side of Man: Tracing the Origins of Male Violence,* Cambridge, Mass.: Perseus Books

Ghiglieri, Michael P., 1988, *East of the Mountains of the Moon: Chimpanzee Society in the African Rain Forest,* New York: The Free Press

Glenn, Andrea L. and Adrian Raine, 2014, *Psychopathy: An Introduction to Biological Findings and Their Implications*, New York and London: New York University Press

Hamilton, William D., 1964, "The Genetical Evolution of Social Behavior," Part I, *J. Theoretical Biology*

Hamilton, Shawn, 2016 December 19, Huffington Post

Hare, Robert D. et al., 1990, "The Revised Psychopathy Checklist: Descriptive Statistics, Reliability and Factor Structure," *Psychological Assessmentl,* **2**, 338-341.

Hare, R. D., 2003, "Hare Psychopathy Checklist-Revised (PCL-R)," 2nd ed., Toronto: Multi-Health Systems

Hare, Robert, 1994, "This Charming Psychopath: How to Spot Social Predators Before They Attack," *Psychology Today*, Jan. 01, 1994. Also at https://www.psychologytoday.com/us/articles/199401/charming-psychopath

Hare, Robert D., 2016, "Psychopathy, the PCL-R, and Criminal Justice: Some New Findings and Current Issues," *Canadian Psychology*, **57**, No. 1, pp 21-34, http://hare.org/

Harlow, John Martyn, 1868, "Recovery from the Passage of an Iron Bar through the Head," Publications of the Mass. Medical Society

Hofstadter, Richard, 1969, *Anti-Intellectualism in American Life*, New York: Alfred A. Knopf

Hyde, Pamela S., 2010, *Report to Congress on Borderline Personality Disorder*, http://namiathensohio.org/~oldsite/pdf/BPD_Congress.pdf

Keeley, Lawrence H., 1996, *War Before Civilization*, New York: Oxford University Press

Kelly, Martha Hall, 2018, "Channeling History," *AARP The Magazine*, Oct., pg. 72

Livitsky, Steven & Daniel Ziblatt, 2018, *How Democracies Die*, New York: Crown Publishing Group

Lukianoff, Greg and Jonathan Haidt, *The Coddling of the American Mind*, Penguin Press,: New York

Lumsden, Charles J. and Edward O. Wilson, 1981, *Genes, Mind, and Culture: The Coevolutionary Process*, Cambridge, Massachusetts: Harvard University Press

Murphy, Ryan, "Psychopathy by U.S. State," 2018 Jun 12, Southern Methodist University, https://papers.ssrn.com/sol3/papers.cfm?abstract_id=3185182&download=yes

Olbermann, Keith, "Could Donald Trump Pass a Sanity Test," *Vanity Fair*, 2016 Jul 21

Palca, J., "NIH wrestles with furor over conference," *Science*, **257**, p739

Price, Roger, 1970, *The Great Roob Revolution*, New York: Random House

Russell, Bertrand, 1903, *Independent Review* (reprinted in *Mysticism and Logic,* 1929, as Chapter 3, New York: W. W. Norton and Company)

Sagan, Carl and Ann Druyan, 1992, *Shadows of Forgotten Ancestors*, New York: Random House

Sandberg, Anders, Eric Drexler and Toby Ord, 2018, arXiv:1806.02404, submitted to *Proceedings of the Royal Society of London A*

Sheaffer, Robert, 1988, *Resentment Against Achievement: Understanding the Assault Upon Ability*, Buffalo, New York: Prometheus Press

Snyder, Timothy, 2018, *On Tyranny: Twenty Lessons from the Twentieth Century*, New York: Tim Duggan Books

Spencer, Herbert, 1892, *The Principles of Ethics*, **1**, London: William & Norgate

Stout, Martha, 2005, *The Sociopath Next Door,* New York: Harmony Books

Thomas, M. E., 2013, *Confessions of a Sociopath,* New York: Broadway Books

Thornhill, Randy and Craig T. Palmer, 2000, "Why Men Rape," *The Sciences*, January/February, p. 30

Turchin, Peter, 2007, *War and Peace and War: The Rise and Fall of Empires*, New York: Plume Books

Ward, Peter D. and Donald Brownlee, 2000, *Rare Earth: Why Complex Life is Uncommon in the Universe*, New York: Copernicus Books

Wells, H. G., 1896, "Human Evolution, An Artificial Process," *Fortnightly Review*, Oct, 1896

Westheimer, Ruth, 1986, *Dr. Ruth's Guide for Married Lovers*, New York: Warner Books, Inc.

Wilson, D. S. and E. O. Wilson, 2007, "Survival of the Selfless," *New Scientist*, Nov. 3, pp 42-46

Wilson, Edward O., 1975, *Sociobiology: The New Synthesis*, Cambridge, MA: Harvard University Press

Wilson, Edward O., 1998, *Consilience: The Unity of Knowledge*, New York: Alfred A. Knopf

Wilson, Edward O., 2012, *The Social Conquest of Earth,* New York: Liveright Publishing Corporation

About the Author

I was born in 1939 in Ann Arbor, Michigan and grew up on a small farm nearby. By age 6 I was smitten by the stars, and astronomy became a life-long hobby. I graduated from the University of Michigan with an astronomy degree in 1961. A 2-year stint at the U.S. Naval Research Laboratory in Washington DC was followed by a brief experience in graduate school at U.C. Berkeley, after which I became employed at Caltech's Jet Propulsion Laboratory. After 2 years I worked briefly at Cornell University's Arecibo Observatory in Puerto Rico, and then returned to work at the Jet Propulsion Laboratory until retirement 32 years later, in 1998.

My 37 years of employment were in several fields: radio astronomy, atmospheric boundary layer remote sensing, aviation safety and airborne atmospheric science. I have about 98 peer-reviewed publications in scientific journals, four patents and numerous awards. The highlight of my pre-retirement career is participation as one of about 17 principal investigators in all of the NASA-led international campaigns of airborne studies of stratospheric ozone depletion – commonly referred to as "the ozone hole." The airborne instrument that I developed contributed to an understanding of the origin of the ozone hole (that man-made chlorofluorocarbon, CFC, was responsible). Another accomplishment during my career was the creation of an avionics instrument for warning and avoidance of "clear air turbulence," CAT.

After retirement I resumed the childhood hobby of astronomy, and moved to Arizona where I constructed a 2-dome observatory in my backyard (described at Wikipedia). My participation in a professional/amateur collaboration (XO) led to co-authorship of discovery papers for 7 exoplanets (planets that orbit other stars). I consulted as a Visiting

Scholar for a university by observing a list of exoplanet candidates and dwarf eclipsing binary stars. Other consulting consisted of observations of ~ 30 Near Earth Asteroids for characterizing their rotational state. My observations of the "zombie" white dwarf WD 1145+017 led to several scientific publications starting in 2015. My observations of "Tabby's Star" (KIC 8462852) during the past 3 years are the most precise ground-based observations since Kepler spacecraft's discovery of it (this is the star that was suggested might be variable due to alien mega-structures orbiting in front of the star).

My publication total after retirement (52) is actually greater than before (46), so in effect I haven't retired.

Resume: http://brucegary.net/resume.html

www.ingramcontent.com/pod-product-compliance
Lightning Source LLC
Chambersburg PA
CBHW082334270726
48658CB00017B/2841